Marc Duval
Director / Directeur
_____ / Community Life
_____niversity of Ottawa

D1284895

3 12174
MD

Making a Difference:

Profiles of Successful Student Affairs Leaders

by Arthur Sandeen

NASPA

Student Affairs Administrators
in Higher Education

Making a Difference: Profiles of Successful Student Affairs Leaders

Making a Difference: Profiles of Successful Student Affairs Leaders. Copyright © 2001 by the National Association of Student Personnel Administrators, Inc. (NASPA). Printed and bound in the United States of America. All rights reserved. No part of this book may be reproduced in any form or by any electronic or mechanical means without written permission from the publisher. First edition.

NASPA does not discriminate on the basis of race; color; national origin; religion; sex; age; affectional or sexual orientation; or disability in any of its policies, programs, and services.

ISBN: 0-931654-29-7

Contents

Preface

L eadership is the subject of much of the professional literature in higher education, management, political science, and other academic fields. Every year, new leadership theories are proposed, extensive organizational studies are conducted, and popular books on the subject are published. A large number of graduate programs are designed to prepare leaders for a variety of professions, and countless organizations conduct workshops and institutes geared to encourage and develop leadership skills. The best social, religious, business, educational, and military organizations recognize that developing effective leadership is the key to their future success.

Student affairs professionals have been very attentive to these developments, and for many years the National Association of Student Personnel Administrators (NASPA) has conducted a wide variety of impressive programs to provide leadership development activities for its members. Both the quality and the quantity of these programs are at an all-time high.

I spent many years as a student affairs administrator and am now a professor in a graduate department of educational leadership. In thinking about leadership in student affairs, I discovered that an important dimension of leadership is missing from the literature—the personal stories of successful practitioners! I knew that extremely valuable insights about leadership could be gained by learning about the diverse personal experiences of successful student affairs administrators. As a result, during the past year I traveled to 15 campuses, from Connecticut to California, and conducted extended interviews with some of the most respected leaders in the profession. This book presents personal profiles of their lives and careers in student affairs.

The chapters in this book reveal a great deal about leadership. Current student affairs administrators and those who aspire to become senior student affairs officers will find insight, knowledge, inspiration, and compassion in these profiles. It is hoped that a new generation of student affairs leaders will learn from the lives and careers of the highly successful men and women described in this book.

I extend my sincere appreciation to President John Lombardi and Provost Elizabeth Capaldi of the University of Florida for their support of this project. I also thank all of the outstanding student affairs leaders who agreed to be the subjects of this book. By sharing their lives and careers in this public way, they are once more extending their leadership in a positive manner to the profession.

Arthur Sandeen, University of Florida

Chapter 1

The Senior Student Affairs Officer in Higher Education

In August 1999, I completed 26 years as vice president for student affairs at the University of Florida. I also served as professor of educational leadership in the College of Education during that time and, when I stepped down from my administrative position, the University granted me a two-semester faculty improvement leave. Having the luxury of some time to think about problems and issues in higher education without having to worry about a demanding administrative role, I pondered how I might contribute something to the understanding of the senior student affairs officer (SSAO) role.

I wrote a book a few years ago, *The Chief Student Affairs Officer: Leader, Manager, Mediator, Educator* (Sandeen, 1991). In this book I described the various roles of SSAOs. I also emphasized their relationships with presidents, provosts, business and development officers, faculty, students, and community members. Improving the educational experiences of students through a better understanding of the leadership roles of student affairs administrators was the overall focus of the book.

During my leave year, 1999–2000, I again reviewed and considered the various leadership and administrative theories that I have studied and taught to students enrolled in the higher education administration graduate program. I have gained valuable insights from the research and writing on organizational cultures (Shein, 1992); resistance to change (O'Toole, 1995); planning and academic strategy (Keller, 1983); leadership challenges (Kouzes & Posner, 1987); visions and strategies (Drucker, 1996); policymaking (Baldridge, Curtis, Ecker, & Riley, 1978); compelling, visionary leadership (Nanus, 1992); the "Fifth

Discipline" (Senge, 1990); situational leadership (Hersey & Blanchard, 1984); and managing and reframing organizations (Bolman & Deal, 1997). The extensive literature on problems and issues in higher education—such as admissions policy (Bok & Bowen, 1998), academic strategy (Rosovsky, 1990), governing boards and change (Kerr, 1989), purposes (Bloom, 1987), academic departments (Bryan & Tucker, 1991), and faculty roles and institutional context (Kernan, 1999)—are also very pertinent in understanding the challenges facing the SSAO. Finally, the excellent research on how college affects students (Pascarella & Terenzini, 1991), the importance of involvement (Kuh, Schuh, & Whitt, 1991), the effect of specific experiences on student learning (Astin, 1993), and the role of assessment (Upcraft & Schuh, 1996) have been very useful to SSAOs in their work.

This extensive writing and research about leadership theories, higher education issues, and student outcomes have been of great value. At the same time, I was struck and intrigued by the extraordinary success of a group of outstanding SSAOs who had worked at their institutions for an extended period of time; moreover, I had real difficulty connecting any specific leadership theory to the activities of these SSAOs. What was it about this group of senior administrators that enabled them not only to survive in their highly volatile positions over many years, but also to have such a positive influence in their institutions? I had known all of them for many years and had admired their work, and now I wanted to examine more closely what it was that made them successful.

The primary questions I decided to explore in this investigation were the following:

(1)   What leadership strategies did these successful SSAOs develop?

(2)   Are the personal backgrounds and professional preparation of these leaders related to their success?

(3)   How did these SSAOs develop the skills that enabled them to have such a positive effect on their institutions?

(4)   How were these leaders able to adjust to the changing needs of students and their institutions over almost three decades?

(5)   Is sustained leadership in a position over many years related to their success?

In order to examine these important questions adequately, I decided to conduct extensive, on-site interviews with all of the SSAOs. I constructed a fairly lengthy interview guide (see appendix A), contacted the senior administrators in advance, and invited their participation. I also requested that they assist me in contacting a variety of people with whom they worked, such as presidents, provosts, business officers, faculty, students, community leaders, and alumni. My method was personal and direct; I spent a full day with each of the senior student affairs administrators, interviewing them on tape about their personal and professional backgrounds, their work at their institution, their accomplishments, their interactions with others, the obstacles they faced, and their strategies for achieving their goals. The several contacts closely associated with these SSAOs during their careers provided additional insight into their work and leadership.

The SSAOs invited to participate in this project all served in their positions at their institutions for at least 20 years, thus fulfilling the condition I wanted to explore regarding sustained leadership at one college or university over a long period of time. All of them had also been recipients of one or both of the most prestigious national awards in the profession: The Scott Goodnight Award for outstanding performance as a dean, and the Fred Turner Award for outstanding service to the profession. Obviously, there are many outstanding SSAOs at other institutions who have also made excellent contributions; I selected this group of 15 because I was confident that they would provide a rich and diverse sample to enable me to explore the questions I posed.

All of the SSAOs accepted the invitation to participate in the study, although many expressed, in their usual modest ways, their surprise over having been asked. In our taped discussions they were open and candid in their remarks about their personal and professional careers, and they freely shared their feelings about the tremendous challenges they faced in their positions. The many faculty, administrators, students, and alumni I contacted were also very generous with their comments, insights, and observations about the SSAOs.

The information I collected in these interviews, letters, institutional documents, electronic mail, and telephone calls was very extensive and detailed. While considerable effort was required to organize it all, there were clear and unmistakable themes that emerged in each institution that reflected the values, beliefs, and styles of the SSAO. This book offers a profile of individual leaders at their institutions over a period of several years. Of course, readers will discover that these SSAOs have much in common, but they will also be impressed with the distinctive cultures at the various institutions and the special abilities of these leaders to adjust to administrative challenges and external changes over the years. How did these successful fits between institution and SSAO occur? All of the SSAOs in this project indicated their enthusiastic support for their college or university as a place they believed in, and indeed, loved. Their own values were in harmony with the educational mission of their institutions. Yet, the profiles of these leaders reveal some daunting challenges, difficult controversies, and vexing decisions that might have caused others to leave their positions.

The most important factor to emerge from this project is that there is no single, fixed formula for successful leadership in student affairs administration. While the profiles of these leaders reveal many commonalities, the overall message is that achieving significant success in student affairs, over time, is the result of highly personalized leadership. The importance of institutional context—understanding the specific nature of the culture of the college or university and learning how to work effectively within this culture—was part of this personalized leadership. Successful strategies for effecting change at one institution might fail in another setting; planning facilities and acquiring resources were often done in different ways at the various institutions; and changing organizational structures and developing new services were initiated in ways that mainly reflected this personalized style of leadership.

The focus of this project was on significant changes in student affairs, observable at actual institutions over time. All of the SSAOs pointed with pride to real accomplishments that were the result of efforts they and others had initiated and planned. These SSAOs were committed to student growth and learning as the fundamental reason for working in their positions; however, they understood that in order for this growth and learning to occur, their leadership was necessary to acquire the necessary resources, build the new facilities, develop the most effective organizational structures, and work in harmony with other administrative officers and the president. What clearly emerged from the work of this project is that these 15 SSAOs are unique individual leaders! As a student of the leadership process, it was necessary for me to understand their personal backgrounds and values and to acknowledge the distinctive differences in the ways they exerted their leadership at their institutions.

The senior administrative officers who participated in this project are a very diverse set of individuals, coming from a variety of educational backgrounds, and representing different philosophical positions about the field of student affairs. Moreover, they represent a wide variety of institutions in terms of size, location, history, academic organization, and type of control. The academic challenges, the financial resources, the administrative changes, the community pressures, and the expectations of the students differed from one institution to another. These SSAOs experienced the effects of the civil rights movement and the Vietnam war during the late 1960s and early 1970s, the Watergate scandal, the oil crisis, the growing drug abuse of the 1970s and 1980s, and the affluence and the computer revolution of the 1990s during their careers. Yet, they all thrived as successful leaders in their institutions during these tumultuous changes, a period of years when many college and university administrators left because the pressures became too daunting.

These SSAOs readily acknowledged the considerable benefits of studying leadership and organizational theories and all indicated a strong commitment throughout their careers to continuing learning. They expressed a genuine sense of excitement about advances in research and professional writing about higher education, and they talked openly about their efforts to read, study, and keep up with the best developments in the profession. All of them were active leaders within the student affairs profession, with several of them serving as presidents of the major professional organizations within the field, recognizing that their leadership responsibilities extended beyond their own campuses. While these SSAOs are a very diverse group, they clearly have in common a strong passion to serve others, a love of learning, and a strong sense of self confidence.

> **The courage to move forward in view of expected controversy and opposition is a clear indication of successful leadership, and the SSAOs who participated in this project all seemed to relish this part of their jobs.**

Evident in the profiles of these leaders and their work at their institutions were three aspects of administrative leadership not very often discussed in the professional literature: ability to deal positively with stress, courage, and integrity. Each of these factors assumed a major role in the success of the SSAOs participating in this project. They are discussed briefly here, but they are most evident in the profiles of each leader.

Serving as an SSAO at a college or university, especially over several years, and during times of major societal change, presents a set of challenges that most people would prefer not to face. It is not a position for everyone! Balancing the competing demands of many constituent groups, including presidents, students, faculty, staff, parents, governing board members, alumni, and community leaders requires patience, intelligence, insight, and wisdom. The volatility of many of the issues and the vociferous demands of some of the constituents make the SSAO among the most vulnerable of institutional leaders.

In describing their experiences during their careers, some of the leaders in this project attributed their survival at times to simple good fortune or their success to the presence or absence of political decisions outside their control. Others suggested that they were able to advance a new policy or major change only because of a highly visible or traumatic incident on the campus. They all readily acknowledged that they served at the pleasure of their presidents, that they were on call 24 hours a day, 7 days a week, and that their futures could easily be determined by the way they responded (or failed to respond!) to a single issue. They were aware that several of their colleagues had been dismissed from their positions at other institutions when pressures from various constituents imposed administrative changes. They were often the objects of vigorous public (and sometimes personal) criticism for the decisions they made, the staff they hired, the policies they enforced with students, and the beliefs they expressed.

Serving as an SSAO does not enable one to lead a predictable life, and all indicated that 60 hours was the minimum they spent on campus each week, with most weekends and nights involving some form of activity. Yet, their personal lives seemed remarkably happy and these leaders expressed their genuine love and excitement for their work. Most of them had other, more lucrative opportunities presented to them during their careers, and all of them declined to leave their positions. There was no discernable pattern in how these diverse leaders dealt with the daunting pressures of their positions; some relied on vigorous physical exercise, some on reading and cultural pursuits, some on travel, and others on community and religious service. After completing the lengthy interviews, I discovered another trait these leaders had in common that was not as evident to me during the many years I had known them: a lively sense of humor! All of these SSAOs enjoyed a good laugh, especially when a joke was played on them. Perhaps this ability to laugh frequently, even in the face of extremely complex and difficult problems, enabled them to survive. Despite the considerable pressures of the position, every one of the SSAOs in this project unhesitatingly responded "Oh, yes, of course!" to my question, "Would you do it all again?"

Being a successful SSAO requires courage. It is surprising that something as important as this is often absent in academic and professional discussions about leadership and institutional change. Effective administration does not consist of timid bureaucrats hiding behind policy or simply fulfilling the minimum requirements of a job description. The emphasis on management in administration during the past several years has probably given some the impression that good management is synonymous with effective leadership. An organization might balance its books each year, staff members might be fulfilling their duties, and the customers might be using the services; but this does not equate with effective leadership. Educational leadership means moving forward; developing new approaches; challenging the status quo; and creating new programs, policies, services, and facilities. Above all, it involves taking risks. Administrators who shy away from controversy and avoid making tough decisions are not leaders. It frequently is tempting for administrators to remain quiet, hoping that problems will go away, choosing what they think is security by not making a decision. Making bold proposals for new facilities, policy changes, new programs, or organizational changes involves risks for SSAOs; their ideas are subject to public criticism, their persuasive powers will be challenged, and their ability to implement the changes will be carefully scrutinized. Moreover, many of the issues and problems (e.g., alcohol policies, rape adjudication programs, student fee assessments for new facilities, admissions and financial aid policies) that SSAOs face in their work are matters of great public interest and attract comments from presidents, governing board members, students, faculty, parents, community leaders, and alumni.

SSAOs know that when they initiate major policy or program changes, make controversial decisions, or hire certain staff, their decisions will generate lots of discussion and debate. The courage to move forward in view of expected controversy and opposition is a clear indication of successful leadership, and the SSAOs who participated in this project all seemed to relish this part of their jobs. They all exuded a quiet confidence in their own abilities to carry out various reforms and improvements, and they viewed such actions on their part as a major reason for remaining in their positions. They also acknowledged that cockiness or arrogance on their own part would be a sure route to failure in initiating change successfully. All had been subjected to vigorous criticism on their campuses at times over the years for decisions made, policies established, staff hired (or not hired), fees established, and public positions taken. However, without bragging, the SSAOs felt confident that they had "done the right thing" and would do it again, even when their proposals for change were not successful. They recognized the risk involved for them in their positions and accepted this risk as part of their responsibility. In exploring with these senior administrators how they developed this willingness to take risks and the personal and professional confidence required to do so, most were genuinely puzzled. "I always had the strength of my own convictions, and I usually can do pretty well in any argument!" was the typical reply.

In discussing this further with the SSAOs, many suggested that it was this ability and willingness to take risks—to demonstrate courage—that most likely attracted them to the senior leadership position in student affairs. It provided them with excitement and challenge throughout their careers. Perhaps because this group of administrators has been so successful at their institutions, they seemed to relish the challenges and were clearly invigorated by the public scrutiny and debate. They indicated that the major satisfactions from their work as leaders often were related to the most volatile situations they had to face. And, they reluctantly admitted, some of these volatile situations were in fact created by their own policy, program, facility, or organizational proposals. The willingness to take risks—to put oneself and one's ideas on the line for public scrutiny—is an extremely important aspect of leadership that deserves more attention by researchers interested in studying how effective leaders develop. In this project with a limited sample of highly successful SSAOs, this willingness to take risks was identified as courage, and it was evident in all of their work.

Acting with integrity is an important aspect of administrative leadership, no matter what the level of responsibility. Acting with integrity means being truthful with others and with the institution. The interviews with the SSAOs and the many comments made about them by staff, presidents, students, faculty, and alumni revealed consistently that the personal integrity of these administrative leaders was an important contributor to their success. The SSAOs who participated in this project earned reputations for honesty and personal integrity on their campuses; and in many cases, it was suggested by others that this trust was often responsible for their ability to gain support for their proposals, policy decisions, and administrative changes.

> **Successful SSAOs cannot operate in isolation from their colleagues in academic affairs, business affairs, and development. Gaining the confidence and support of these key institutional leaders is critical to the success of student affairs programs and policies.**

There was no evidence that any of the SSAOs preached about morality on their campuses, or attempted to set themselves up as personal models; to the contrary, they simply tried to treat others with fairness and consistency, shared problems openly, involved others in decisions, and always told the truth. Former students, who in their undergraduate years had been active in protest movements and had clashed with their SSAO, frequently commented that "I strongly disagreed with her position on the issue, but I knew she was telling the truth." Faculty members and presidents also suggested that the long-time reputation of the SSAO for being honest and fair was a great asset to the institution—students and others were much more likely to accept and believe what was said by this leader. Some of the SSAOs were aware of their reputations in this regard, especially after a number of years in their positions; as a result, they made special efforts not to misuse this asset and tried very hard not to appear pompous.

Some of the SSAOs were very explicit in their views about integrity; they stated that if they had not been forthright and honest with students, staff, or others, they would have lost their credibility and thus their effectiveness. Without this, they suggested, they would have had to resign. Others mentioned the importance of describing problems and issues as they are, and the difficulties that result from exaggeration. Sometimes these SSAOs observed other administrators who consistently embellished problems and issues, most likely to enhance the importance of the challenges they were facing; inevitably, such misrepresentations resulted in a loss of credibility for the administrator and ineffective leadership. Acting with integrity is necessary for all administrative leaders, and SSAOs have no corner on it. While perhaps not surprising, it clearly emerged as a key factor in the long-term success of this group of senior leaders and was confirmed repeatedly by those who worked with them.

Without exception, the SSAOs who participated in this project emphasized the importance of the president in their work. Most identified it as the most critical factor in their success. Having the confidence of their president enables SSAOs to make decisions, submit proposals, hire staff, allocate resources, and decide division priorities with the assurance that they will be supported in their work. This freedom to act was extremely important to the SSAOs, and they suggested that their jobs would be intolerable and unworkable without it. They readily admitted, however, that they had to read their presidents very well, understand the pressures their presidents were facing on certain issues, and adjust their actions accordingly. None of the SSAOs claimed they ever had (or deserved) complete freedom to act or speak on any issue at their institutions; however, their own beliefs and values were closely in line with the missions of their institutions and with their presidents, and they found their situations acceptable most of the time. They also emphasized the importance of being forthright with their presidents about their views on issues and problems, although they said such discussions should be conducted in private. The SSAOs were quite willing to disagree with and challenge their presidents in private, but they were well aware that it was their role to support the president's decision in public. "I don't always get my way, of course, but I am almost always heard by my president on an issue," was a typical comment made by an SSAO.

Serving in their positions for more than 20 years at the same institution presented these SSAOs with an additional challenge: changes in the presidency! Some had worked with as many as six different presidents during their tenure as SSAO. Their comments about these critical transitions were candid and reveal their ability to adjust to changing priorities and administrative styles. Some presidents were very comfortable with students, enjoyed the stage, and loved to engage students with issues; others avoided such contact at all costs and expected the SSAO to handle all such matters; others had virtually no knowledge or experience with student affairs prior to becoming president and needed a gently planned "orientation" from the SSAO. Some presidents simply did not do well with students, and the SSAO consciously protected these presidents from situations or issues that might embarrass them. No matter what the style, priorities, or knowledge of the president regarding student-related issues, the support of the president was considered crucial to the success of the SSAO. These leaders understood clearly that they served at the pleasure of the president and that it was their obligation to support their president. All of them stated that they were fortunate during their careers to work with presidents they could support (some more than others!) and that they would have resigned their positions if the gap between their beliefs and those of the president became too great.

SSAOs work as part of a team on their campuses, placing them in daily contact with the senior administrative officers for academic affairs, business affairs, and development. On some campuses, there may be senior officers for medical affairs and research as well. While SSAOs often compete with their administrative colleagues for resources, they are expected to work as a team, collaborating and cooperating to accomplish the objectives of the president and the mission of the college or university. Successful SSAOs cannot operate in isolation from their colleagues in academic affairs, business affairs, and development. Gaining the confidence and support of these key institutional leaders is critical to the success of student affairs programs and policies. The SSAOs who participated in this project emphasized the importance of developing this support and understanding; and at the same time, they expressed more frustration about this aspect of their jobs than any other. Planning and building a new recreation center or residence hall or creating a new student fee to support a child care center necessarily involves agreement with the senior business officer; proposing a new academic advising program, a change in undergraduate admissions policy, or a new orientation course for credit must involve collaboration with the senior academic affairs officer; and proposing a parents association or a fund raising effort for student leadership retreats will have to include the senior development officer.

Some SSAOs in this project stated that they had worked to win the support of students, staff, faculty, and others for various proposals, but then encountered serious opposition from their senior administrative colleagues in academic or business affairs and development. Sometimes these disagreements had to be resolved by their presidents, but most SSAOs preferred to work these matters out with their administrative colleagues themselves. All of them described strategies for involving their senior colleagues in the activities of the division, being convinced that such involvement would increase the likelihood of their support for their proposals. Inviting their senior colleagues to student leadership retreats, engaging them in direct discussions with student groups, asking them to advise student organizations or to speak at student banquets, and seeing to it that they are recognized by student groups often contributed to the success of their own programs. Many of the SSAOs chuckled about these actions and confessed that they were, at times, bordering on manipulation, but nevertheless, they were effective methods of gaining support for their programs. Especially in times of crises, such as natural disasters, student deaths, or disruptive protests, the support and understanding of these senior institutional colleagues is critical to the SSAOs. The profiles of the SSAOs reveal specific instances where this support and cooperation made the difference in the institution's ability to respond effectively to a crisis situation. The SSAOs acknowledged that there may be differences among the senior institutional officers, but they need each other in order to be successful. All of them commented on the necessity to learn as much as possible about the other major areas of the institution; and the need to negotiate, bargain, trade, cajole, and compromise.

The student affairs staff at any college or university comprises a small percentage of the institution. These successful SSAOs recognized this fact, and moreover, knew that working in isolation as a staff was impossible and indeed, counter productive to their goals. As a result, all them commented extensively on the importance of involving faculty in their various activities, programs, and policy initiatives. This sometimes required student affairs staff to invent ways to convince faculty to assist with a campus program, but it was usually accomplished by personal invitations to faculty to share their expertise or lend their professional advice. Many of the SSAOs had devised faculty recognition programs for those who had made outstanding contributions to student life; others created faculty advisory committees or faculty associates programs; still others found ways to convince faculty to serve as sponsors of student organizations. When faculty members served as masters in a residential college, volunteered as mediators in adjudicating discipline cases, provided professional advice in setting up a child care center, or advised a student political group, they were usually more sympathetic to the needs of student affairs on the campus and might even be counted on for support when needed. Most important to the SSAOs in this project was the increased attention to the personal needs of students that faculty could offer by being involved in student life programs.

One of the recurrent themes that emerged during this project was the strong dedication of these SSAOs to the development and growth of their own staff. Without exception, comments from former staff revealed this commitment, and many of these staff attributed their own subsequent professional success to the personalized care and guidance provided by these SSAOs. The SSAOs admitted that they were often demanding and uncompromising in their standards for their own staffs, and none apologized for this. At the same time, they often described what they called their "obligation to teach" regarding their staff. When they recognized high ability in their staff, they pushed them hard, prodding them to complete graduate degrees and to accept new challenges. Indeed, some of the SSAOs indicated that one of their roles was to get their staff to do more than they thought they were capable of doing. All of these SSAOs served as mentors to many of their staff, whether consciously or not. In the process, over the years, they developed very strong bonds of loyalty and reputations for genuinely caring for and developing their staff. As a result, many talented young professionals sought positions on their staffs, eager to learn from them. Caring for the lives and careers of their staff was a sincere and continuing effort by these SSAOs, but it was also a very effective way to build a successful team that could achieve success in campus programs. There are dozens of SSAOs and other senior administrators at colleges and universities throughout the country who served as staff members for the SSAOs in this project. Their success is another indication of the effective leadership of these SSAOs.

Effective leadership is an art, not a science; and it was evident in this project that the SSAOs had become very proficient in this art. Remaining in the same position at their institution for many years enabled them to know its history and culture; to understand how decisions were made; and to know who the most influential people were, both on the campus and in the community. This knowledge and experience made it possible for them to avoid many problems in their efforts to change policies, propose new facilities, or introduce new programs.

Many of the SSAOs emphasized the importance of another aspect of leadership not often discussed in the professional literature: timing. They often attributed the success they achieved on a project to their decision to postpone an initiative due to various conditions that prevailed at the time on the campus or in the community. A key administrative appointment might be in the process of being made; a student organization election was taking place, and a change in priorities was likely to occur; a budget cutback was going to be announced in the next month; or the president was in the middle of a difficult fight with some governing board members at the moment—the SSAOs cited such examples as factors to consider in deciding the appropriate timing of important changes they intended to make. The wisdom to know when to proceed and when to delay certainly is enhanced by years of experience in the same position at one institution, but it was apparent in the interviews with these SSAOs that this wisdom does not develop on its own.

Each of these leaders indicated that they worked hard at understanding their institutional cultures throughout their careers. They did this primarily, they said, by listening carefully to faculty, students, alumni, their own staff, and community members. They all regularly engaged in "walking around management," emphasizing the importance of getting out of their offices and spending time in a large variety of settings on and off the campus. Not only did such activity make them more visible and well known, but also it provided them with understandings and insights about their institutions that they could not gain in any other way. It was striking how much each of these SSAOs stressed the value of attending faculty seminars, student organization meetings, community programs, public lectures, athletic events, weekend retreats, and a variety of other gatherings. They all stated that there was no substitute for being there, knowing that their presence was always noted in some way, especially by students and their own staff. But most important, they said, was the insight and understanding they gained by doing this themselves. It enabled them to know the several cultures that exist on their campuses and in their communities, and thus to know how and when to move forward with their various initiatives. When asked about the huge demands on the time required to engage in this informal activity, all of the SSAOs had essentially the same response: "Sure, this was difficult, but it was really very enjoyable, as we knew we were building support for the initiatives we wanted to take."

Every one of the SSAOs participating in this project expressed genuine enthusiasm and affection for students. Indeed, everything they did in their positions was done with student growth and education in mind. They emphasized that they never felt bored in their jobs, despite spending more than two decades in them on the same campus; and this was due to their commitment to students. They took the greatest pride in the success and accomplishments of their students, and all of them talked in detail about the scores of former students with whom they still correspond. This dedication to students and affection for them has been returned in many ways, and the profiles of these SSAOs reveal several permanent tributes to them on their campuses from students.

> *These SSAOs viewed themselves primarily as teachers and change agents; and they never lost their excitement for the programs, policies, and facilities they were working to create.*

The conversations with these SSAOs revealed a strong faith in the essential goodness of students and a determination to assist them, despite obstacles that would discourage others from even trying. While perhaps viewed by some people on their campuses as mild mannered and laid back, the truth about these SSAOs is that they are highly competitive, determined advocates who love to argue for the rights of individual students against any form of bureaucracy. It was fun to tease them that they spent many long hours developing equitable policies for their campuses and then were quite willing to grant an exception to these same policies when it might benefit an individual student. These SSAOs were proud of the accomplishments of their outstanding students, and they were always present to cheer them on and recognize them. However, they mostly enjoyed helping the down-and-out student, the underachiever, the student who was not a natural star. They never were bothered by the debates about the legal status of the in loco parentis concept; they simply viewed students as people and did whatever they thought was necessary to help them succeed. Based on many reports from former students collected during this project, these SSAOs leaders had a profound and positive influence on their lives. Every one of these SSAOs said that working with students gave them their greatest satisfaction during their careers.

Serving as SSAOs during parts of the last four decades of the 20th century, these leaders were visible participants in the highly volatile debates about social issues on their campuses. During their careers, tremendous changes occurred in American society; and college campuses were often the primary stage where such critical issues as race, gender, sexual orientation, and access were to be tested. These SSAOs were not just participants in these issues; they were often outspoken advocates, willing to take public positions before others in their institutions did, and sometimes at a personal price. While all of these leaders rejected vigorously any notion that they were the "conscience of their campus," they saw it as their responsibility to advocate for individual human rights, and they did this throughout their careers. Some of the SSAOs in this project served as chairs of campus and community human rights committees during the most volatile periods of the civil rights movement. For these SSAOs, it would have been unthinkable not to be directly involved in these critical social issues, and they all viewed such involvement as part of their leadership responsibilities.

What was it about this group of SSAOs that made them so successful at their institutions? No single administrative strategy, no clearly defined leadership theory, and no simple formula emerged that might easily explain their success. From the discussion presented in this chapter, it is clear that they had much in common regarding their beliefs, commitments to students, and passion for education. However, this group of 15 SSAOs mainly revealed their diversity of styles and their individuality of method. Theirs was a highly personalized form of leadership, exercised over time, with lasting effects. It was impossible to separate their personalities from their positions. Most of what they were able to accomplish was a function of their personalities and courage, not just the random convergence of times and circumstances. They all borrowed liberally and consciously from the variety of administrative and leadership theories they read, but all remained eclectic in their approaches to their work, using knowledge and experience from whatever source they could to accomplish their goals. They all readily acknowledged their commitment to a team approach to leadership, discounting their own roles relative to the work of their staff. Yet, on every campus, those who knew them and observed their work strongly argued that none of the success would have been achieved without their presence and their personal leadership.

These SSAOs viewed themselves primarily as teachers and change agents; and they never lost their excitement for the programs, policies, and facilities they were working to create. They were among the most competitive, determined, and tenacious persons one can imagine. They loved building and improving things and approached their work with a passion. Their jobs were an extension of their values and presented them with the best opportunity to express their basic beliefs. To a person, they deeply loved their work!

In the individual profiles, readers will become closely acquainted with the personal backgrounds and styles of these outstanding SSAOs. By their willingness to reveal the details of their successful careers at their institutions, these leaders are continuing the teaching roles so important to them!

There are many ways to learn about leadership. Reading and debating leadership theories, attending conferences and workshops, studying for advanced degrees, doing research, and discussing case studies all are valuable approaches to helping others learn to become successful leaders. This book is intended to introduce an additional opportunity to learn about leadership. It is not intended to be a substitute for the more traditional methods listed above, but as one more way to gain insight into the leadership process. By learning about the actual personal and professional lives of highly successful leaders, it is hoped that new understandings and skills might emerge.

I am greatly indebted to the 15 outstanding SSAOs who graciously gave of their time to serve as the participants in this study. By agreeing to do so, all of them are continuing to serve the profession and the education of students.

Chapter 2

Donald V. Adams
Drake University

Imagine a summer orientation session in an auditorium at Drake University, filled with newly admitted freshman students and their parents….Don Adams is speaking to the group about the institution, its history, values, and educational mission. Even though he has done this several times per year for more than 25 years, his voice begins rising, his gestures become animated, and his enthusiasm is unbounded. The audience of students and parents is enraptured by his message and, after giving him a rousing ovation, is absolutely convinced that Drake University is the perfect institution for them!

Don Adams has been an ambassador and a supersalesman for Drake University for more than three decades. His enthusiasm and dedication are legendary on the campus and since joining the staff as vice president in 1969, few people at the institution have had a greater effect on students.

Donald V. Adams earned his B.A. in business education in 1957 from the University of Northern Iowa, his M.A. in guidance and counseling in 1961 from Michigan State University, and his EdD in higher education administration from Michigan State University in 1965. He was director of the freshman men's residence hall at the University of Northern Iowa in 1957–1958; and he taught disadvantaged students at Washington Junior High School in Clinton, Iowa during 1958–1959. He was the head resident adviser in Rather Hall at Michigan State University from 1959–1961, and then the head resident adviser in South Case Hall, the first living and learning center at Michigan State University in 1961–1962. He became the director of residence hall programs at Michigan State University in 1962 and served in this position until 1969. Later that year, he was appointed the first vice president for student life at Drake University in Des Moines, Iowa. In 1985, his position was expanded and his title was changed to vice president for student life and enrollment management. In 1995, he was appointed executive assistant to the president and secretary of the university, a position he continues to hold. He has taught graduate courses in higher education and student affairs since 1963, has served as a consultant to over 60 colleges and universities, and has been a frequent speaker and presenter at professional conferences. He has been a consultant and a commissioner-at-large with the North Central Association of Colleges and Schools, served on a special team of consultants to the American Council on Education, and in 1991 was selected as a Fulbright scholar in Germany. He chaired the National Association of Student Personnel Administrators (NASPA) Governance Committee from 1971–1973 and served as the associate editor of the *NASPA Journal* in 1981–1983. He was a regional vice president of NASPA from 1974–1977 and was elected president of NASPA in 1977–1978. In 1984, he received the Fred Turner Award from NASPA for outstanding service to the profession, and in 1989 he received the first Distinguished Professional Award from the Iowa Student Personnel Association. NASPA presented him with its highest honor, the Scott Goodnight Award for outstanding performance as a dean, in 1992.

Donald V. Adams was born in 1935 in a farmhouse just outside the small town of Liscomb, Iowa. He jokes now that he was delivered by a midwife who was a close friend of the family and who consequently kept close tabs on his activities all during his life. Don and his identical twin brother, Deane, were the only children in this very close, extended rural family. They lived in the house of Don's grandparents until 1940. The Adams family had immigrated from Holland and England and came to Iowa via Pennsylvania and Ohio, having homesteaded in Iowa during the 19th century. Neither of Don's parents had been to college and were natives of Liscomb. Don's mother was a homemaker; and his father held various jobs in Liscomb and Marshalltown until World War II, when he obtained his own garage and worked as a highly skilled mechanic, repairing cars, trucks, and farm equipment. Don's father was an extremely hard worker who put in long hours every day at his job and earned the trust and respect of all who knew him; it was from his father and grandfather that Don learned these same values that were to guide his own life and career. His father also served for 22 years as an elected member of the city council and was the chief of the volunteer fire department. Don remembers when he learned about Carl Rogers' "unconditional positive regard" in graduate school—it was the same concept he had observed in his grandmother's relationship to him. He stressed how fortunate he was to be a part of such a close and supportive family. Their protestant church was a central part of their lives; Don remembers at least five members of the extended family being in church every Sunday, and his grandmother taught Sunday school and played the piano at church during her entire adult life. In 1942, when Don was 7 years old, his father contracted spinal meningitis and was in a coma for 50 days. After being almost completely paralyzed for a year, he recovered. A young man at the time, this disease prevented him from serving in the Army during the war. This experience brought the family even closer together and convinced Don that almost anything could be accomplished with hard work, encouragement, and determination.

Life in the small, north-central town of Liscomb, Iowa was very pleasant during Don's youth, despite the fact that most people were poor by today's standards. Don was a child of the Great Depression and remembers being selected to ring the bells in his church in 1945 when World War II ended. Don and his twin brother, Deane, remember taking $50 from each of their savings accounts when they were 13 to give to their father and mother to help pay the costs of heating oil for the house. Don and Deane had accumulated this money by working in odd jobs around the town during the year and from their work on the farm. Don, Deane, and their friends were all active in the 4-H organization, and Don and his brother sang in a quartet in church and played musical instruments in the school band. But Don's first love was baseball, and he played this and many other sports every chance he had while growing up. He used to listen to Chicago Cubs' games on the radio, keeping very well organized score cards of each game—which Don thinks explains his later decision to major in accounting in college!

Don began working in part-time jobs in his small town when he was only 10 years old, and he does not remember another time during his life when he was not working. His father made him a lawn mower by mounting an old washing machine engine on a hand mower, and Don became quite an entrepreneur as a youth! He also was hired to maintain the grounds at a local school, and he worked on his uncle's farm. He was an outstanding baseball pitcher and played in American Legion games throughout the area. He was a good student in high school; and, like his father and grandfather, he had so much energy that he had to find outlets for his many interests. He was the captain of his basketball team, president of the student council, editor of the yearbook, and president of his 4-H club. His role models were his father and grandfather, whose hard work, community service, and leadership inspired Don in all of his activities. Don also was fortunate to have a coach who pushed him to do his best in school and encouraged him to consider going to college. Don later joked that there were only 12 students in his graduating class in high school. "We were so small that everyone had to be involved, or nothing would have happened!"

Few members of the extended Adams family had attended college, and all members of the family lived within a few miles of one another. When Don attended the state fair with his 4-H club and visited Iowa State University for 4-H activities, it was the farthest away from home he had been. His involvement in baseball and his admiration of his coach made Don think he wanted to become a coach himself someday. While working at the school during high school, Don had lots of informal contacts with teachers, and they encouraged him to go to college. Don laughs now as he remembers traveling the 45 miles to Cedar Falls, Iowa to visit Iowa State Teacher's College during the summer of 1953; he and his two friends got lost on this big excursion from home! But he liked what he saw in Cedar Falls, and he knew he wanted to be a coach. Most of his friends stayed at home to work on farms or to work in the local Lennox Furnace factory. Don wanted something beyond all of this, and coaching was his ambition.

When Don went away to college and left the extremely close family, it was a very difficult experience for everyone. Don and Deane had done everything together for 18 years; and Deane's choice was to stay at home and continue with farming, while attending a short course in farming at Iowa State. But Don was determined to strike out on his own, and with his family's support he went to Iowa State Teacher's College in Cedar Falls in the fall of 1953. Coming from such a small town and high school, the college seemed large and chaotic to him and he didn't know anyone at the institution. He remembers being confused with the orientation and registration process and not wanting to admit to anyone that he did not understand anything about college. Don had been in his residence hall for only 3 days, but he became so upset at registration that he decided he would leave college and return to his home in Liscomb. He decided he could not make the transition from high school to college. But the resident assistant (RA) on his floor, Neil VerHoef, noticed that things were not going well with Don and spent several hours with him, helping him with the details of registration, with the result being that Don decided to stay in college. Neil was to become a fraternity brother of Don's and many years later, when Don was the vice president at Drake University, Neil's daughter enrolled as a student at Drake! This experience in Don's first 3 days at college in 1953 convinced him of the importance of the transition from high school to college and the need for institutions to pay close, personal attention to the needs of its students. Don became an RA during his sophomore year and never lost the passion or focus that he learned from this experience as a new student.

In his freshman year, Don was a member of the baseball team, worked in the dining hall, was active in a local church, and was on his residence hall judicial board. Most important, he did well in his classes and gained the confidence that he could succeed in college, while majoring in accounting. He joined a fraternity, Sigma Tau Gamma, and later became its vice president. He was selected as an RA in the freshman residence hall, and together with a tuition scholarship (he had finished second in his high school class), the free room and board he earned from his RA job enabled him to pay his college expenses. He was fortunate to be able to work summers during college in Marshalltown, Iowa, only 14 miles from his home, as a playground supervisor. Don was assigned to the most difficult young people in the city, but the experience proved to him that he could work effectively with young people. There were college students from other institutions working in similar positions in this summer program; and Don rediscovered that he not only could compete successfully with them, but also that he could excel. Don's supervisor in this job was Dick Jordan, who was to become his long-term mentor, giving Don encouragement and confidence in all of his activities. The example that Jordan set for Don was to become a model for his own work as a student affairs professional later in life—providing close, personal encouragement to students in all of their work.

During his sophomore year in college, Don met Carol Gaunt, a freshman student from Clemons, Iowa. They dated throughout college and were married in 1958 after Carol earned her degree from Iowa State Teacher's College. Don continued to love his total experience as a student, was elected vice president of the student body, and became the chair of the all-campus judiciary board. College graduation was a very happy day for the Adams family, all of whom were present to cheer for Don. He was presented with three job choices—the dean of students, Paul Bender, invited him to become the director of the freshman men's residence hall; his faculty advisers in accounting encouraged Don to accept a position with the federal government in Denver, Colorado; and his friends and coaches urged him to accept an offer to teach business courses and to coach baseball and basketball at an Iowa high school. Don was flattered with all the attention; and after talking the situation over with his family, he decided to remain in Cedar Falls and become the director of the freshman men's residence hall. It was 1957; Don had just turned 22 and found himself with a good deal of responsibility and with a staff of his own. He loved the job, learned a great deal about working with other people, and understood that he needed to trust in others to accomplish many of his goals.

Don's excellent leadership and ability to work with students were recognized quickly, and the dean of students offered him a promotion to remain another year and the opportunity to pursue a master's degree. But Don had a military obligation, and thus his plans were to join the Army in the summer of 1958. After consulting with his draft board back home, he was told that the need for teachers in the state was so serious that they would defer his military obligation for a year if he accepted a teaching position. Don decided to accept a position as a teacher of disadvantaged students, some of whom were just released from reform school or prison, at a junior high school in Clinton, Iowa in the fall of 1958. It was a difficult decision for him to make, as he loved his work at Iowa State Teacher's College and was doing very well there, but he also felt an obligation to serve in the Army. However, he had always wanted to be a teacher and a coach, and Carol had accepted a position as a speech therapist in Clinton, so he accepted the position. He and Carol were married in June 1958 and both began their positions that fall. Don found his work with the disadvantaged students so challenging that he worked very long hours, trying to help the often violent students, many of whom came from very dysfunctional families. He worried so much about his job that he contracted ulcers and consequently was exempted from the military draft. Don was very committed to this job and was determined to succeed with his students, but he was unsure about the benefits of working there another year.

While he was serving as director of the freshmen men's residence hall at Iowa State Teacher's College, Don worked closely with Ruth Renaud, who directed the freshman women's residence hall. Renaud was a young master's degree graduate from Syracuse University's well-known program in student personnel administration, and she and Don had remained in contact after he left Cedar Falls. She and another Cedar Falls friend, Len Froyen, urged Don to consider the graduate program at Michigan State University, due primarily to its strong affiliation with its residence hall program. In the spring of 1959, Don drove to East Lansing and met with Wayne Tinkle, who was in charge of the program at Michigan State. After meeting Don, he was very impressed and offered him a position as director of Rather Hall, a large residence hall of over 450 students. He was also admitted to the master's degree program in student personnel administration. Don had worked extremely hard to help the disadvantaged students in his teaching job in Clinton, and it was a difficult decision to leave that position. However, he and Carol decided to go to East Lansing, with Don working in Rather Hall and Carol teaching in the public schools of St. Johns, Michigan, in September 1959. This represented another major transition for Don, as the idea of being away in Michigan was a difficult decision for his family back in Iowa to understand.

> **Don was well known at Michigan State for his incredible energy, his willingness to deal openly with difficult issues, the long hours he worked, and his honest dedication to students.**

Although Don was assigned to Rather Hall, which had a reputation for serious disciplinary problems for several years, he felt very fortunate to be at Michigan State and was excited about the opportunities there. Through his hard work, caring attitude, and willingness to make tough decisions, he earned the support of the students and the respect of his supervisors, Wayne Tinkle and John Truitt. Michigan State had been admitted to the Big Ten conference only a few years before Don arrived in East Lansing. The institution was growing very rapidly and because of its dynamic president, John A. Hannah, was among the most innovative large universities in the country. Don was very stimulated by the quality of the student affairs staff and thrived on the fast-paced activity at the institution. When Michigan State opened Case Hall, a new facility for 1,200 students in 1961, Don was selected as the first head resident for South Case Hall. The innovative hall included 12 regular classrooms, science teaching laboratories, 18 faculty offices, and a branch of the university's main library. It was a bold and exciting new venture in higher education, and it attracted considerable attention throughout the country. Freshmen and sophomores lived in the hall and took at least half of their general education courses from faculty who taught in the hall and were officed there. Don loved working with the students and faculty in this new living-learning facility, and his ability to develop positive relations with faculty in Case Hall served him very well in his future career as a senior student affairs officer (SSAO). During an incredible period of the next 8 years, Michigan State was to construct eight more of these large, living-learning residence halls, a decision that was to transform the way undergraduate courses were taught at the university, and one that was to affect the development of student affairs on the campus as well.

After only one year as head resident adviser in South Case Hall, Don's supervisor, Wayne Tinkle, left Michigan State to become dean at Marquette University; and to Don's surprise, Don was selected to succeed him as director of residence hall programs in the summer of 1962. He had only completed his master's degree at Michigan State in 1961, and there were others within the large residence hall staff who had more years of experience than Don. However, those who had observed Don's work, especially in South Case Hall, were impressed with his organization, his positive relations with faculty and students, his ability to develop programs with staff, and his hard work. President John Hannah was strongly committed to the idea of the living-learning residence halls, and he knew that Don Adams was the person to lead this exciting and growing program. By the time Don left Michigan State in 1969, Michigan State had the largest residence hall program in the country, providing housing to 22,000 students; and Don supervised a staff that included more than 350 RAs and over 100 professional staff.

During the years Don was at Michigan State, the institution also created three undergraduate residential colleges—James Madison College, Lyman A. Briggs College, and Justin Morrill College in the residence halls. Due to Don's leadership, the student affairs staff and functions in these residential colleges were well represented, and Don was intimately associated with the academic programs and deans of these new endeavors. This experience proved to Don that teaching and student development were compatible, and it provided him with valuable lessons in how to work with Provosts and faculty later in his career.

Don's wife, Carol, gave birth to their first two sons, Greg and Garth, in 1961 and 1963 in East Lansing. Their third son, Matthew, was born in 1971 after Don and Carol were at Drake. At the same time, Don was pursuing his doctoral degree at Michigan State, which he completed under the direction of Walter F. Johnson in 1965. His dissertation focused on the student subcultures at Michigan State and the learning opportunities in residential settings, an idea that was to become an important part of his work throughout his career.

Don was well known at Michigan State for his incredible energy, his willingness to deal openly with difficult issues, the long hours he worked, and his honest dedication to students. He hired a large number of professional staff during the 8 years he served as the director of residence hall programs, many of whom went on to distinguished careers in student affairs and higher education. Don was very close to students and staff, being convinced that this personal approach to his work was a key to his success. Some of his supervisors warned him of the dangers of getting too close to students, but Don knew how he could best do his work, and he took pride in knowing the names of hundreds of students. These were fast-moving times in higher education; there was turmoil in the country with the civil rights movement and the war in Vietnam, enrollments were exploding, and professional opportunities opened up rapidly. Before Don completed his doctoral degree, his former supervisor, John Truitt, had left for Indiana State to become vice president for student affairs; and he asked Don to join him as dean of men in 1963. Don declined, but he now understood that others viewed him as an excellent leader. A short while later, Michigan State created a new branch institution close to Detroit (now Oakland University), and Don was invited to become its first vice president for student affairs. He was tempted by this offer; but the size, growth, and excitement of his position at Michigan State caused him to remain as director of residence hall programs. Michigan State's enrollment increased from 16,000 students in 1958 to 44,000 students in 1969, and Don could not imagine anything more challenging than this dynamic institution.

Don experienced some very tough problems at Michigan State, especially in the watershed year of 1968. The emotionally draining issues demanded long hours; and sometimes ugly confrontations took place among students, police, and university officials. As usual, Don was a very visible leader, one of the few among the administration who were trusted by students. By 1969, John Hannah had retired as president, and it was in many ways the end of an era at Michigan State; the residence hall building period was over, excellent programs and staff were in place, and Don was ready for a new challenge. Many of his colleagues urged him to remain in East Lansing, as they were convinced he would eventually become the vice president for student affairs there. However, even though Don was young, he had established a firm principle for himself in his career—he would never wait for any position. He wanted to determine his own career, on his own terms, and was confident that he had the background and the experience to do this. Among several opportunities that were presented to him that year, a call from Dr. Paul Sharp, president of Drake University in Des Moines, Iowa intrigued Don the most. He knew about the institution, of course, in his home state; and as a private, urban institution, it was very different from Michigan State.

Moreover, Don was very impressed with President Sharp and when he visited the campus, he quickly realized that it presented a unique set of challenges to him. Students and faculty he met during a second visit to the Drake campus were so impressed with Don that he received several phone calls from them when he returned to East Lansing, urging him to accept the position. He knew he was ready to be an SSAO, and he was very enthusiastic about the opportunity. In the late spring of 1969, he decided to accept the position as vice president for student life, and he and his family moved to Des Moines, Iowa. He was 33 years old.

When Don assumed his duties at Drake in 1969, there was great unrest in the country. Drake had already experienced its share of student protests and turmoil, and relationships between students and the institution were characterized by distrust and anger. Located in an urban setting, Drake's relationships with its African American students and the local community were also strained. The student affairs staff was relatively small and did not have a history of reaching out to students beyond traditional settings. When Don had visited the campus for his interviews, he had spent many hours with various student groups and knew the students had very high expectations for him. As soon as he arrived at Drake as the new vice president, he began meeting with students from all areas of the campus, in a variety of settings, on and off the campus. He listened carefully to their concerns, talked about the mission of the institution and how the students could be involved in institutional affairs, and especially shared his own values and thoughts about higher education with them.

Keenly aware that Drake was a private institution and that all of his experience had been in large, public universities, Don worked hard to understand the history, culture, and traditions of his new institution. He found that the same values of hard work, honesty, openness, and trust were the key to his success as a leader. In only a few months at Drake, Don had won the confidence and trust of most of the student groups and their attitude toward the institution became much more constructive. This proved to be critically important in the spring of his first academic year at Drake, as the May 4, 1970 Kent State shootings occurred; and without the base of support Don had built with key student leaders and student groups, the institution surely would have had to cancel its classes for the remainder of that year. He spent much of his time trying to bridge the communication gap between students and other administrators, and especially between students and the board of trustees. He was able to convince President Sharp and the board to establish a standing committee on student life; and through this group, he, the board chair, and the student body president began a constructive process of increasing understanding between students and board members.

Don's basic faith in the willingness of young people to do positive things when treated with respect and trust paid off. When there were raucous discussions on campus Don assumed the role of mediator and conciliator. He never lost his faith that if people—young and old, black and white, male and female—could get to know each other well in the spirit of trust and honesty, then genuine friendships would result. He became well known as a tireless, enthusiastic, and positive leader who literally willed good things to happen by his determination and his belief in others. He got to know large numbers of students personally, and he often challenged them individually to take responsible action. Don was also not hesitant to confront students when their behavior violated stated rules and regulations. He made it clear that he expected high standards and held students accountable when they did not meet these standards. A former student body president of that era commented many years later, "We admired Don Adams because of his honesty and his commitment to our activities; we sometimes disagreed with him, but we always knew exactly where he stood. His personal interest in each of us made a big difference in our lives."

> **After many years of success as vice president for student life, the program at Drake became well known and Don was frequently sought after by other institutions as a consultant in their student affairs programs.**

Don was so visible and enthusiastic in his first year at Drake as vice president that he made some of his own staff feel unsettled. He had no intent on usurping their roles with students; but he wanted his own actions with students, faculty, and staff to serve as a model for how they should reach out to the campus and community. For some of them, Don's presence stimulated them to do new and positive things as professionals; for others, the expectations for change were too dramatic and they decided to step down or sought other, less daunting assignments. Don left no doubt about what he expected from his staff, and these were the same things he expected from himself—hard work, honesty, long hours, and a positive approach to students. Drake was a fine institution; but as a private university located in a relatively small state, it needed to work extra hard to attract and retain outstanding students. Don knew that if Drake were to continue to succeed, it would have to offer a high quality of student life, and he was determined that this would be the case— from new student orientation all the way to graduation!

In his first 2 years at Drake, Don was able to revamp the orientation program, expand financial aid and scholarship programs, renovate residence halls, revive the Greek system, and streamline the organizational structure of the student life division. He became a trusted leader on the campus and, most importantly, helped to build positive student–institution relationships during a time of great unrest. He loved the challenges at Drake and believed that more good things could happen in the future. Then President Sharp left to accept the president's position at the University of Oklahoma, and he wanted Don to join him as the new vice president for the university community. In addition to student affairs, Don would have responsibility for the large intercollegiate athletic program at Oklahoma. Don had only been at Drake for 2 years—he had not come to Drake with any plan to go elsewhere and had no time for those who used one institution as a "stepping stone" to another. He loved working for President Sharp and was flattered at the offer, but after thinking about what he had started at Drake, and especially about his many close relationships with students, he knew he wanted to remain in his current position and continue to improve the student life program at Drake. It was a very difficult decision for Don, but afterwards he knew he had done the right thing. He would have many other invitations to become an SSAO at other institutions in the years ahead, and opportunities to become a president as well, but Don declined to leave Drake, knowing that his own priorities were with students and with the mission of the institution.

After many years of success as vice president for student life, the program at Drake became well known and Don was frequently sought after by other institutions as a consultant in their student affairs programs. In 1985, Don was asked by his president, Dr. Michael Ferrari, to assume responsibility for admissions, registration, financial aid, recruitment, and retention; and his title was changed to vice president for enrollment management and student life. This function was critical to the future of Drake, especially with rising costs and competition from other public colleges and universities in the region. Don did not have direct experience in enrollment management, but President Ferrari had confidence in his leadership and knew that Don would achieve success in this important responsibility. After visiting with the best enrollment management authorities he could find and studying the limited amount of useful research available, Don established a program that involved every person at the university in a coordinated effort to build positive relationships with students and their parents. He argued that "there were not tasks to be done, but relationships to be built!" During the next 10 years, Drake met and exceeded its enrollment and retention goals and, equally as important, developed positive relationships with its students, creating very loyal and supportive alumni in the process. The enrollment management program at Drake became widely known and respected, and many other institutions visited the campus to learn about how they could improve their own efforts.

During his years as vice president at Drake, a university center, a recreation center, athletic facilities, Greek houses, two multicultural centers, and career development programs were built. The student life program was closely linked to the academic mission of the institution, and relationships between students and the university were greatly enhanced. Don knows that his longevity in his position made it possible for him to accomplish many of the things he did, and the support and freedom given to him by the four presidents with whom he worked enabled him to exercise his own special style of personalized leadership.

While Don was building the highly successful student life program at Drake, he somehow found the time to be a prominent national leader in the profession as well. He was very active with the North Central Association of Colleges and Schools, serving as a consultant evaluator at over 25 institutions, and then as commissioner at large during 1984–1988. He was invited by the American Council on Education to serve as a consultant to dozens of colleges and universities about financial aid policy and practices, and he was selected to participate in the Fulbright Commission to study universities in Germany. He was a frequent keynote speaker at regional and national conferences and was presented with the first Distinguished Professional Award from the Iowa Student Personnel Association in 1989. He was the associate editor of the *NASPA Journal* in 1981–1983, a regional vice president of NASPA from 1974–1977, and chairman of that organization's governance committee in 1971–1973. This latter assignment was especially challenging, as NASPA was in transition and there were various groups within the organization with strongly opposing views about its future direction. Don was asked to chair this 2-year effort because of his reputation for fairness, honesty, and ability to bring people together effectively. In 1977–1978, Don was the elected president of NASPA. He was presented with the Fred Turner Award for distinguished service to the profession in 1984; and in 1992 NASPA bestowed its highest honor on Don, the Scott Goodnight Award for outstanding performance as a dean. In the year 2000, the Drake University Athletic Association established a special award in Don's name, called the "Donald V. Adams Spirit of Drake Award," to be presented to an outstanding faculty member who demonstrates the same qualities of enthusiasm, dedication, and commitment to the university that Don has. At the annual Drake Relays this spring, the largest event of the year on the campus, a group of former students announced the creation of a special educational endowment in Don's name, to be used to support student leadership programs at the institution.

Don Adams is perhaps the epitome of a student affairs administrator who leads with the heart. One of his presidents, Dr. Michael Ferrari, said of Don,

> This is a man who does not covet the limelight. He has always been ready to give credit to his staff, even when he was the driving force, not they, for a project. Yet, he was always ready to accept blame when things went occasionally awry. He is a thoroughly decent, honorable, and honest person. He sets the

standard very high for himself and models and encourages others to meet or exceed it. His word really is his bond. One may disagree with him but never seriously question his motives. He has never forgotten his friends and colleagues and has never forgotten his roots. At many institutions, there are always a few people—very few—who have had a significant role in the life of the university over an extended period of time. When it comes to Drake University, it is embodied in the life of the sustained high quality and selfless service of Don Adams. His impact for the last third of a century at Drake has made it the strong university it is today as much as any single person or factor (Personal communication to author, May 15, 2000).

In 1995, after serving for 26 years as the SSAO at Drake, Don stepped aside from this position and was appointed executive assistant to the president and secretary of the university. He works directly with the board of trustees, with key alumni and donors, and with community leaders in continuing efforts to enhance the university's programs. Many of Drake's graduates have become state and national leaders; with the university located in the capitol of Iowa, it is in the center of public activity. When I visited with him on his campus in March 2000, he had just returned from a meeting with a former governor, two chief executive officers of Fortune 500 companies who are members of the board of trustees, and the Drake president. I could not help remarking, "Don, it's been a long journey for you from that tiny town of Liscomb, Iowa to that meeting!" Indeed it has, and along the way thousands of students have benefited from being part of Don's exciting journey as well.

Chapter 3

David A. Ambler
University of Kansas

As Dave Ambler walks into a room in the Kansas Union where 15 student leaders are engaged in a raucous debate about a campus issue, almost immediately, the noise level decreases and the students walk over to greet him. He smiles, shakes their hands, calls each student by name, and invites them to sit down for a discussion. There is an obvious respect among the students for Dave Ambler. During the 2-hour meeting, Dave is very quiet, but his presence encourages the students to work out their differences. Later that evening, Dave and his wife, Mary Kate, host these same students at their house for dinner. On the beautiful campus of the University of Kansas in Lawrence, Dave Ambler's thoughtful, considerate, and gracious leadership as vice chancellor for student affairs has benefited students for the past 23 years.

David A. Ambler earned his B.S. degree in business administration from Indiana University in 1959, his masters in public administration and political science from Indiana University in 1961, and his EdD in higher education administration from Indiana University in 1966. After serving for 6 months in the U.S. Army Reserves, where he ultimately achieved the rank of captain, he became the head counselor in the Graduate Residence Center at Indiana in 1961 and, for the next 2 years, served as program assistant and then assistant director in the Residence Halls Counseling and Activities Office at Indiana. In 1965, he was a research associate for the survey team for the Kentucky Commission on Higher Education. After completing his doctoral studies at Indiana in 1966, he was appointed dean of men at Kent State University. The next year he served as the associate dean of students and director of residence halls at Kent State. In 1969–1970, he was the assistant vice president and dean for student residence life at Kent State, and from 1970–1977 he was the vice president for educational and student services at Kent State. In 1977, he accepted the position of vice chancellor for student affairs and associate professor of education at the University of Kansas. He has taught graduate courses in higher education at the University of Kansas; and his writing on organization, management structures, and model practices have contributed to the professional literature in student affairs.

Dave Ambler has been the elected president of both the Ohio and the Kansas Association of Student Personnel Administrators, and he served as chairperson of the National Association of Student Personnel Administrators - American College Personnel Association (NASPA-ACPA) Joint Task Force on Professional Preparation and Practice in 1987. He has been a member of the executive committee of the Student Affairs Council of the National Association of State Universities and Land Grant Colleges, a member of the *NASPA Journal* editorial board, and the ACPA Monograph editorial board. He has served as the coordinator of the National Vice Presidents for Student Affairs organization, and from 1996–1998 he was the president of the NASPA Foundation board of directors. In 1987, he received the Robert H. Shaffer Distinguished Alumni Award from Indiana University, and in 2000 he received the Fred Turner Award for Outstanding Service from NASPA. He has also served as a consultant to several colleges and universities and is a frequent presenter at regional and national conferences.

Dave Ambler was born in Hammond, Indiana in 1937. Located in extreme northwest Indiana, Hammond was an industrial city with a diverse, working class population. Dave was the third of four children in his family, and both of his parents grew up in the area and graduated from high school in 1929 and 1930. Dave's father obtained a job with the Sinclair Refining Company in Hammond after high school, and he worked there for 44 years until he retired. Dave learned a strong work ethic from his father, who also sold insurance at night and trained himself to repair watches at home. Dave's mother worked in the high school library and was also a school secretary. His parents were able to remain employed during the years of the Great Depression. Neither of them completed college, but Dave's father enrolled for some courses at the Indiana extension center in the area. Dave is quite interested in genealogy and knows that the Ambler family was in Virginia by 1710, eventually moved to Ohio, and then to Indiana, where they pursued farming. He plans to meet relatives he has identified in England sometime during the next year. Dave's family was quite typical of those living in Hammond. Although they did not have much money, Dave never thought of himself as poor. His parents were active socially and were both involved in community leadership and service. His mother was president of the PTA for many years and an officer in the Girl Scouts. His father was the head elder at his church for many years, so Dave understood the value of involvement early in his life, although he emphasized that his parents never pushed him into any activity.

Dave remembers World War II, as one of his uncles went overseas; and he recalls the blackouts and air raid practices, which were considered very important in Hammond due to the large concentration of oil and steel production facilities. Dave has kept some of the ration books used by his family as mementos of that time. During his youth, Dave's activities reflected the values of hard work of his family. He worked in various part-time jobs and delivered the *Hammond Times* for 4 years as a paperboy. His father was an avid fisherman and hunter and loved the outdoors, and consequently Dave became a member of the Boy Scouts. He loved camping and scouting trips to area lakes, and he excelled in his scouting work. Although he liked sports, he preferred camping and fishing, and he and his family enjoyed vacations in Ludington, Michigan during many summers. The Ambler family was always active in their church and Dave became an excellent singer as a member of his school choir for years. He later joined an octet, and this interracial singing group performed at many locations in the area. One day, while he was still a young teenager, Dave's octet was invited to sing for a function at a private country club; when some members of the club discovered that three members of the octet were African Americans, they told them they were not welcome there. When all members of the octet refused to perform that day and walked away, it was a defining moment for Dave. He had learned basic values of fair play and consideration for others from his mother, and consequently Dave was always very sensitive to and respectful of others' feelings. Dave grew up in a very diverse community; and although it was not always peaceful, he learned about human differences at an early age and about the values of tolerance, understanding, and patience.

In high school, Dave's ability to work hard was rewarded when he was appointed the editor of the school newspaper when he was just a sophomore. The thoroughness that he would become well known for as a senior student affairs officer (SSAO) was evidenced in his job as editor. He would pick up the 1,500 copies of the weekly paper at the printer's, take them home on the bus, fold each paper individually, and then make sure they were distributed at school the next day on time. He also worked 3 nights a week at a local diner and during one summer, at the local telephone company, replaced old phones with the new dial phones of the time. In this job, he found that much of his time was spent listening to people talk to him about their problems. His warm, friendly, and nonjudgmental approach to others was already recognized and appreciated. He was active in school activities, especially in student government and music, and discovered early in life that he was successful in human relations—he seemed able to bring others together, help them become friends, and simultaneously help them accomplish their goals. He became the elected president of the Christian Youth Fellowship and attended brief church summer camps during his high school years. For a while during high school, Dave thought he might want to become a minister, as he had been involved in community service activities and genuinely liked the idea of helping others. In his senior year, was elected to the position of director of student activities for his high school of 2,000 students. Dave later joked, "I didn't know it at the time, of course, but this was my first job in student affairs!" He was a good student in high school, but he said that it was his older sister whose excellent academic work served as the primary stimulus for his achievement. She was the first member of her family to go to college, and it was her influence that caused Dave to follow her to Indiana University in the fall of 1955.

Dave had the support of his family to attend college, but he never felt any pressure from them to do so. He knew he would need to provide the bulk of his college expenses himself, so he used the money he had made while working during his high school years, and he continued to work while he was at Bloomington. He was not sure about what he wanted to study in college, so he enrolled in business administration, assuming that this major might lead to a good job after graduation. Having been so involved in student activities in high school, and not very confident about his academic ability, Dave was determined as a college freshman to concentrate on his studies and not to join any student groups. He worked hard on his studies, but his interest in service and his love of social interaction quickly got him involved in campus life. He was elected vice president of the freshman class at Indiana, became an officer in his residence hall, and was active in his ROTC unit. When rushed by the fraternities, Dave declined their invitations, as he saw elitism and separatism there and did not want to be a part of it. Later that year, he participated in a small demonstration with some friends, protesting a racial discrimination policy in a local Bloomington business. Dave was never an aggressive flag waver on social issues, but his basic sense of fairness and respect for others continued to guide his actions. With his interest in music and singing, Dave was greatly stimulated by the world-class performing arts programs at Bloomington; and he took advantage of the many opportunities to attend concerts, plays, and the opera. He remembers being invited to a special dinner as a student, where he found himself sitting at a table next to Rudolf Bing of the Metropolitan Opera! Dave said, "Higher education worked its magic on me—I was a first-generation college student, and I was awed and stimulated by my classes and by the extracurriculum!" Dave has never lost his enthusiasm for the uplifting, liberating force of higher education and, as a student affairs leader, has always worked to provide students with the same exciting experiences he had as a student at Indiana. Dave's leadership was recognized by others as a student when he was elected president of his large residence hall and later was an officer in the campus-wide residence hall association. In his senior year, he was selected to be a residence hall counselor and worked for James Lyons, who was the associate resident head counselor. Lyons was later to become the SSAO at Stanford and a close colleague of Dave's. Dave worked about 10 hours a week throughout college in the dining hall and during the summers, in the refinery back in Hammond.

Dave did well in his business administration classes; but he found that he strongly preferred his psychology, political science, history, and philosophy courses. He spent some time in college wrestling with his own religious and philosophical beliefs, and this experience later convinced him of the importance of the values clarification process for many undergraduate students. When he was ready to graduate from Indiana University in 1959, he was unsure of his future direction. He was fortunate to have had an excellent mentor, Robert Crane, who was later to become a student affairs dean at Miami University in Oxford, Ohio. Dave worked for Crane in the residence hall program at Indiana, and he was introduced to the field of student affairs by his mentor. But Dave had also completed 4 years of the ROTC program, and at graduation he was commissioned as a second lieutenant in the United States Army Infantry. He was assigned to a 6-month program and was sent to Ft. Benning, Georgia and then to Ft. Knox, Kentucky. Dave's experience in the Army was quite positive and, among other things, he used that time as an opportunity to consider what his future might be.

Dave applied to law school at Indiana and was accepted, but then he decided to enroll in the master's degree program in public administration in the political science department. He completed his master's degree at Indiana in 1961, and he helped support himself by working in the residence halls. By this time, he was convinced that a career in student affairs was what he wanted; and he received a lot of encouragement in this regard from Betty Greenleaf and Bob Shaffer, both of whom became mentors and close friends of Dave's in future years. Betty, who directed the residence halls at Indiana, offered Dave a position as the head counselor of the large Graduate Residence Center. Dave also was admitted to the doctoral program in higher education administration. But at this same time, he received a phone call from the president of Bethany College in West Virginia, inviting him to come to the campus to consider becoming the dean of students! Dave knew of the college because it was associated with his Disciples of Christ Church, and his mentor, Bob Crane, had recommended Dave. Dave was astounded that he might be considered for such a position, given his young age and the fact that he only had very brief experience in residence halls. He decided to decline this opportunity and accepted the head counselor position in the Graduate Residence Center at Indiana, and he began his doctoral program.

Dave was excited with his work at Indiana and, as he became more involved with his graduate study, was convinced he had made the right career decision by selecting student affairs. After only a year and a half in the Graduate Residence Center, Betty Greenleaf invited Dave to become the assistant director of residence hall counseling and activities, a job he accepted and held until completing his doctorate in 1966. He was responsible for 12 large residence halls, as well as the hiring of all staff and the professional development program. During the first year of his doctoral program, in 1962, Dave met Mary Kate Harris, a Marshall University graduate who received her master's degree in remedial reading at Indiana, and they were married in the summer of 1963. They moved into the married student housing apartments at Indiana, and Mary Kate taught at the university lab school.

These were very busy times for Dave and Mary Kate, as Dave continued his active reserve status with the Army, which involved summer and weekend obligations. He also had the opportunity to work with M.M. Chambers on a statewide study of higher education in Kentucky, and his own dissertation was a part of this large investigation. By the time Dave completed his graduate work in 1966, the country was in social and political turmoil, and he had already witnessed a good deal of campus unrest at Indiana. He had also established a reputation as a thoughtful, caring, and effective leader; and he was in demand for professional positions at several institutions.

After thinking about various professional opportunities, Dave decided to visit both Colorado State University and Kent State University and was offered a position at each of these institutions. He liked both of them but finally decided in the summer of 1966 to go to Kent State; now, reflecting back on that decision, Dave suspects that he and Mary Kate went there because it was closer to both of their homes in Indiana and West Virginia. Dave loved Indiana University and was offered a position to remain there after completing his graduate program, but he knew the best thing for his career was to move to another institution. Kent State University had experienced phenomenal growth, with its enrollment having increased from 6,000 to 18,000 in less than 10 years. Some outstanding staff had worked in student affairs at Kent State, but when Dave arrived in 1966 as the assistant dean for residence halls changes were taking place rapidly, and within 6 months he was named acting dean of men, and then named dean of men. In the next year, he was asked to move to the position of associate dean of students and director of residence halls, and in 1969 he was appointed as the assistant vice president and dean for student residence life. Dave's impressive skills in human relations were quickly recognized by Bob Matson, the SSAO, and by Robert White, the president.

Kent State University is located in an industrial quadrant of Northeastern Ohio, and in the late 1960s many of its students were the sons and daughters of working-class citizens. Almost 20 percent of the students were minorities, and Dave's background in Hammond, Indiana was quite similar to that of much of the student body. He developed close and personal relationships with many students and was strongly committed to assisting them on the campus. Dave had been at Kent State for only a few weeks when he discovered that the same difficult social problems and issues he had been dealing with at Indiana were also at Kent State. The African American students, declaring that Kent State was a "white supremacist" institution, staged a walk out, resulting in new efforts by the university and student affairs staff to establish a human relations program, something in which Dave was a key participant. Because most of Kent States' students came from working-class families, many of them had relatives or close friends who were in Vietnam, or who had already returned from a tour of duty there. Moreover, most of the male students had deferments from the military draft simply because they were in college, and these factors combined to create extremely bitter feelings toward the U.S. government. Dave and many other student affairs staff were spending many nights on the campus, sleeping in their offices, in efforts to keep the volatile protests from getting completely out of hand. The university itself was an available target of the "establishment" for the students, especially anything at the institution thought to be directly associated with the war effort, such as ROTC or scientific research. The year 1968 had been one the most tumultuous of the century, with Martin Luther King, Jr. and Robert F. Kennedy being assassinated, the Tet Offensive in Vietnam, and the divisive election of Richard M. Nixon as president. As the 1969–1970 academic year began, Dave and his student affairs colleagues at Kent State, along with many others around the country, worried about the future as protests against the war on the campuses and in the cities became larger and more violent.

> **His ability to work hard, his basic faith and trust in the goodness of most people, and his determination to help students and the university succeed in this crisis enabled Dave to make the decision to stay.**

It is perhaps ironic that with so much national attention being paid to the student protests of this period that many very positive educational developments were taking place on the campuses at the same time, but received very little coverage in the media. At Kent State, the enrollment continued to grow, new academic programs were created, new academic and student affairs facilities were built, many outstanding new staff were hired, and new student service programs (e.g., child care, drug abuse prevention) were established. It was an extremely busy and challenging time for Dave, who had assumed substantially more responsibility in just 3 years. Moreover, his wife had given birth to their two daughters, Laura and Sarah, in 1966 and 1969. As Dave joked years later, "I was extremely fortunate to have such a supportive wife, as I was not home very often and rarely saw my daughters go to bed at night."

Dave was responsible for hiring many professional staff at Kent State during his first 3 years there, especially when he became the assistant vice chancellor. He said that traditional job descriptions were set aside during those years, and a typical question he asked candidates for positions was "how much black coffee do you drink?" If staff were not inclined or able to deal with the long hours and the emotionally draining challenges of working in student affairs, Dave knew they should not be hired. Years later, reflecting his typical compassion, he said, "For many staff during these years, the pressures were just too great, and they left their positions; this did not mean that they were not good professionals—not everyone was well suited to work in such difficult, and sometimes dangerous, circumstances."

The tragedy that took place on May 4, 1970 at Kent State, resulting in the deaths of four students and the wounding of nine others, produced unprecedented national turmoil and continues in the nation's collective consciousness now, 30 years later. The incidents of that terrible day have been chronicled in great detail and need no repeating here. Dave Ambler was the assistant vice chancellor at Kent State at the time, and of course various political agendas in the state and nation at the time resulted in the Ohio National Guard being placed in charge of the campus, with university personnel removed from any role in deciding the fate of the institution. Nevertheless, Dave and many other staff were on the campus, working around the clock with students and student leaders. Following the incident on May 4, the university closed for the rest of the semester, the National Guard remained on the campus, and the students were all ordered to go home. Everyone wondered what the future of the university might be and whether it would be possible for the institution to resume operations again.

National attention focused on the tragedy at Kent State and, during the summer of 1970, Dave and other student affairs staff met frequently to do what they could to assist the university to open classes in the fall. Bob Matson, the vice president for student affairs, resigned on August 1 to become president of a small northeastern college, and President White asked Dave to serve as the acting vice chancellor. Dave had only been at Kent State 4 years, and he was just 33 years old. It was the most difficult period of Dave's career, and he honestly wondered if he was up to the challenge. He also wondered how he happened to find himself in this situation, certainly one of the most difficult ever faced by any student affairs leader. After meeting with the student affairs staff and talking the situation over in great detail with his wife, Dave decided to accept the position as acting vice president for student affairs in August 1970. His ability to work hard, his basic faith and trust in the goodness of most people, and his determination to help students and the university succeed in this crisis enabled Dave to make the decision to stay. He could have turned his back on this situation and easily could have found another student affairs position at another institution; however, he felt a moral obligation to face the issues and to work toward a reconciliation among the many factions of dissenters. Dave knew the students, had faith in their willingness to move forward, and knew that these students needed strong and dependable leaders to help them in the years ahead. Looking back on those years now, Dave reflects, "There was no place to hide, and my commitment to democratic values was so strong that I refused to believe that we could not bring about an eventual reconciliation."

With the entire country watching, Kent State resumed classes in the fall of 1970, and it seemed that every week there was a national report on television about the several inquiries and investigations being made of the tragedy. But on the campus itself, the faculty, staff, and students worked very hard to make the institution whole again, to begin the healing, and to concentrate on the educational process. The controversies about the May 4, 1970 event continued for many years, involving politics, legislation, law suits, contested memorials, and court decisions. Dave was viewed by students, faculty, and staff as a trusted, thoughtful, and caring administrator who did a great deal to help people come together during the difficult 1970–1971 year; as a result, he was asked to become the permanent vice chancellor for student affairs in November 1970. Dave was strongly committed to the university and its future, and he decided to accept the appointment.

It is doubtful that any new senior student affairs officer has ever faced such a daunting set of challenges as Dave Ambler did at Kent State, beginning in the fall of 1970. Dave called a meeting during the opening of the semester of a large group of student leaders and the entire student affairs staff. He did not know what to expect in terms of the attitudes of the students after they had been away for 4 months. It was a highly emotional meeting, where Dave shared his thoughts, faith, and hope in the future. His empathy for the students, his reputation for honesty and fairness, and his ability to listen and respect others' views were greatly appreciated by everyone. The meeting was televised and parts of it appeared on the network television news. Dave's determined and compassionate approach won wide support and gave this 33-year-old SSAO added confidence that he could provide the needed leadership. Dave also met with alumni groups around the state in efforts to increase understanding and gain support for the institution. These sessions were often difficult, but they demonstrated that the university was genuine about its efforts to communicate openly with its constituents.

Kent State University survived this terrible tragedy, and by 1976 its enrollment was slightly larger than it had been in 1970. Glenn Olds became its new president in 1972 and was an excellent leader who helped students, faculty, staff, and the community come together. Dave benefited from working for President Olds and received his support for the many positive things he was able to accomplish in the student affairs division. A new student center was built, residence halls were constructed, a new student life program was established, and special services for minority students were created. Dave became a highly visible and respected leader at Kent State as vice president. In 1977, University of Kansas Executive Vice Chancellor Delbert Shankel urged Dave to come to Lawrence, and later commented, "One of the major reasons we hired Dave Ambler as the vice chancellor for student affairs was the impressive way in which he had restored student confidence in the aftermath of the tragedy at Kent State. I know of no other chief student affairs officer who had led his area of responsibility so effectively" (Personal communication to author, April 19, 2000).

In February 1977, after serving as vice president for student affairs at Kent State University for almost 7 years, the University of Kansas recruited Dave, and after two visits to the campus he accepted the position of vice chancellor. Leaving Kent State was not easy, as Dave was very close to students and staff and had a very large emotional investment in the institution. But he had positive feelings about what he had accomplished at Kent State, and he decided it was an appropriate time to move to a new setting. The University of Kansas had excellent resources as an institution, and Dave was attracted to the position because he was comfortable with the university's mission and felt it was possible to make major improvements in the student affairs program. He and his family moved to Lawrence in the summer of 1977.

Dave was the first SSAO at Kansas who was a career professional in the field, and he described the vice chancellor's job there as a "golden opportunity." The staff and students were eager for leadership and were very happy to have Dave there. There were 15 departments in student affairs, and all of these units reported directly to the vice chancellor when he arrived. Kansas was one of only a few large institutions whose student affairs programs was still organized around gender in 1977, and Dave began a process of changing this. He established three separate task forces—on mission and goals, on student databases, and on personnel matters. He visited individually with all the college deans, the other vice chancellors, key faculty leaders, many student leaders, and most of the members of the student affairs staff. He listened carefully to these people for almost a year before streamlining the student affairs organization, reducing the number of departments, establishing two deans' positions, and bringing into the division some new areas of responsibility. In the next few years, he was able to hire several new staff, and the outstanding professionals he has hired remain his proudest accomplishment at Kansas, as Dave believes that more than any other factor it is the high quality of his staff that have enabled the division to do positive things.

During his years as vice chancellor at Kansas, several new, small group residence halls have been constructed and others renovated; a complete renovation was made to the student union; a state-of-the-art student health center was expanded; a multicultural resource center was established; and the construction of a new student recreation center was approved. The food service, which the university runs itself, was revamped and modernized; a centralized career development center was created; and the Raymond F. Nichols League of Former Student Leaders was established. The Nichols League is a fund raising program in student affairs, which supports special leadership development opportunities for students and already has raised more than $250,000. As one of several ways to enhance better relations among students, faculty, and staff, Dave created the President's Roundtable, where each month major student leaders meet for dinner with the president, other key administrators, student affairs staff, and selected faculty to discuss campus issues and problems. In his first year at Kansas, Dave established a professional development committee, and to this day it is one of the most comprehensive staff continuing education programs in the country. He and his staff recently received approval for their proposal to create an academic minor in leadership studies for undergraduate students in cooperation with the Department of Communication Studies at the university. Courses will be taught by student affairs professionals and by faculty from communication studies in this 19-credit academic program.

In his 23 years as vice chancellor at Kansas, Dave has worked for four chancellors, with five chief academic affairs officers, and several senior business officers. He emphasized the importance of understanding the beliefs and special skills of chancellors and adjusting to these in ways that benefit the institution and place the chancellor in a favorable light with students. Dave's work with senior business officers was enhanced by his own undergraduate degree in business administration and especially by the sound fiscal management of residence halls, the student union, the food service, and other major units within student affairs. He felt very comfortable in his relations with the five academic officers with whom he worked, always seeking ways that student affairs could be supportive of the academic mission of the institution, not competitive with it. He was well respected for his ability to get along with everyone, his ability to get things done while at the same time bringing people together, and for his sincere dedication to students. Dave continues to attend student senate meetings, which often continue until 1:00 in the morning. "With students, we say a lot to them about how much we care about what they are doing just by being there," Dave said.

While he was building the highly successful student affairs division at Kansas, Dave was also a very visible leader within the larger profession. His colleagues elected him president of the Kansas Association of Student Personnel Administrators in 1982. He served as a member of the NASPA Journal editorial board from 1987–1990, and he chaired the NASPA-ACPA Joint Task Force on Professional Preparation and Practice from 1987–1989. He was selected for this latter role because of his outstanding ability to bridge the gap between groups with different perspectives and simultaneously achieve very substantive results. He was elected to the executive committee of the Student Affairs Council of the National Association of State Universities and Land Grant Colleges; and he has been a very active member of the NASPA Foundation board of directors, serving as its president from 1996–1998. He has been a member of the National Vice Presidents Group for 16 years and serves as its coordinator. He has been a consultant to several colleges and universities and was honored by his Alma Mater, Indiana University, with the Robert H. Shaffer Distinguished Alumni Award in 1987. He received the first Citation for Leadership and Achievement in Student Services Award from the senior class at the University of Kansas in 1987, and he was named a "Pillar of the Profession" by NASPA in 2000. At the national conference in March 2000, NASPA presented Dave with the Fred Turner Award for outstanding service to the profession. He has also been an active community leader, serving on the boards of the Lawrence Chamber of Commerce, the Friends of the KU Theatre, the Hilltop Child Care Center, and the United Way of Lawrence. He also served as the president of the Rotary Club of Lawrence in 1988.

Dave had several opportunities to move to other institutions during his years at the University of Kansas, including invitations to consider presidencies. But he decided to remain in Lawrence, feeling very committed to the mission of the institution and to his staff and students. He is convinced that being in his position for 23 years enabled him to accomplish many things he might not have been able to do without the perspective of time. He became an effective leader by his hard work, his care for others, his integrity, his willingness to listen, and his ability to make decisions that improved the quality of life at the university. He is widely known and respected for his kind, considerate, and quiet approach to others; his modesty; and his habit of always giving credit and thanks to others. Behind his genuinely calm demeanor is a man with passionate views about higher education, high ethical standards, and a tenacious determination to do positive things for students. Reflecting on his modest roots in the industrial city of Hammond, Indiana, Dave said, "I have been blessed by the liberating and uplifting world of higher education!" In turn, thousands of students at the University of Kansas have been blessed by the work of David Allen Ambler.

Chapter 4

Carl Edwin Anderson
Howard University

C arl Anderson and Howard University are almost synonymous. Few individuals in the university's history have been known or admired by more students. Carl's intelligence, wit, humanity, and energy are legendary on the campus. Even a decade after his retirement, most people cannot keep up with his many activities as he continues to work for the benefit of the institution, its students, and the community.

Carl Anderson earned his B.A. degree in political science in 1956 from Southern Illinois University, and his M.A. degree in student affairs in higher education in 1958 from the same institution. While working at Howard University, he completed his EdD degree in higher education administration at the University of Maryland in 1969. He worked in the residence hall program as a graduate assistant at Southern Illinois University for 2 years. After graduation, he took a position in residence life at Howard University. Two years later, in 1960, he became director of student activities at Howard and served in that position until 1965, when he was appointed associate dean of students. From 1969 until his retirement in 1990, Carl served as the vice president for student affairs at Howard University. He was a leader in National Association of Student Personnel Administrators (NASPA), having served on its national board of directors. He received the Scott Goodnight Award from NASPA for outstanding performance as a dean in 1990. He worked with the Ford Foundation for many years and was instrumental in the establishment of that organization's national graduate fellowships for minority students. He served on the board of directors of the American College Personnel Association and as president of the Kappa Scholarship Endowment Fund, Inc.

Carl was born in St. Louis in 1934. He was the sixth of 11 children, his father was a church sexton, and his mother was a homemaker. Neither of his parents had graduated from high school, and Carl was their only child to go on to college. He attended the segregated Dunbar Elementary school as a young boy and immediately was identified by his teachers as bright and hard working. Carl described his youth as happy, with relatives and friends everywhere. His teachers knew his parents and often came by the house, encouraging Carl in his schoolwork. "It was almost impossible to get into trouble when I was a kid— everyone in the neighborhood knew you and kept track of you!," he said. He began working after school at age 10, and as he joked recently, "I never stopped!" Carl delivered newspapers, organized talent shows in the neighborhood, delivered packages for a drug store, worked as a car hop, sold tickets for a variety of community and school events, mowed lawns, and sold flowers on Mother's Day. It seemed to everyone that Carl had boundless energy and an entrepreneurial spirit. He said his family was poor, but he never thought of himself in that way. Carl was determined to excel in all that he did, and said even as a young boy that he only wanted something if he deserved it.

Carl was an active leader in his church, and he was often called upon to represent his school and speak at public meetings. He was highly competitive, excelled in his academic work, and loved athletics. Carl was a leader in all aspects of school; this became most evident at Charles Sumner High School in St. Louis, where he was president of the student council, active in many speaking and community activities, twice elected president of his class, and elected to Boy's State in Missouri. Carl recalled that when he attended Boy's State in Jefferson City, the state capitol, the African American student delegates were not able to stay in the same hotel with the other students. They were allowed to attend the meetings; at one of the banquets when a state legislator made disparaging remarks about African Americans, Carl led the African American students as they walked out of the banquet room in protest. It was 1951 and, while the major events of the civil rights movement were still years in the future, Carl had the courage of his convictions and as a 17-year-old high school student acted upon them. The student body at Sumner High School voted to give Carl their highest award for outstanding service to the school.

Later during his career, Carl devoted a great deal of time and energy to the establishment of college scholarships for several organizations; this was inspired by the actions of so many friends and neighbors in St. Louis, who helped him with his expenses as a student at Southern Illinois University. Carl was the pride of the neighborhood, and his family and friends knew it was the right thing to do to invest in Carl's future. He remembers the scene in his neighborhood when he left for college; family and friends were all present, and Carl's minister offered a prayer for his safe journey and his success in college. Carl moved into a residence hall at Southern Illinois University as a freshman in 1952, with $130 to his name. He was eager, willing to work hard, and ready to learn.

Carl was a good student at Southern Illinois, but mostly he loved being involved in student life on the campus. He became the president of his fraternity (Kappa Alpha Psi), president of the Interfraternity Council, and vice president of the student body. He worked in various jobs in college to earn money to support himself; he raked leaves for the physical plant, worked in one of the campus stores, and he later joked that he was "Colonel of the Urinals" for a year in one of the campus academic buildings. He was also an resident assistant (RA) in the residence halls, a job where he learned that he could have a very positive effect on the lives of young college students. Carl was the first African American student to serve as an RA, and his success in this job in 1955 enabled many other African American students to follow him. Carl was also the chairman of the homecoming celebration on the campus; and because of his leadership, he was often invited to have dinner at the home of university's president, Deleyte Morris. Such occasions represented major events in the life of this young man from such a modest background in St. Louis, and Carl used them to urge the president to recruit more African American students to Southern Illinois University. Carl was good friends with a classmate who was to become famous, Dick Gregory, and they were active in social issues together in Carbondale. During his time in college, one of Carl's brothers was killed in the Korean war, and of course Carl returned home for this sad event. Carl continued to receive great encouragement from his family and often said, "I was blessed, because I had so many family, friends, and teachers who always were encouraging me." Carl used this phrase throughout his career, giving others credit for his accomplishments.

While still an undergraduate at Southern Illinois, Carl met Clark Davis, the dean of students. Carl was president of his fraternity (Kappa Alpha Psi), and his organization had no residence facility. Dean Davis helped Carl and his fraternity rent a house close to the campus, but located in a white neighborhood. Carl then negotiated a loan from the alumni chapter of his fraternity in East St. Louis, Illinois to purchase furniture; and he and his 18 fraternity brothers moved in the house, paid off the debt for the furniture, and established the first African American fraternity house at Southern Illinois University. It was 1954, and this was highly unusual; but it was made possible by the support of Dean Davis, a person who had a major influence in Carl's life. The dean's faith in Carl and his willingness to support him and his desire to have a house became a model for the way Carl himself was to work with students throughout his career. Carl expressed confidence in young people, accepted the fact that they were not perfect, and did everything he could to help them achieve success. Despite the terrible racism of the time in the country, Carl found Southern Illinois University to be a supportive and friendly place where he was not only accepted, but also where he became the most well-known student leader on the campus. The city of Carbondale was still not integrated, however, and Carl became active in the Congress of Racial Equality. He remembers a Sunday morning when the group marched to a traditionally segregated Baptist church; upon their arrival, they were greatly surprised and pleased when they were warmly welcomed by the congregation into the service.

Carl also met a young member of the student affairs staff at Southern Illinois, Bob Etheridge, who was an assistant dean. Bob quickly recognized Carl's excellent ability as a leader and encouraged him to become involved in campus life. They were to become close friends, and of course both became major national leaders within the student affairs profession. Carl and Bob both received the profession's highest honor, the Scott Goodnight Award for outstanding performance as a dean, and they remain close colleagues today, 48 years after first meeting at Southern Illinois.

One of his most vivid recollections was the day he was asked by Dr. Max Turner, the associate dean of arts and sciences, if he was receiving any scholarship aid at Southern Illinois. When Carl replied that he was not, Dean Turner invited him to come to his office; and in the second quarter of his freshman year, Carl was awarded a full tuition scholarship that enabled him to continue his studies. It was another example of Carl being convinced that "he was blessed." Dean Turner's actions also influenced the way Carl reached out to students during his career and what he expected his staff to do as well. In his senior year, Carl was awarded the Service to Southern Illinois University Award and the Most Valuable Fraternity Man Award for his contributions to the institution. He remained on the honor roll throughout his undergraduate program and was elected to Pi Sigma Alpha, the political science honor society, in his senior year.

Carl was now ready to graduate from Southern Illinois, and what he really wanted to do was to run for public office and to have a career in public service. But he was being pulled in several directions, as others thought so highly of his ability; he was offered a position with the Urban League in St. Louis, a teaching job in a high school, and a position on the student union staff at Southern Illinois. Dr. Maude Stewart, who headed the new master's degree program in student personnel work at Southern Illinois, offered Carl a graduate assistantship as a hall director; after a great deal of soul searching, Carl decided to accept and enrolled in the master's degree program. Carl's family was very supportive of his decision, and it was at this time that Carl and Ida Bass, a close neighborhood friend since grade school, decided to get married. They lived together in the residence hall, where Carl worked with the students and pursued his graduate degree. When Dr. Stewart left Southern Illinois for Ohio State University, Dr. Dennis Trueblood became the new faculty coordinator of the program. Dr. Trueblood also recognized Carl's ability and strongly encouraged him to pursue a doctorate and become a college president. But Carl loved what he was doing in the residence halls; he especially enjoyed working directly with the students and was convinced that he wanted a career in student affairs.

When Carl was about to complete his master's degree, he was still in close touch with Dean Davis at Southern Illinois. The dean encouraged Carl to consider a position at Howard University in Washington, D.C. Dr. Armour J. Blackburn was the dean at Howard and a close colleague of Dean Davis'. Carl had never been to a national professional student affairs meeting. Dean Davis thought it was important for Carl to do this, so he provided Carl with the funds necessary to attend the NASPA conference in French Lick, Indiana. Carl met Dean Blackburn at the conference and was awed by the outstanding leaders in attendance. He knew about Howard University, of course, and was extremely flattered when Dean Blackburn offered him a residence hall director's position. Carl still likes to joke about the fact that he was the first graduate of Southern Illinois' master's program—because his last name began with "A!"

Carl made the decision to accept the job at Howard University. He, Ida, and their young son, Carl, Jr., moved to Washington, D.C. in 1958, and Carl became the head resident of Cook Hall on the campus. They lived in the hall apartment for 2 years; their second child, Rhonda, was born while they were in Cook Hall. Reflecting his competitive spirit and his desire to succeed, Carl was determined to make Cook Hall the best residence hall at Howard. He found that his own enthusiasm and support for the students resulted in positive activities in the hall; and the residents excelled in various social, service, and athletic events.

In recalling his long days and nights on the campus during those years, Carl said that he relied almost entirely on his personal relationships with students to earn the trust needed to do his job and keep the institution open.

Carl's work was so outstanding that Dean Blackburn, who nurtured his career, asked him to become the director of student activities at Howard University in 1960. Student activities at this time were highly volatile, as the country was engaged in the civil rights movement. Howard University, the nation's best known and most prestigious predominately black institution, was not only located in the nation's capitol, but also was expected to assume a major leadership role in addressing the nation's most pressing problem. All of the most important national civil rights leaders often appeared at Howard, of course, to speak and to lead marches. Dr. Martin Luther King, Jr., H. Rap Brown, Stokely Carmichel, Roy Wilkins, and Malcolm X were among many leaders who came to the campus. In the middle of all of this activity, of course, was Carl Anderson, who also held passionate views about the social revolution taking place in the country. But Carl was the director of student activities, so much of the responsibility for maintaining civility on the campus rested with him. He was strongly dedicated to the rights and freedoms of students to speak out on any issue and to engage in the critical events of the times; sometimes clashed with the views of the older, more conservative academic leaders at Howard on these issues.

In only his 3rd year as director of student activities at Howard, Dr. King's famous "I have a dream" speech took place in Washington, D.C., and President Kennedy was assassinated. Carl was only 29 years old, and he found himself in a highly responsible position at Howard University in Washington, D.C. during one of the most difficult and challenging times in the nation's history. In recalling his long days and nights on the campus during those years, Carl said that he relied almost entirely on his personal relationships with students to earn the trust needed to do his job and keep the institution open. He added, there were students being arrested, buildings being taken over, and demands being made that the institution could not possibly meet; but I knew so many students that I could call most of them by name, and they knew what I believed and what I expected of them. As a result, we were able to engage in honest conversation and in most cases, resolve the issue at the time.

Carl became very visible at Howard, even though he was a young man and not yet a senior administrator. But not all of his work as student activities director had to do with the civil rights movement; he and Ida still lived on the campus in a university house, so Carl was available 24 hours a day. Since he had been used to working hard all his life, he loved the opportunity to be engaged with students.

Carl loved to see students create positive programs, and his experience as homecoming chairman at Southern Illinois caused him to challenge the Howard students to develop an exciting homecoming program. In a few years, this became the finest tradition at Howard; it is now among the most outstanding homecoming programs in the country, annually attracting 35,000 alumni to the campus for the various events.

Carl was extremely busy during this period, and his close association with Dean Blackburn had convinced him that he wanted to pursue a doctorate in higher education. Thus, he enrolled in the graduate program at the University of Maryland and somehow found the time to attend classes in College Park on a part-time basis, usually at night. He was appointed associate dean of students in 1965. In 1968, when Dean Blackburn suffered a stroke, Carl became the acting dean of students for a year. As an indication of how emotional the times were that year, Howard was faced with a group of approximately 20 student Vietnam war protesters who disrupted a speech by General Hersey, head of the Selective Service Commission. These students, over the objections of Dean Blackburn, were expelled from the university. Dean Blackburn told Carl that it was the most difficult day of his career, and later that night at home he had a stroke. Blackburn was a role model and mentor for Carl and all of this happened in 1968, the same year that Dr. King and Robert F. Kennedy were assassinated. Carl and Ida now had three children, he was acting dean of students at Howard during the most traumatic year of the decade, and he was trying to complete his doctoral dissertation.

Carl had always been able to succeed by working very hard and by putting in long hours, but these demands were too much even for him. When Dean Blackburn returned, Carl was granted a 6-month leave, with full pay, to complete his dissertation at the University of Maryland. Ironically, Carl's dissertation topic was on the psychological and social correlates of student protesters and nonprotesters at Howard University. He later joked that the data for his dissertation was almost lost when a group of student protesters seized the computer center building where his data was stored, and so he thought he would lose his work of several months! Luckily for Carl his data survived, and he was awarded his degree in 1969 at the University of Maryland. Carl's mother and mother-in-law came to College Park from St. Louis for the ceremony, which was a very happy day for the entire family.

When Dr. James Cheek became president of Howard University in 1969, he asked Carl to accept the newly established position of vice president for student affairs. Dean Blackburn had retired, and his long-time mentor and friend urged Carl to accept the position, which he did. Carl was only 35, which made him the youngest senior administrator at the institution. But Dr. Cheek had great confidence in this bright and vigorous young man and was very pleased when Carl agreed to accept. Carl had the utmost regard for Dr. James Nabrit, Jr., the previous president of Howard University, who had served as one of the attorneys in the landmark *Brown v. Board of Education* case in 1954. Moreover, Dr. Cheek was one of the most dynamic and nationally prominent educators and civil rights leaders in the country in 1969, and Carl again said to himself, "I am blessed!" He had come a long way from his poor, segregated neighborhood in St. Louis, and he was determined to prove himself worthy of the trust so many people had placed in him.

Carl was very excited about the challenges facing him as Howard University's first vice president for student affairs. He had been at the institution for 9 years; knew the faculty, staff, and students well; and had studied the history and traditions of this unique university. He enjoyed the support of a very strong president and was fully aware that it was in 1969, the high point of the Vietnam war protest movement and the continuing struggles with civil rights, that he was assuming his position. Howard University, as the leading African American institution in the country, located in the nation's capitol, subjected Carl and student life to constant public scrutiny. Network television reporters were common on the campus, and Carl became a frequent spokesperson for the university. He joked later in life that all of his experiences speaking to groups in Boy's State, the high school student council, his college fraternity, and college student government had prepared him to do quite well in front of the television cameras!

Howard University had a tradition of a rather conservative and sometimes paternalistic way of relating to its students. Students were treated with respect by faculty and administrators, but they were not involved in the decision-making process at any level of the institution; and when they encountered difficulties in their personal lives, many of them perceived that they were handled in a rather authoritarian manner. Carl was well aware of this situation, of course, but realized that he, as the youngest and newest vice president at the institution, would face substantial resistance to any changes he might propose. He was also aware that his staff, and especially the students, had high expectations for him and that they viewed him as their best advocate for change. Carl understood as well that he would not be able to make all the changes he wanted in his first year, and that he would have to be very thoughtful about when to proceed with his various plans.

The first changes Carl decided to address were the old parietal rules, especially those that pertained to women's hours in the residence halls. Howard University is private, and its long-time, conservative approach to such rules was supported by most parents of the students, but certainly not by the students themselves. Carl was convinced that the best way for students to learn responsibility is to have it, and then to prove that the students can handle it well. After arguing successfully for a change in these rules with the other vice presidents and President Cheek, Carl faced the more daunting task of helping to convince Howard's board of trustees. Carl argued that students do not grow when they live under constant restrictions, and he suggested that the college experience should be liberating for students—not just intellectually, but also socially. He knew the students well, and he was also confident that he could count on the cooperation and support of the students to affirm his statements to the board with their subsequent behavior. Carl believed in students and knew they could handle more responsibility, and with their trust he was successful in his advocacy before the board.

Carl was also convinced that if student government was to become a positive learning experience for students, it was necessary to grant them more autonomy and responsibility. He again developed plans with student leaders, won their support and that of his president, and went to the board to ask their permission to allow student government to allocate student activity fees. This represented a major change at Howard University, and it took Carl almost 3 years of working with the board and its committees before it became a reality. Carl laughingly described himself as an "information freak" to the board, as he presented them with lots of information from other campuses, results of studies done at Howard, articles from professional journals, and results of national research surveys. "I got to know members of the board very well," Carl said, "and I knew that some of them wanted hard data, some wanted personal contacts with me, others wanted direct contact with students, and of course, some just didn't want to deal with our issues!" But he was determined to move ahead, convinced that the changes he was proposing were positive for student learning and good for the university.

Perhaps most challenging of the changes Carl wanted to see take place during his first few years as vice president for student affairs was increasing the role of students in campus governance. Students were not represented on any campus committees, councils, search committees, or the board of trustees; and Carl was strongly committed to getting them involved. He knew that they had useful ideas to contribute, but he understood that the major benefits of this were students' own learning and their increased commitment to the institution. He and his staff spent a good deal of time working with students, explaining major university departments, divisions, committees, and governance structures. Carl wanted to be assured that if the governance process was opened to them, they would be prepared to contribute in useful and thoughtful ways. After a period of about 4 years, and with the support of Dr. Cheek, Carl and his staff succeeded in this major change at Howard. Now students are represented at every decision-making level of the institution, on all committees and councils, and there are two student voting members on the university's board of trustees. Almost everyone at Howard attributes these changes to Carl's leadership, his confidence and trust in students, and his ability to deliver positive results.

Carl had supported President Cheek's decision to establish a standing board of trustees committee on student affairs, and of course this was the primary group of board members with whom Carl worked for many years. He always reminded this group (as he did with student leaders) of the history of Howard University, and that the institution represented liberation and freedom for its students and faculty. Within this context, Carl argued, how could the board deny current students the opportunity to be free, to experience real responsibility, and to take on major challenges? Through his work with students, other administrators, the president, and the board, Carl was able to transform the student newspaper (*The Hilltop*), the yearbook (*The Bison*), and other aspects of student life so that they not only were true reflections of students' ideas and values, but also positive learning experiences for students because they had actual responsibility for them. In achieving autonomy for student government in the allocation of fees, Carl challenged the students each year to contribute something lasting and positive to the educational program at the institution. Thus, a fine tradition was established that continues to this day, as the students have made real improvements to the library, campus cultural life, international programs, and the aesthetics of the campus. The student government, responding to information they learned by increased involvement in campus governance, voted to tax all students in order to create a special scholarship program for needy students at Howard. Seeing this substantial and ongoing commitment by the students themselves, the board of trustees was moved to invest substantially more money in the scholarship program.

As vice president for student affairs at Howard University, Carl had responsibility for recruitment, admissions, registration, financial aid, counseling, housing, career planning and placement, student activities, veteran's affairs, international student services, campus judicial affairs, student recreation, the student union, and intercollegiate athletics. He informally shared responsibility for the student health service with the vice president for health affairs. With such a large administrative portfolio, Carl had to push himself very hard to remain knowledgeable about all aspects of his division and to stay in personal contact with staff in every department. His own leadership style was direct and personal, and he insisted that all staff directors and deans report to him. He was out of his office more than he was in it during the day, and he was known personally by all of the staff in the various offices. He found his supervision of admissions and intercollegiate athletics to be especially time-consuming because of the intense interest of so many people in and out of the institution in those areas. "I couldn't believe the outlandish requests and claims of some people who wanted the university to do various things in these areas," Carl said, "but I learned very quickly the art of listening and the value of diplomacy!"

During his 32 years as an administrative leader at Howard University, Carl hired all of the directors and deans of the various student affairs departments. He emphasized the importance of the hiring process and said that he sought professionals who were willing to work hard, who had already demonstrated their care for students, who had personal integrity, and who wanted to improve student opportunities to learn. Carl hired many outstanding staff, some of whom became national leaders within the profession. However, with his typical honesty, Carl admitted to the difficulty of knowing what staff might actually fulfill the expectations he had for them. "All the best information in the world cannot accurately predict how people will perform," he said. "Most of the time, my decisions were the right ones, but good administrators who hire lots of professional people know that this process is an art, not a science."

When Carl Anderson moved into Cook Hall as the head RA in 1958, Howard University's enrollment was 3,000. In 1990, when he retired as vice president, the enrollment had grown to 13,700. This was in part a direct result of his leadership of the recruitment and admissions office, of course, but he attributes this growth primarily to the overall commitment to excellence throughout the institution. "It was incredibly exciting to be involved in the rapid development of this university," Carl said. His proudest achievement is what he calls the transformation of student life at Howard, which has resulted in a positive and open environment for learning. He and his staff were largely responsible for "liberating" the students and opening up the institution to the full participation of students in its work and life. He argues strongly that such a positive campus environment needs constant nurturing and leaders who continue to advocate for its benefits. "Without strong leadership, it is relatively easy for institutions to revert back to old practices, ignoring learning opportunities for students. This is one of the primary leadership roles for the student affairs vice president—to see that this does not happen!" Carl asserts.

Carl is also very proud of the building of the impressive university center, which he worked for many years to create and became a reality in 1979. He insisted that it be located in an area of the campus that overlooked the city reservoir, a place consistent with the most cherished phrase in the university's alma mater, "High Above the Lake So Blue Stands Old Howard, Firm and True." Most important to Carl, he was successful in convincing the president and the board of trustees to name the university center after his long-time friend and professional mentor, Dean Armour J. Blackburn.

With its location in Washington, D.C., acquiring space for expanded housing and other facilities was a very difficult challenge and was also very expensive. Carl was asked by his president to explore what might be possible, as the institution was growing rapidly and needed more land. In his search for off-campus accommodations for student housing, Carl found several sites that the university purchased, which eventually became satellite campuses. One site now houses the university's law school, and the other houses the university's school of divinity. The two sites comprise over 43 acres of prime real estate in the District of Columbia.

Carl Anderson was recognized by many organizations in and out of higher education for his leadership and service. When he received the Scott Goodnight Award for outstanding performance as a dean from NASPA in 1990, Carl emphasized that "leadership is not accomplished by any one person, but by lots of people working together." He was presented with the Distinguished Alumni Award from Southern Illinois University and has been given over 100 awards by students, staff, faculty, and community organizations. His leadership was direct, honest, face-to-face, and always focused on improving student learning. A year before he retired, some 600 people paid $100 each to attend a testimonial dinner in Washington, D.C. to honor him. His friends established a scholarship program in Carl and Ida's names for Howard University students; and for this man who had grown up in a poor, segregated neighborhood in St. Louis, he knew he had traveled a long way.

Chapter 5

William R. Butler
University of Miami

A tall, outgoing, athletic looking man is walking briskly across the campus of the University of Miami (U.M.); he is wearing white trousers, a dark green sport coat, an orange and green striped tie, and white bucks...it is Dr. William (Bill) Butler, the vice president for student affairs! Any student, faculty, or staff member on this lovely Coral Gables campus would instantly recognize Bill, whose name and presence are synonymous with U.M. Many simply refer to him as "Mr. Miami," as he wears the university's colors. He tells students the colors refer to the orange tree—orange for the fruit, green for the leaves, and white for the orange blossoms.

Bill Butler served as vice president for student affairs and professor of higher education at U.M. for 32 years, from 1965 to 1997. Before moving to Miami, he served as a teaching and research fellow in the department of human relations at the University of Kansas (K.U.) from 1951–1953. In 1953, he became the assistant dean of men and foreign student adviser at K.U., until 1957 when he accepted the position of dean of men at the University of Wisconsin-Milwaukee (UW-M). In 1959, he became dean of men at Ohio University (O.U.) and was promoted to dean of students there in 1962. He resigned from O.U. in 1965 to accept the position as vice president for student affairs at U.M.

Throughout his 46 years in higher education, Bill enjoyed a highly successful and challenging career and was recognized by student, faculty, trustees, local and international governments, and professional organizations for his leadership and service. He was elected the president of the American College Personnel Association (ACPA) in 1971, and he was the 1997 recipient of the Scott Goodnight Award from the National Association of Student Personnel Administrators. In the late 1960s, he was appointed to the Florida Student Financial Assistance Commission, was its chair and vice chair for 7 years, and was a member for 19 years. In 1984, Bill was invited by the Chinese government to present lectures on American higher education at six universities in China. He was honored that same year with the Commander's Cross of the Order of Merit by the president of the Federal Republic of Germany for his contributions to German-American understanding. He became a Fulbright Exchange scholar in Germany in 1994. He served as the chair of the City of Coral Gables Community Relations Committee and was one of the founders of the National Vice Presidents' Group in 1967, which was dedicated to the exchange of information. U.M. honored him by naming the William R. Butler Student Volunteer Center in recognition of his long commitment to students and community service. Also at his retirement in 1997, the U.M. trustees named the beautiful atrium in the Smathers Student Wellness Center in his honor.

Bill Butler was born in Robinson, Illinois in 1926. The population of Robinson was 3,500 at the time, a town located in the rural belt, some 150 miles south of Chicago. Bill likes to say that Robinson is known as the home of the Heath candy bar and the birthplace of James Jones, the author! Bill's father, George, was a wholesale truck driver in Robinson; and his mother, Blondell, was a piano teacher. Robinson, Illinois was a very homogeneous town; and with so many of Bill's aunts, uncles, and cousins living there, Bill was well known in the community. He greatly enjoyed the informal and secure 1930s atmosphere of his hometown. Bill was athletic and learned the values of thrift and hard work during his youth, which coincided with the years of the Great Depression. He mowed lawns to earn money and delivered the *Robinson Daily News* to 144 customers each day. His high school science teacher, S.R. Bradley, also the local Scoutmaster, encouraged Bill to join and become active in the Boy Scouts. Through his scouting experiences, Bill learned the value of solving problems in a logical and responsible manner, a skill that was to serve him well throughout his professional life. Bill's first aid Scout team competed at the University of Illinois in 1942, and it was recognized as one of the best in the state. His skills as a problem-solver and leader were already evident to several of his teachers and peers.

Bill was expected to become a medical doctor (M.D.) by his relatives and close friends, because one of his uncles and two of his cousins were already M.D.s. Yet Bill did not spend much time as a young boy thinking about his future academic pursuits, as he was primarily interested in sports, work, scouting, and leisure time activities. After Bill's junior year in high school, a major change occurred in Bill's life. His parents decided to move to Newark, Ohio with Bill and his younger sister, Alice. At this time, Bill's father was to take charge of Butler Bakery, a business started in 1895 by Bill's grandfather, William Butler. Bill assisted in the business by selling and delivering bread, cakes, and pies and working long hours during his senior year in high school. Newark's population in 1943 was 50,000—a much larger and more diverse city than Bill had experienced in rural Robinson, Illinois. But Bill made the necessary adjustments regarding academic work, his new friends, and his on-going interests in athletics.

It was 1943, and the country was very much at war, so Bill enlisted in the U.S. Navy Reserve at the age of 17, 1 month before high school graduation. Upon receiving his high school diploma, he was sent to the Great Lakes Naval Training Station in Chicago. Only 7 weeks later, he was on a troop train heading to Treasure Island in California. Shortly thereafter, he embarked with 6,000 other troops on a Liberty Ship bound for New Guinea. Bill had just turned 18, and he understood well that the situations he would now face were far removed from those in his rural hometown of Robinson, The torrid, wet, and mosquito-infested life in New Guinea was dangerous and difficult, especially while living in the open, awakening nearly every morning with 4 inches of water in his tent.

In October 1944, he was shipped to Brisbane, Australia, where he was assigned to the Radio, Radar, and Harbor Defense Warehouse for military communication supplies. He worked and lived in Brisbane for nearly a year. After President Roosevelt's death in 1945, Bill was shipped to the Philippine Islands along with his warehouse unit, since the war in the Southwest Pacific had moved much closer to Japan. Bill served as a second class storekeeper technician while in Subic Bay and until the war ended in August 1945. When the peace agreement was signed, Bill was 19, yet he was offered a promotion to the rank of chief petty officer if he agreed to re-enlist in the Navy for an additional period of 4 years and remain in the Philippines. In recalling this experience, Bill joked, "Here I was in the Philippines, the war over, and because some Navy officers thought I had something on the ball, I could have reached the top of my profession as a chief in the Navy at age 19!" He declined the offer and several months later was shipped back to the states, where he was discharged from the Navy in May 1946. Now, Bill had to decide what to do next with his life!

Bill returned to his parent's home in Newark, Ohio, and he knew he had always been expected to go to college. Like thousands of other veterans of World War II, he decided to take advantage of the G.I. Bill of Rights. He had been an average, not an outstanding, student in high school; he had come from a very ordinary and modest family background; but he knew the values of hard work and taking on new challenges. O.U., located in Athens, was just 75 miles away, so Bill decided to enroll as a freshman in the fall of 1946. Because of the huge enrollment of veterans, there was no room available in a campus residence hall, so Bill and three other veterans found an apartment over a restaurant in town, and he lived there during half of his freshman year. Bill and his fellow veterans loved their new freedom in college, and the monthly check from Uncle Sam made life quite enjoyable. Bill did not devote much time to his studies and his apartment became well known as a good place to "hang out!" In those days, noisy behavior, even off campus, was sufficient cause for the university to intervene, and Bill and his roommates were summoned to the dean of men's office at the end of the first semester. The dean informed them that because of complaints received from neighbors and other people, they were to move to an on-campus residence hall immediately. Bill strongly objected by saying that he had been overseas during the war and could take care of himself. The good dean cut him off abruptly and told him that he had no choice if he wanted to remain as a student at O.U. Bill left the dean's office in anger, as he did not appreciate either the dean's message or his manners. He well remembers muttering to himself as he stormed out of the office, "I could do that job a hell of a lot better than he did!" Little did Bill realize that he would replace the dean and have that very job at O.U. 13 years later! During the remainder of his undergraduate years, Bill became friends with John Baker, O.U.'s president; and it was President Baker who met Bill in Chicago in 1959 for the purposes of inviting him back to his alma mater as dean of men.

In the spring semester of 1947, Bill took the dean of men's advice and moved into a campus residence hall, but he found this did not change his lack of enthusiasm for pre-medical studies. He decided to take a short break from classes, and so he hitchhiked to Washington, D.C. to visit a close buddy from his overseas Navy days. After several days of partying, Bill decided it was time to do something more positive with his life, so he returned to O.U. and began applying himself to his studies. He changed his major to psychology since he had enrolled for a course in human relations, which had sparked his interest in human behavior. His grades soared, and he soon became very involved with his new academic interests.

Bill joined a local fraternity, Sigma Theta Gamma, which became the campus Sigma Chi chapter just 2 years later. Bill was asked to serve as the pledgemaster but told his fraternity brothers that he would do so only under the condition that he would be allowed to eliminate all hazing practices of pledges. After a hotly contested chapter debate, the fraternity accepted his new approach, and he structured a study program every night at the university's main library for the pledges as well as himself. By the semester's end, all 25 pledges made their grades and were initiated into Sigma Chi. Bill already was setting high standards, developing new programs, and working hard to assure that they were carried out in the manner he felt was educationally sound—a method of administrative leadership he was to follow for the rest of his career.

Bill graduated from O.U. in 1950 and was encouraged to continue his studies there for a master's degree in psychology, leading to certification in the state of Ohio as a school psychologist. So Bill enrolled in graduate school and, while studying for his master's degree at O.U., he continued to test his ideas about problem-solving techniques through thesis research. Bill completed his master's degree in 1951 and assumed he would pursue a position as a school psychologist in a large public Ohio high school. However, one of Bill's professors who had close ties with the doctoral program in Counseling and Clinical Psychology at K.U. intervened and, with his encouragement and support, Bill was awarded a research and teaching fellowship in the Department of Human Relations at K.U. But before he did, he and his college sweetheart, Virginia (Ginnie) Ault, were married in the summer of 1951 in Cleveland. They moved to Lawrence, where Bill began his doctoral studies and Ginnie continued her career as a business representative with the Southwestern Bell Telephone Company, after a transfer from Ohio Bell.

> *Living on the campus meant that Bill was easily accessible to both students and the president around the clock, and his energy and enthusiasm for his work became a model for the rest of his staff.*

After 2 years of teaching and pursuing graduate study, Bill and Ginnie had their first child, Michael, and Bill suggested to his adviser, Dr. Gordon Collister, that he needed a better paying job in order to support his family. Bill was soon recommended for the newly created position of assistant dean of men and foreign student adviser; and when the position was offered to him, he accepted. He fell in love with student affairs work and applied the same analytical planning and determination to his work with students that had worked so well at O.U. He particularly enjoyed working with the international students and hired buses to take them on excursions to government offices (including annual personal meetings with former President Truman), to small Kansas towns, and other places of interest in the area. Bill dubbed this program "Operation Friendship," reflecting his determination to create positive learning experiences for students. The values of fairness and openness, which Bill had learned from his family and from growing up in a small town, together with his experiences gained overseas during the war, made him very sensitive to racial prejudice and intolerance. Through his student affairs position at K.U., Bill quickly understood the challenges facing him in this important area of human relations, and this was to be a focus of his work throughout his career. His work with international students at Kansas was a transforming experience for Bill and, despite the obstacles to understanding throughout American society, Bill remained convinced that positive outcomes would result from educational experiences. Bill was also responsible for the fraternities and the residence halls program at Kansas (he remembers helping a Kansas student by the name of Wilt

Chamberlain acquire a custom made, longer bed!) and, by the time he completed his doctorate in 1956, the Butler family had been blessed with their second child, Barbara.

Dr. Martha Peterson, who was serving as the dean of women on the K.U. student affairs staff with Bill, was named dean of women at the University of Wisconsin in Madison (she was later to become president of Barnard College). When the dean of men's position became open at the University of Wisconsin's campus in Milwaukee, Martha called Bill and urged him to apply. Bill could have become a school psychologist at this time, of course, but he loved the challenges of administration, and he felt ready for the new dean's responsibilities in Milwaukee. He and his family moved to Wisconsin in 1957.

Bill served as the UW-M's first dean of men, enjoying being a pioneer and a builder of new programs for students. He met his daily challenges with high energy and enthusiasm and reached out to students in all areas of the campus. He was able to develop new educational programs and student services at this urban campus, which was searching for a sense of academic identity and pride.

But, new opportunities arose for Bill after only 2 years at Wisconsin. In 1959, John Baker, president of O.U., telephoned Bill and asked to meet him in Chicago, as he wanted Bill to return to Athens as dean of men and assistant professor of human relations. Bill liked the opportunities he saw at his alma mater and accepted President Baker's offer. Prior to the move, the Butlers became parents of their third child, Jennifer.

After Bill and his family arrived in Athens, Ohio in the summer of 1959, Bill understood well the importance of networking with colleagues, and he knew the student affairs program at O.U. needed new ideas and new staff. He traveled to Indiana University to consult with Dean of Students Robert Shaffer and to Miami University in Oxford, Ohio to consult with Dean Robert Etheridge, both of whom were organizing their programs in ways that Bill thought had promise for his plans in Athens. It was the beginning of the 1960s decade and, with all the social turmoil in the country, there existed a climate for needed and dramatic change.

Vernon Alden, a young Harvard Business School dean was named the new president at O.U. in 1962 when President John Baker retired. He invited Bill to accept the responsibilities of the newly created position of dean of students, and Bill would then have responsibility for building a comprehensive student affairs program for both men and women. He relished the challenge. Bill and his family lived in the dean's house located in the heart of the campus, next to the president's residence. There was daily excitement and high morale on the campus. Bill undertook the planning for new residence halls, the hiring of outstanding staff, the creation of new student life programs, the revision of existing policies pertaining to student rights, and the building of a new administrative organization that fostered positive relationships with students. Living on the campus meant that Bill was easily accessible to both students and the president around the clock, and his energy and enthusiasm for his work became a model for the rest of his staff. Bill assembled one of the most talented student affairs staff ever to serve on one campus during his years at O.U. Tom Dutton, Bill Sheeder, Dennis Madson, Annette Gibbs, Richard Correnti, Dale Mattmiller, Jim Whalen, Bob Hynes, Doug Woodard, Ed Birch, and Johan Madson were hired by Bill at O.U.; and they all went on to very distinguished and successful careers in higher education.

This was the period of the civil rights movement, and students were eager to challenge existing policies and question traditional ways of administering university affairs. Bill vigorously defended the right of students to invite controversial speakers of their choice, such as George Lincoln Rockwell, who spoke on the O.U. campus despite vehement opposition from many students, faculty, and community leaders. For a World War II veteran who himself had been overseas, defending the right of a proclaimed American Nazi to speak on campus was a true test of Bill's commitment to the principles of freedom of expression. Walking across the campus one morning with a student, Bill looked up and noticed that he had been hanged in effigy from a tree. The student remarked, "Well, Dean Butler, I see you're getting up in the world these days!" Bill smiled and replied, "Yes, O.U. students have unique ways of showing their affection!"

Bill achieved success at O.U. through his highly energized, planned, and thoughtful style of campus leadership. Reflecting on his early experiences in using the case method of analyzing problems, Bill would gather his staff together to review and critique problems in detail, developing various assumptions and approaches for their solution. Vigorous staff debate occurred prior to deciding on a course of action. Bill believed in involving his staff in most of the major decisions he made. He was convinced that this resulted in better decisions and stronger commitment to their implementation. The process also contributed substantially to the learning and development of his own staff. As Johan Madson, now the associate provost and dean of students at Vanderbilt University, and one of Bill's staff at O.U. at the time said, "Bill Butler hired me for my first student affairs job and for over 30 years has been a mentor, adviser, friend, and colleague. He is truly a dean's dean!"

Bill was also willing to take clear stands on issues, based on his strong sense of values and personal beliefs. When asked many times by students, faculty, and staff why he made a decision, especially when he knew he would be bitterly criticized for doing so, Bill simply replied, "Well, it was the right thing to do!" His standards were based on high educational and personal expectations for students, honesty, fairness, and above all, civility in the treatment of others. Behind the warm smile and ready laugh of this highly popular leader was a fierce and dedicated fighter for his beliefs and for the educational rights of students.

At O.U., Bill gained a well-deserved reputation for hiring some of the most outstanding student affairs staff in the country. When asked how he was able to identify such excellent talent, he said that he looked for professionals who were enthusiastic and eager to serve, who loved to work with students, who did not care about long hours, and who knew how to get things done. Bill asked a great deal of his staff, and his staff learned from seeing Bill's untiring, enthusiastic leadership. Bill was very proud of the many accomplishments at O.U. regarding new facilities, revised polices, positive attitudes, and a new organizational structure; however, he was most proud of the outstanding staff he hired and the legacy they created at O.U.

Bill was active in the American College Personnel Association and in the National Association of Student Personnel Administrators during these early years in his career as well as for many years thereafter. He was well known to his colleagues throughout the country, and they frequently called on him for his counsel and advice. So, in 1965, it was not a surprise when President Henry King Stanford at U.M. phoned Bill and invited him to come to Coral Gables for a visit to consider filling the newly created position of vice president for student affairs. Bill thanked Dr. Stanford for his interest in him but said he really was not ready to leave O.U., his alma mater. Moreover, he explained he had no prior experience in a private institution and had never really considered leaving the midwest. But Dr. Stanford was insistent, and Bill and Ginnie agreed to fly to Miami for a visit. Bill was immediately impressed by President Stanford's personality, leadership, and his plans to move this struggling private university forward. President Stanford realized that the student affairs program at U.M. was very underdeveloped, needed strong leadership, and was far behind what Bill had already accomplished at O.U. Bill returned to Athens, flattered with the offer, but not totally convinced that he should make this move. During the ensuing weeks, however, he and Ginnie decided to leave O.U. and move to U.M. in July 1965. He informed President Alden of his decision to leave and was extremely pleased when Dr. Jim Whalen, a staff member Bill had recruited to O.U., was named as his successor. Bill was only 39 when he left for Florida, but already he had enjoyed 14 years of professional experience at three different universities. He was ready for the new vice presidential challenges in Coral Gables. The Butler family increased to four children when Rebecca was born shortly before they left for Florida.

Since Bill was to become the first vice president for student affairs at the institution, he was granted a great deal of freedom in building a new administrative team. This was the perfect opportunity to initiate new and innovative programming that was student-centered. He began to develop ways for his staff to support the university's academic missions of teaching and research. This was the midpoint of the 1960s decade, and great changes were occurring in all of American higher education. The city of Miami was often in the national news due to the rapid changes taking place with the influx of Cuban exiles and the unrest in the

African American community. Bill, in his usual optimistic way, saw nothing but opportunities. He knew he had made the right decision to move to Miami, and he relished the challenges of building a model student affairs program based on this newfound diversity of students from around the world.

Bill once again decided to invite consultants to Miami, hired new staff, established new programs, advised the president and trustees on the need to build new residence halls and other student facilities, and began building his team. As a professor of education himself, he was influential in convincing Dr. Bernard R. Black, an outstanding higher education faculty member at O.U., to come to Miami to establish a graduate program in student personnel administration. Together with President Stanford, Bill established biweekly breakfast meetings and other open forums on campus with students, which during those days of unrest proved to be most effective in improving institutional communication and understanding. Bill emphasized the great importance of the support that President Stanford had given him in leading the student affairs division. Bill soon learned that he had earned the confidence of President Stanford because of his dedication, teamwork, good judgment, organizational skills, and his close relationships with students and faculty. It was the 1960s, and there was considerable turmoil on most campuses. U.M. President Stanford depended on Bill to oversee the difficult problems and crises on campus associated with war protests and civil rights. Dr. Stanford was an extremely popular and visible president with his students and faculty, as well as within in the greater Miami metropolitan area. But Bill and his staff knew they needed to address and resolve most of the difficult campus and political protests before they escalated to the president's office. By working many long hours with students from many ethnic and racial backgrounds and political persuasions, key members of the student affairs' staff were able to open up and maintain positive communications. Bill personally agreed with many of the social issues of the times about which students were protesting, but he was a vigorous advocate of equal opportunity for all students to be heard. He organized seminars and discussion groups between student groups and members of the board of trustees in efforts to improve communications and understandings, as well as to educate the trustees about the complex needs of the students of the 1960s.

Reflecting his long-standing commitment to international education and understanding, Bill initiated a recruitment program to increase the number of international students at U.M. and to make them an important part of the campus community. Wherever he found prejudice and intolerance—and during the 1960s decade there was far too much of both— Bill worked hard to bring people of different backgrounds and persuasions together, always convinced that by creating situations where people can know one another better, friendships and understanding would occur. He and his wife hosted dozens of student groups and staff members for this purpose at their home over the years, and Bill gained a well-deserved reputation as an ambassador of good will for all students.

The tragedy at Kent State University in May 1970 resulted in many major protests on American campuses, including U.M. Due to the effective leadership of President Stanford, other key administrators, the faculty senate, and student government, the protests were brought to a peaceful conclusion. Bill and Fred Lewis, the dean of the U.M. law school, worked over the summer to rewrite the conduct rules and due process procedures, and this new code became a model for other campuses.

Soon thereafter, Bill also initiated actions to enhance student participation in the decision-making processes of the university, and President Stanford approved a new charter for the undergraduate student government. This system, ensuring an important student role in campus governance, has worked very well at U.M. for nearly 30 years. Early in that decade as well, Bill was influential in creating an "ombudsman council" to help resolve student problems. As a result, a "troubleshooter" position has been in place since 1973.

> *Bill was well known by everyone on the campus for his witty remarks, his smile, and his warm and gracious personality.*

During these tumultuous years on American campuses, Bill was among the first student affairs leaders to formally recognize the need for colleagues to share their experiences and learn directly from one another as the profession struggled with the difficult social and political issues of the times. Reflecting his lifelong commitment to networking with colleagues, Bill joined with Charles Lewis of Penn State, Robert Ross of Nebraska, and Robert Callis of Missouri in inviting an initial group of 15 senior student affairs officers from public and private institutions to meet. The purpose was to discuss various administrative organizational models, as well as student problems that they were all facing. The initial meeting in 1967 on the Penn State campus proved to be so valuable that the group agreed to continue meeting twice each year. The group later expanded its membership to 25 student affairs vice presidents. Most of the participating members commented in later years that these meetings of the National Vice Presidents' Group were among their most beneficial professional experiences. The group still exists today, after 33 years, a tribute to Bill and the other foresighted founders of 1967.

U.M. has truly become an independent global institution today and has transformed its educational image dramatically during the past 35 years. Once known affectionately as "Sun Tan U.," it is now a highly selective, diverse, internationally oriented, private research university. It enjoys several distinguished professional schools, such as medicine and law; and has nationally renowned academic and research programs in oceanography, psychology, biology, engineering, and medical science. As the city of Miami has grown and has become one of the most international of all U.S. cities, U.M. has become its leading educational and research university with a nationally renown medical center. Participating in this exciting growth and development of the university for 32 years, from 1965–1997, was exactly what Bill Butler loved the most. He rose to the challenges of building new programs, attracting students worldwide, creating new living and learning opportunities, constructing new facilities, and working closely with the many diverse student groups. During the years that Bill served as vice president, the number of international students increased from 200 to 2,200, and international post-doctoral scholars increased from 5 to 550. Coupled with the growth of international students from over 110 countries, African American, Hispanic, and Asian American enrollments also more than quintupled. It is this dramatic increase in diversity and the climate of mutual respect that developed on the Miami campus that Bill is most proud of in terms of his long tenure at that institution. When Edward T. Foote II became Miami's new president in 1981, Bill was delighted to learn of President Foote's strong commitments to international education and family ties with international education and student diversity. President Foote's wife, Bosey, was Senator J. William Fulbright's youngest daughter. The institution's commitment in these areas accelerated significantly during President Foote's long and very successful tenure at U.M.

President Foote encouraged Bill to find new ways to strengthen the "living-learning" environment for students living in the residence halls. It was largely through President Foote's personal undergraduate experiences at Yale University that Bill, his staff, and other key academic officers proposed to the president and the U.M. board of trustees the establishment of the nationally known system of residential colleges. The creation of five residential colleges represented a major financial, as well as educational, commitment by the trustees to undergraduate education at Miami. The colleges improved the nature and quality of each student's campus life experience. Each of the residential colleges enjoys a live-in senior faculty master and family, as well as two senior faculty associate masters and their families. Bill and his staff worked closely with the 15 masters living on campus in the colleges to make the residential programs truly special as living-learning centers.

With the support of President Foote, Bill worked with student government in the 1980s, and a new U.M. Student Honor Code and Honor Council were established and approved by the board of trustees. He also stimulated the development of a dynamic new student volunteer program, and in 1989 the U.M. Student Volunteer Services Center was officially opened. By 1999, 53 percent of the student body was participating. The trustees recognized this significant legacy of Bill's by naming the center in his honor upon his retirement, and the U.M. Alumni Association created the William R. Butler Community Service Award to recognize distinguished alumni who have demonstrated a special commitment to volunteerism.

Bill frequently was able to understand what the students' needs were before others had seriously thought about them. Indeed, much of his strategy as a senior leader was to demonstrate to the university community what should be essential for a quality education at U.M. To aid in this process, he often persuaded the president and trustees to establish new student fees, after securing student support through campus-wide student referenda. The most recent example was the building of a state-of-the-art $20 million Student Wellness Center, an innovative facility that has attracted national attention for its design and its inclusion of health, diet, cultural, exercise, and recreational opportunities for students. Upon Bill's retirement in 1997, the trustees named its beautiful atrium in his honor.

Besides the construction of the Student Wellness Center, fees were increased for the creation of the five residential colleges, a new rathskeller, the renovation of the Student Health Center, and a new Career Planning and Placement Center. Funds were also obtained from the central administration to renovate and upgrade each of the student organizational offices and the various student affairs departmental offices, including installation of the latest computer technology.

Before the advent of the federal legislation that culminated in "Title IX," Bill, after listening to the plight of female student athletes, became a vigorous advocate for women's athletic scholarships at Miami. President Stanford supported Bill in presenting a proposal to the board of trustees for this purpose in 1973. He not only won the support of the trustees with 15 initial scholarships for female athletes, but also initiated the most successful women's athletic program in the nation at the time. It is also noteworthy that Bill convinced President Stanford and the board of trustees to establish a permanent trustee committee on student affairs in 1968. Over a period of many years, this committee has become a valuable vehicle for addressing university-wide student needs and all policies affecting student life.

Bill has always given credit for the many student affairs accomplishments at Miami to his staff. He is especially proud that so many of his former staff members have gone on to significant leadership positions in higher education at other institutions. Several individuals at U.M. who achieved outstanding prominence in their fields are Patricia Whitely, Don Kubit, Jerry Askew, Jim Grimm, Chuck Lynch, Joel Rudy, Bill Sandler, Nick Gennett, Fred Kam, Bill Mullowney, Craig Ullom, and Aley Kosy. Rick Artman, a former student affairs staff member at Miami, and now president of Sienna Heights University, said, "Bill created a special bond among those of us who served as his assistants during his tenure at the university, a special relationship built on mutual trust and common mission. I've never worked for anyone as courageous or as astute as Bill Butler" (Artman, personal communication, 2000).

Bill was well known by everyone on the campus for his witty remarks, his smile, and his warm and gracious personality. Yet he was a man of steely determination regarding the needs of students, and he always insisted on the highest professional and ethical standards by his staff. He was never one to shy away from problems, no matter how difficult, and he had the courage to speak out and take whatever action was necessary on issues that most others were usually hesitant to address. He viewed himself as an "active listener" whose responsibility it was to act on behalf of students' education. At times, this stance made him unpopular or controversial on campus, but when Bill was convinced that "it was the right thing to do," he would take steps to initiate a new program, proceed with a new policy, or a tough decision regardless of the opposition.

Bill Butler was a futuristic dreamer for the student affairs profession, and he was almost always ahead of his time. Unlike other dreamers, he was a superb planner who was very effective in involving a large number of others in his leadership efforts; and he had the courage, ability, and determination to follow through to get things accomplished. He frequently told his staff that if they stopped growing as professionals and delayed earning advanced academic degrees, they would soon become ineffective. He tried his best to set an example of self-renewal.

Bill developed considerable self-confidence, over many years of service, which helped make it possible for him to understand and articulate the educational needs of students. He loved U.M. and decided to continue as its vice president and professor despite several offers to move elsewhere, especially as a president. His first love was the education of students, and his long career as a leader at Miami offered him the opportunity to play a significant role in the lives of thousands of U.M. students. When Bill retired in 1997, he had served as vice president during 45 percent of U.M.'s existence.

In reflecting on his professional and family life, Bill felt that his early worldwide interests motivated him to travel, which in turn enhanced his international understanding. He traveled to Central and South America to recruit international students to U.M. in the late 1960s. He traveled to Germany in the early 1970s to develop educational exchange linkages with Dr. Ulrich Littmann, executive director of the German Fulbright Commission, and with other key German educators and politicians. In 1984, he and his son traveled to China to recruit Chinese graduate students and post-doctoral research scholars. In 1987, he was invited to attend, along with 500 other scientists and educators from 25 countries, a world conference in Moscow, Russia to deal with alternatives to the world's depleting energy resources. While there, he met with American Ambassador Foy Kohler and also with key Russian politicians in the Kremlin for purposes of beginning new educational exchange opportunities between the United States and Russia. All four of Bill and Ginnie's children have become engaged in international affairs and issues, in travel, overseas study, professional employment, and in language proficiency. In short, in addition to Bill's personal and professional growth, all members of the Butler family, in a sense, have become "citizens of the world" as Bill increased his global travels and developed international friendships.

Even though Bill retired from U.M. in 1997, at the age of 71 after serving as vice president and professor for 32 years, he still remains active today in university affairs. He is currently working with his successor, Dr. Particia Whitely, who served most ably on Bill's staff for 16 years, on the planning and construction of a $3 million Student Islamic Center, a project that was initiated some 25 years ago. A donor has been identified and the center is expected to open on campus in 2002. Bill is also involved in the raising of private funds for the William R. Butler Student Volunteer Center and the funding of academic scholarships for U.M.'s School of Nursing. He serves on the ACPA Educational Leadership Foundation, and he will return to China later this year with his son to revisit the universities where he lectured in the 1980s.

One of his Miami colleagues, Edward Coll, now president of Alfred University, summed up Bill's impact very well when he said, "Bill Butler was the most effective student affairs leader I have ever served with in nearly 4 decades in higher education. An outstanding planner, he was a motivational force that was felt from the governing board to the physical plant staff. His record of achievement at U.M. might be unparalleled in the history of higher education in this country" (Coll, personal communication, 2000).

Chapter 6

Thomas B. Dutton
University of California at Davis

Walking across the beautiful campus at the University of California at Davis (U.C.D.), evidence of Tom Dutton's influence is everywhere: a large, state-of-the-art recreation center, including extensive outdoor facilities for students; graceful residence halls; a centrally located student union; a modern and accessible student health center; and the new Thomas B. Dutton Hall, providing easy access for many student services—most all of these first-class facilities are there because of his foresight and leadership as the university's first full-time vice chancellor for student affairs. During his 21 years as vice chancellor at U.C.D., Tom Dutton built one of the most comprehensive and successful student affairs programs in the country.

Thomas B. Dutton earned his B.A. degree with highest honors in history and political science in 1954 from the University of California at Berkeley. He received his two graduate degrees from the same institution; his master's degree in educational curriculum in 1956, and his EdD in educational administration and higher education in 1961. He served as assistant football coach at the University of California at Berkeley from 1954–1956. Then, while he completed his master's degree and from 1956 to 1962, he served as the assistant dean of students at Berkeley, with responsibilities for student residential groups and fraternities. In 1961–1962, he also was lecturer in education at Berkeley. In 1962, he moved to Athens, Ohio, where he served as the dean of men and assistant professor of human relations at Ohio University and remained in that position until 1965. He then moved to Oakland University in Rochester, Michigan, and became that institution's senior student affairs officer (SSAO), as dean of students and associate professor of education. In 1969, he was named vice chancellor for student affairs and associate professor of education at Oakland. In 1970, he moved back to the West Coast and was appointed vice chancellor for student affairs at U.C.D. He remained in this position until 1991 and then served for 2 years as senior adviser to the chancellor before retiring in 1993. He was very active in the National Association of Student Personnel Administrators (NASPA), and he served as the director of research and program development for NASPA from 1967–1969. He directed the national conference for NASPA in 1970 and was elected president of NASPA in 1972–1973. In 1976, NASPA presented him with its highest honor, the Scott Goodnight Award for Outstanding Performance as a Dean. He served as the chair of the student affairs council for the University of California System from 1979–1988, and he was a member of system-wide Task Forces on Admissions Practices and Processes, Affirmative Action, Services to Students with Disabilities, and Financial Aid Policy. He was also a member of the National Vice President for Student Affairs Group from 1972–1991. He assisted other colleges and universities by participating on accreditation teams, and he served as a consultant to many institutions and their student affairs programs. He was co-author of the NASPA publication *Pieces of Eight* in 1978; and has published articles and monographs on institutional policies, adjudication of student misconduct, assumptions and beliefs of members of the academic community, conflict and change, organizational structure, and fiscal management.

Tom Dutton was born in 1932 in Alhambra, California, a city of about 20,000 residents at the time, located in the southern part of the state. He was the youngest of seven children of Clare and Elizabeth Dutton. The Dutton family had come to this country in its early years and eventually migrated to Kansas. Tom's mother was a schoolteacher in Kansas, where she met Tom's father and then married him in Portis, Kansas. The family moved to southern California in the early 1920s, and Tom's father began a painting contracting business in Alhambra. Tom joked that "it was a challenging environment for me to grow up as the youngest of seven children!" In this friendly and highly supportive family environment, Tom learned the values of hard work and respect for others that were to characterize his career. All during his youth, Tom and his two brothers worked in the family business; and Tom said he washed, sanded, and painted hundreds of walls—all before he was 15 years old! Although Tom's father had not been to college, he was a collector of books and an avid reader, especially of history; consequently, education was emphasized strongly in the family. Even though Tom was born early in the Great Depression, there were many books and magazines available in the house, and reading and discussion of ideas were frequent activities. His father's love of history stimulated Tom to major in history in college and to become a lifelong student of the American Civil War and American history in general.

The Dutton family worked very hard during the Depression years, and Tom's father's business survived those difficult times. Tom's memories of his family life are very positive. On Tom's birthday, he recalls getting a whole egg for himself—an example of the careful attention families paid to food during those years. Most of all, Tom and his older brother, Bill, loved sports. At an early age, Tom loved to play football, even though he was not big for his age. Having to compete with his older brother made Tom very competitive and determined! He attended the Central Grammar School and was a very good student. Tom remembers Pearl Harbor and the rationing and fear during World War II in California. Another of Tom's brothers, Dan, was in the Army and fought in Europe, and Tom remembers reading daily accounts of the war and listening to radio reports with his family. Tom was only 13 when the war ended in 1945, but he remembers a Japanese family in the neighborhood that was ordered by the government to move to one of the infamous camps during the war; seeing this happen bothered Tom's sense of fairness and justice, even at such a young age. Tom's parents were kind, compassionate, and caring; and Tom's life and career reflected these values. He learned what was right and wrong, and the moral compass he developed in his home played a critical role throughout his life.

After the war, the explosive growth of southern California enabled the Dutton family business to thrive. Tom attended Alhambra High School and continued to work for his father after school, on weekends, and during the summer. He was a very good student in high school and excelled in his first love, football. He played guard in the popular single wing formation of the time, and linebacker on defense, and was named to the all-conference team in both his junior and senior years. Although he weighed only 185 pounds, Tom was named to the all southern California first team as a senior in 1950, and his team won the area championship. Tom was active in other activities in high school as well, but he spent a good deal of his time working in his father's business when he was not studying or playing football. In his younger years, he was part of a group called the "Woodcraft Rangers" that went camping and performed service activities. His family bought some land in Arizona, and Tom and his family enjoyed spending some time on this "homesteading" site during vacations.

Tom's superior athletic and academic achievements were recognized; he was recruited by California, Stanford, Southern California, UCLA, and Washington. Because Alhambra was close to Los Angeles, many people assumed that Tom would attend UCLA. But one of Tom's high school coaches convinced him to visit the Berkeley campus; and after meeting the students, faculty, and coaches, Tom decided to accept the academic and athletic scholarships at Berkeley. His brother, Bill, transferred from a community college to Berkeley and played football there with Tom. Tom's family was supportive of his decision, although they were a bit apprehensive about Tom being 400 miles away and at a university nationally known for its liberal, and sometimes extreme, activities. Tom was most impressed with the academic opportunities at Berkeley, and his scholarships recognized both his academic and athletic accomplishments.

Tom was highly motivated to succeed in college and was determined to prove himself in football as well. As a freshman at Berkeley, he joined the Psi Upsilon fraternity and found this experience important in the transition from high school to college. He liked the discipline required by being on the football team, and he appreciated the academic support programs available. These experiences influenced his commitment to similar transition services for students later in his career. Tom put himself through college not only with his scholarships, but also by working on campus in the athletic equipment room and in the family business during summers. Tom had a very successful first year, both as a student and a football player. After his freshman year, he returned to his home in Alhambra, but he got sick that summer and, after losing considerable weight, worried if he would be able to return to college in the fall. He regained his strength, though, and enjoyed a successful sophomore year at Berkeley, earning a starting position as guard on the football team. His travels with the team to other campuses broadened Tom's horizons, and he enjoyed the close friendships he developed on the team. Near the end of his sophomore year, Tom had a "blind date" with Eina Anderson, a student at UCLA, and they fell in love almost right away! They were married in 1953, when Tom was in his senior year of college. Eina took a leave from her studies at UCLA and worked in the Registrar's Office at Berkeley.

> **Tom developed a comprehensive, written plan for success in the fraternity system at Berkeley, emphasizing educational programs and workshops on a variety of topics.**

Tom continued to work in college and excelled in his studies. His leadership was recognized in his senior year when he was elected captain of the football team. He was also selected as a member of the Academic All-American Football Team. A tradition at Berkeley was to have the football captain talk to the fans in the stadium after each home game; since the team did not win all its games that year, Tom later joked that he learned some valuable diplomatic skills by doing this! Clark Kerr was the chancellor of the Berkeley campus at the time, and he invited Tom to speak to some alumni groups, representing the student body. Although Tom always appeared poised, well prepared, and confident before large groups, he was actually quite nervous about public speaking; and he gave his wife, Eina, a great deal of credit for encouraging him and supporting him in these efforts. He was also selected for Berkeley's top honorary society, the Golden Bear, and received one of the institution's highest honors by being invited to deliver a valedictory address at his graduation exercises. He did not seek this honor and was reluctant to compete for it but, again, Eina's encouragement resulted in a very well-received address on "The Importance of Community Colleges." At commencement, he spoke of the challenges and opportunities confronting his graduating class, with emphasis on achieving permanent peace in the world. It was a big day for the entire Dutton family! Tom graduated with highest honors, receiving his B.A. degree in June 1954 from Berkeley, majoring in history and political science.

Tom's role model in college was Pappy Waldorf, the legendary football coach, and Tom decided that he wanted to become a teacher and a coach himself. He earned his teaching certificate, and a faculty adviser convinced him to remain at Berkeley and earn his master's degree. Tom was hired as an assistant football coach at the university, while he worked on his master's degree in educational curriculum and completed the program in 1956. Eina continued to work in the Registrar's Office at Berkeley during these years as well.

Tom loved coaching football and had considerable responsibility for such a young man at this major institution. But others also recognized his outstanding leadership and scholarship, in particular, Hurford Stone, the dean of students at Berkeley. Stone and the dean of men, Bill Shepard, contacted Tom and invited him to become the assistant dean of students, with responsibility for student residential groups and the 52 fraternities on the campus. Tom was also encouraged to enroll in the doctoral program in educational administration and higher education. Although Tom had excelled in student life and leadership as an undergraduate, he had no actual experience in student affairs. Moreover, his master's degree at Berkeley prepared him for teaching and, with his 2 years as an assistant football coach, Tom was a very attractive candidate for teaching and coaching positions. After a discussion with his wife, Eina, Tom decided to accept the position of assistant dean of students at Berkeley in the spring of 1956 and, at the same time, to enroll in the doctoral program in the school of education. He was also awarded two Woodrow Wilson grants for his doctoral research. This was obviously a major career decision for Tom; looking back on it now, he still is not sure of why he chose the direction he did. It seemed like the right thing to do at the time; so he did it!

Tom was fortunate to work with Deans Stone and Shepard. With their assistance, he became part of NASPA and learned everything he could about student affairs. He was very engaged with his doctoral course work and, as a result of his own leadership and involvement as an undergraduate, he knew a lot about the problems and challenges facing the large fraternity system. Tom's own values caused him to fight against hazing, alcohol abuse, and the exclusivity of some of the groups as well. Using the same highly organized and thoughtful approach that was to characterize his later career, Tom developed a comprehensive, written plan for success in the fraternity system at Berkeley, emphasizing educational programs and workshops on a variety of topics. Tom had worked hard all his life; so the long hours, nights, and weekends spent in the 52 fraternities and other living groups did not seem all that unusual to him. Moreover, his competitive drive that had made him so successful in football resulted in a strong determination to reform and improve the fraternity system. He was very effective in resolving conflicts and handling difficult situations, and he earned the respect and admiration of the students and other student affairs staff for his hard work and talents. He and Eina were thrilled when their two sons, Tyler and Ward, were born in 1958 and 1962. But when Tom completed his doctorate at Berkeley in 1961, the long hours of work and graduate study caught up with him and he contracted mononucleosis. Especially as a highly successful athlete, Tom expected that his energy was without limits, so he greatly disliked the time away from his job while recovering.

During his doctoral program at Berkeley, Tom worked closely with such nationally prominent faculty as Paul Heist, T.R. McConnell, and Leland Medsker. When he completed his doctorate, he had many professional opportunities available to him. The system-wide university relations office was interested in Tom, as was the office of vice chancellor for business affairs at Berkeley. But Tom's 6 years as assistant dean of students at Berkeley had convinced him that student affairs was the right career for him, and he decided to continue with it. In the spring of 1962, Tom received a letter from Dean of Students Bill Butler at Ohio University in Athens, Ohio, inviting Tom to consider the dean of men's position at that institution. Tom admitted later that he had never heard of Ohio University but, after some encouragement by his wife, Tom and Eina agreed to visit the campus and found the small town and the campus to be very attractive and welcoming. Tom was a native Californian, and Eina had lived there since she was 3 years old, so the idea of moving to a small town in southern Ohio represented a major change in their lives! Ohio University, founded in 1804, was an excellent institution, and Tom was very impressed with its young, new president, Vernon Alden, and its dynamic young SSAO, Bill Butler. Tom saw this as an exciting opportunity, so he decided to accept the position of dean of men and assistant professor of human relations at Ohio University in the summer of 1962, and he and his family sold their house in the Bay Area and moved to Athens, Ohio. Tom was only 30 years old.

Tom found Ohio University to be a very warm and accepting campus. It was much more conservative, of course, than Berkeley, although civil rights and racial issues were emerging as problems in Athens, Ohio in 1962 when he arrived. As dean of men, Tom enjoyed the support of Bill Butler and President Vernon Alden and was excited to be part of an institution that was growing and changing in many ways. Tom was highly visible on the campus with students and faculty, and as dean of men he helped attract many new and outstanding staff members, many of whom later became national leaders in student affairs. His ability to identify, hire, and develop talented professional staff was amazing; and this ability served him extremely well throughout his career. Many of the student issues Tom dealt with at Ohio University were the perennial problems of alcohol abuse, hazing, and student misbehavior. However, he and his staff developed excellent educational, social, and service programs that attracted large numbers of students; and Tom again earned high respect and admiration from students, faculty, and staff. Tom and his family were well established in the community of Athens and enjoyed the small town atmosphere. Tom was already an elder in his church and had no plans to leave, when in the spring of 1964 he received a call from Woody Varner, the chancellor of Michigan State University's new branch campus in Rochester, Michigan, inviting him to consider becoming that institution's SSAO. Tom had become very active in NASPA activities and had impressed many of his professional colleagues with his leadership abilities, and Chancellor Varner learned about Tom from them.

Michigan State University-Oakland had been established in 1957 as an innovative, public institution where an outstanding faculty had been recruited to build an educational program that would emphasize liberal arts, student creativity, and an appreciation of the performing arts and music. Tom's background at Berkeley, together with the excellent reputation he had established as an administrator there and at Ohio University, made him a strong candidate for the position. When Tom agreed to visit with Chancellor Varner in Rochester, Michigan, where Oakland was located, Tom discovered that the new institution was struggling, its students were unsettled, faculty were in conflict with administrators, and the former SSAO had just left his position after serving only a short period of time in it. Moreover, there was little structure in the student life program, and simple things like rules and regulations were very vague and undeveloped. Tom laughed later about this situation, since he viewed himself as a conservative, well-organized administrator, and most of the faculty and staff at Oakland appeared to be very liberal and casual. He wondered if he might fit at such an institution.

Tom liked Chancellor Varner and was excited about his plans for Oakland. When the chancellor offered Tom the position of dean of students and associate professor of education, Tom said he felt obligated to Ohio University, where he had only been dean of men for 2 years. President Varner knew Tom Dutton was an outstanding leader, and he said he would keep the position open for a full year, hoping Tom would accept it during the summer of 1965. After discussing this with his family and his dean at Ohio University, Bill Butler, Tom decided to accept President Varner's offer. In looking back at this decision many years later, Tom realizes he accepted the position because it was a tremendous challenge, it was a senior student affairs position, it was a new and exciting institution, and because he was so impressed with Chancellor Varner. Tom and his family sold their house in Athens, Ohio and moved to Rochester, Michigan, not far from Detroit, and he began his duties as dean of students at Oakland in the summer of 1965.

Tom immediately began to build a student affairs division at this new institution, where many of the students were suspicious of authority and highly individualistic. Many of the faculty were also wary and distrustful of administrators and resisted any initiatives that appeared to be controlling in nature. Tom knew Oakland's culture was different, but he had spent many years at Berkeley and was neither surprised nor intimidated by it. To the contrary, he found the students and faculty to be very stimulating and challenging; and his honesty, his straightforward way of dealing with problems, his respect for others, and his willingness to listen earned their understanding and respect. He again hired some very outstanding staff members at Oakland, including James Appleton, Edward Birch, Fred Smith, Douglas Woodard, Thomas Zarle, and Patricia Houtz. Most of Tom's key staff later became college presidents, SSAOs, or provosts at other institutions. With the excellent staff Tom was able to recruit, the student affairs program became well known for its innovative approaches to handling student problems and its ability to work positively with the diverse students on the campus. It was the late 1960s, and the terrible Detroit riots of 1968 reflected the tense racial problems in society and on the campus. Tom and his staff dealt with student unrest and protests regarding the war and racial issues, and with the daunting problems of alcohol and drug abuse.

The university grew rapidly, became independent of Michigan State University, and was named Oakland University. Tom was responsible for admissions, orientation, financial aid, registration, housing, and student life; and he developed well-organized programs to ensure success in these vital areas. He and his staff also saw the need for special support services for many students (for example, women, minorities, and older students); despite some resistance on campus, they were able to create successful programs in this area as well. He developed and implemented a new and comprehensive student conduct code and judicial system, assuring students fair treatment and shared responsibility. He managed to build a new student health center, a counseling center, and new residence halls. At the same time, Tom was becoming a national leader in NASPA and was appointed the director of the Division of Research and Program Development during 1967–1969. Under his leadership, the Division produced three widely used monographs during that time on "Institutional Policies on Controversial Topics," "Institutional Approaches to the Adjudication of Student Misconduct," and "Assumptions and Beliefs of Selected Members of the Academic Community." Given the problems faced by student affairs professionals during that tumultuous decade, it is no surprise that these publications were eagerly received and appreciated. He was also invited to become the director of the national conference for NASPA in Boston in 1970, which occurred, of course, in the same spring as the killings at

Kent State University. Oakland University recognized Tom's outstanding work and national reputation, and they changed his title to vice chancellor for student affairs and associate professor of education in 1969. He had built a highly successful student affairs division at Oakland, had hired a tremendous young staff, and was at the top of his profession.

Tom was a leader who gained quick respect from others because of his ability to speak clearly and honestly about issues, to work effectively with people, to organize well, and to get things done. It was thus no surprise that in 1969–1970 he received invitations to consider becoming a college president from several institutions. In his usual modest way, Tom never sought such a position and had not really thought about becoming a president. He did agree to pursue one of the invitations at a private institution in another state. As usual, he was enthusiastically received by students, faculty, staff, and the governing board; but he decided to decline the offer to become the college's president. Later, he understood that this experience helped him to clarify his own professional priorities. He enjoyed working directly with students, and he found the many challenges in student affairs to be a good match with his own values and abilities.

Tom and his family had now been in the Midwest for 8 years, and they loved the community of Rochester, Michigan and the exciting challenges at Oakland University. Moreover, Tom was very proud of the strong student affairs program and staff he had built and he had no plans to leave! Then Dr. James Meyer, chancellor of U.C.D., called Tom and asked him to consider the position of vice chancellor for student affairs. Tom had completed 5 highly successful, but stressful years at Oakland, and he and his family enjoyed their life in Michigan. But U.C.D. represented a unique opportunity, as it was a prestigious campus of the University of California system, and it was located close to the area where Tom and Eina had lived in Berkeley several years earlier. When Tom agreed to visit in Davis with Chancellor Meyer, he was most impressed with the comprehensive plans for the campus, the resources of the U.C.D. system, and the opportunity to build a first-class student affairs program. Tom felt very comfortable with the mission and values of the U.C.D. campus, and was enthusiastic about the support and leadership ability of Chancellor Meyer. He was also struck with the turmoil on the campus, and the unrest among students throughout the state. After careful consideration and discussion with his family, Tom decided to accept the position, and in the summer of 1970, during a period of great social turmoil in the country concerning the Vietnam war, Tom and his family moved from Rochester, Michigan to Davis, California, and he became the vice chancellor for student affairs and lecturer in education.

The Davis campus of the University of California is large and beautiful. Its traditional emphasis on agriculture, veterinary medicine, and the physical and biological sciences was expanding rapidly in the late 1960s and the early 1970s, and it eventually included schools of medicine and law, as well masters' and doctoral programs in many other academic disciplines. Tom was a recognized national leader in student affairs, and Chancellor Meyer was very supportive of Tom's plans to create a comprehensive and high-quality student affairs program. When Tom arrived at Davis, the student affairs program was limited in scope and decentralized under two administrative officers, both of whom reported to the chancellor. Right away, Tom worked to integrate all student services into a coherent and well-organized administrative structure to provide for the needs of existing and future students. Tom was given the authority to consolidate and expand services and programs, and he was asked to coordinate programs in his division with the undergraduate colleges, the graduate division, and the professional schools in the areas of academic support, retention, student affirmative action, student conduct, due process, and student-related legal concerns. In all of his professional positions, Tom had recognized the importance of a supportive, visionary president; and at Davis he felt very fortunate to work with Chancellor Meyer, whose notion of a "constructive learning environment" for students clearly reflected Tom's own educational values.

Tom was a strong advocate of planning and of involving staff, students, and faculty in his efforts to create effective service and educational programs for students. Perhaps most important, Tom knew that his success as a leader depended on understanding and support of basic ideas and assumptions about student learning. He was very effective in articulating the purposes and goals of the student affairs division as a natural and necessary part of the U.C.D. educational mission. An excellent listener, Tom was also a very persuasive presenter and speaker and was highly visible with students, faculty, and staff at Davis in his efforts to build the student affairs program. He was highly organized and developed written program statements and academic plans, distributing these documents widely on the campus, and encouraging open discussion and debate about them. He again demonstrated his talent to identify, hire, and develop very outstanding staff; and he attracted many nationally prominent professionals to Davis. Among the important documents Tom was involved in developing at Davis was the U.C.D. "Principles of Community," in which the institution's commitment to human dignity, freedom of expression, civility, and diversity was clearly stated.

The student affairs program at Davis became well known as perhaps the most comprehensive in the country during Tom's 21 years as vice chancellor. Tom eventually had responsibility for some 30 programs, which he organized under three vice chancellors for enrollment, advising, and academic support services; student life; and student relations. He was also in charge of intercollegiate athletics, which included some 20 sports for men and women. Tom was responsible for a budget of more than $120 million by 1991. His access to special student registration fees, in cooperation with the associated students of U.C.D., enabled Tom to create new programs, services, and facilities, especially during years when legislative appropriations were limited. Tom and his staff, through his open, honest, and personal work with students, were able to establish trust with student leaders and gain their support. Especially during the early 1970s, this was a very impressive achievement and resulted in much success in student life at Davis.

> *Tom began his work at Davis in 1970, one of the most volatile years of the century. Through his leadership, he brought structure, confidence, and a sense of trust and community to the student life program at the institution.*

As a result of Tom's leadership, the Davis campus now includes some of the best physical facilities for the support of student affairs programs of any campus in the country. A state-of-the-art student health service, a large recreation building, a learning skills center, a women's resource center, a child care center, a student union, cultural centers, residence halls, and the Thomas B. Dutton Student Services Center provide marvelous learning and service opportunities for Davis students. Among Tom's many accomplishments at Davis, the creation of the student affairs research and information office is one of the most outstanding. Tom was able to achieve funding for this office and staff it with several professionals early in his tenure as vice chancellor. He was convinced that systematic, reliable, and longitudinal information was critical to the university's ability to understand student needs and experiences and to improve the quality of student learning. The publications of this office were regularly distributed to faculty, administrators, parents, and others and remain today as a vital component of the overall student affairs program. Certainly related to Tom's leadership and his strong emphasis on planning, community, and assessment, the Davis campus consistently had rates of student retention, graduation, and student satisfaction that were among the highest in the University of California system.

As a leader, Tom knew that understanding of and support for student affairs was dependent on high performance, excellent staff, and effective services. To ensure that these goals would be realized, he was involved in establishing and maintaining advisory committees for financial aid, recreation, athletics, the student union, registration, the student health service, student affirmative action, disabled students, and international students. Most importantly, he involved many faculty and staff outside the division in these committees, and he took very seriously the advice that they offered. He found it very natural to work closely with the vice chancellor for academic affairs in establishing educational support programs for students, and his excellent record of performance usually resulted in Tom becoming responsible for administering the program. At the same time, Tom was able to convince the entire institution to open its various committees and councils to important student involvement, something that is now taken for granted on the Davis campus, but which was the result of years of hard work by Tom and his staff. It was certainly one of many reasons why the U.C.D. campus was selected as one of the 14 institutions from around the country as models for the important student affairs book, *Involving Colleges,* in 1991.

Tom also emphasized the importance of courage and good judgment for successful leadership. He often had to make difficult and unpopular decisions as a leader and had the fortitude to break new ground at Davis in such areas as race relations, gender equality, and freedom of expression. He openly challenged policies that needed change, and he was willing and able to accept the criticism that inevitably was directed at him.

Tom began his work at Davis in 1970, one of the most volatile years of the century. Through his leadership, he brought structure, confidence, and a sense of trust and community to the student life program at the institution. He was also able to adjust to the changes that came later in that decade and to the issues of the 1980s decade, which was especially challenging in California, with economic pressures and the rapidly changing demographics of the state. His clear value commitments to honesty, hard work, trust, freedom, and student learning placed him in a highly visible and important role at his institution, and his longevity as vice chancellor enabled him to achieve great success at Davis. He also emphasized the importance of teaching throughout his career, which he felt helped him to clarify the principles and values in his work with students. He was also very frank about the reality of stress for such major leaders as SSAOs; and he stated that he was able to survive, despite the unrelenting pressures, because of time away from the campus and the support and love of his wife, Eina.

Tom was an advocate of confronting problems directly, and he urged his staff not to ignore the effects of stress in their work. His hard work and attention to excellence in all that he did was developed early in his life, through his family and especially with his father. As a teenager, Tom learned that if the family business was to remain successful, he would have to pay close attention to the needs of his clients and to deal with them in an honest, open, and fair manner. The values he developed at this young age were to serve him extremely well throughout his student affairs career. In 1991, after serving as the vice chancellor at Davis for 21 years, Tom decided to step aside from his position. He served the Davis chancellor as senior adviser for the next 2 years and then retired in 1993.

The high regard that his professional colleagues felt for Tom was recognized in 1972–1973 when he was elected the president of NASPA. This was an intense period for many SSAOs, and Tom's thoughtful, vigorous, and sensitive leadership proved very valuable for the association and its members. While Tom approached issues and problems in a quiet and considerate manner, he was a very strong advocate for the values and beliefs he held and was tenacious in his determination to get things done. He was presented with NASPA's highest honor, the Scott Goodnight Award for Outstanding Performance as a Dean, in 1976. He chaired the Student Affairs Council of the U.C.D. System from 1979–1988, was a long time member of the National Vice President for Student Affairs Group, and was a frequent presenter and speaker at national and regional conferences.

One of Tom's chancellors at U.C.D., James H. Meyer, said of Tom, "One of the best things about Tom was that he worked cooperatively with others. He communicated extremely well with student and faculty leaders. He involved himself in other academic and nonacademic matters and was always looking to help prevent problems and to keep issues from being misinterpreted, rather than waiting until problems needed to be solved. "I really can't say enough good things about Tom. He was one of the best vice chancellors I ever hired!" (Meyer, personal communication with author, 2000).

Thomas B. Dutton was born in 1932 in southern California and achieved an amazing record at the University of California, Berkeley as a student and as a star football player and leader. He returned to his home state in 1970 and established one of the most successful student affairs programs in the country at U.C.D. His leadership at that institution and within the student affairs profession made a tremendous impact on the education of students and the development of staff. Throughout his career, Tom remained firmly committed to his basic values of honesty, hard work, trust, and respect for others. In the process, he became one of the most admired and most successful senior student affairs leaders in the country.

Chapter 7

Robert F. Etheridge
Miami University

Strolling through the beautiful Miami campus in Oxford, Ohio, Bob Etheridge says in a matter of fact way, "You know, this is Camelot!" A legend among students, faculty, and staff at the institution he loves so dearly, Bob is an enthusiastic advocate for Miami. When he joined the Miami staff in 1958, it was a perfect institution–person match, and this match flourished for the benefit of students' education for the next 30 years.

Robert Etheridge, an Illinois native, earned his B.S. and M.A. degrees from Southern Illinois University and his EdD from Michigan State University. He served as assistant dean of men at Southern Illinois University and as assistant dean of students at Michigan State University before being appointed the dean of men at Miami University in 1958. He became dean of students in 1959 and served as the senior student affairs officer (SSAO) at Miami from 1959 until his retirement in 1989. His title was changed to vice president for student affairs in 1967. Bob developed one of the country's most admired student affairs programs, well known for its extensive involvement of students in all aspects of the institution. He was elected the vice president of NASPA and was the person most responsible for establishing the now highly successful regional structure of that organization. He also served as the president of the Ohio Association of Student Affairs Administrators and as the president of the Association of Naval Reserve Officer Training Colleges and Universities. He served as the chair of the Student Affairs Commission of the National Association of State Universities and Land Grant Colleges, and he was the 1983 winner of NASPA's Scott Goodnight Award for outstanding performance as a dean. He was honored by both of his alma maters, Southern Illinois University, and by Michigan State University as a distinguished alumnus. His former students and colleagues established the Robert F. Etheridge Center for Reflective Leadership at Miami; only 10 years after his retirement, this endowment has grown to more than $1 million, a tribute to his tremendous leadership at the institution. Miami University named Bob an honorary alumnus and inducted him into in the Hughes Society, honoring educational leaders who have made an especially outstanding contribution to the institution.

Bob likes to describe how he was born on a kitchen table in the small, farm town of Fairfield, Illinois in 1925. There was no hospital within miles, and Bob, his older brother Bill, and his father were all born in the same house. As the family faced the Great Depression and very hard times in rural America, Bob's father, unable to find work, went to Detroit in 1931 to find employment in the auto industry. But his father disliked city life and missed his family, so he returned to southern Illinois, where he found a job with the postal service. Almost everyone was very poor in that area during the 1930s, and Bob grew up with a keen understanding of the value of hard work. As a young boy, he worked on the farm and remembers having to prove that he could lift and throw a certain amount of hay before he could get paid! To a young boy who already loved challenges and was very competitive in everything he did, Bob was up to the task. His family was close and there was no confusion about what values were important, with honesty emphasized most of all. Bob remembers a time when, at age 6, he naively took a harmonica from a local store; when his mother discovered what he had done, she marched Bob back to the store for a full confession. His commitment to honesty and fairness was strongly reinforced!

While the Depression years were tough, there was great love in the family and Bob and his older brother, Bill, enjoyed their small town, especially all the activities in which everyone was involved. Bob was a star athlete, became the captain of his high school football team, and was named to the all-state team. He also played basketball and was the valedictorian of his high school class, graduating in 1943. The country was at war, of course, and Bob was 17. Bill was already in the Air Force, and Bob wanted to follow him, so he went to St. Louis, Missouri and took an examination that might qualify him for that service. But he was also recruited by the University of Illinois to play football; after having been awarded an academic scholarship, he enrolled in classes in the summer of 1943 in Urbana-Champaign. He immediately was "put to work" as an athlete in the Illinois Union, setting pins for 30 cents an hour! But after only 3 days in classes at the University of Illinois, Bob received a letter, ordering him to report for military duty at Milligan College in Tennessee. Hundreds of college and university campuses were used as training sites during the war, of course, and Milligan, Tennessee was the furthest Bob had ever been from home. Bob had signed up for the ROTC program at the University of Illinois and now he was in a Navy officer flight training program at age 17. While he had obviously been an outstanding student in high school, he now encountered many other young men who were equally bright in this selective, highly competitive program. After 8 months of intensive training, he was sent to another training facility in Norman, Oklahoma. He also was assigned to posts in Wooster, Ohio; Iowa City, Iowa; Corpus Christi, Texas; and finally, in Kingsville, Texas, where he was awarded his wings. At that time, the war had ended, and although Bob had the opportunity to remain in the Navy as a pilot, he declined, left active service, was placed in the Naval Reserve, and returned to his home in Fairfield, Illinois. During his almost 3-year service in the Navy, Bob again proved to himself that he could compete with the best and the brightest, and his love of sports continued as well, as he played on highly successful service football teams during this time. He was now 20, had earned his wings, and was eager to move ahead with his life.

Bob had known a young girl by the name of Veda Hallam in his hometown since he was 7 years old. She was a talented and successful young woman, and when Bob returned from his Navy service on Christmas day, 1947, they were married. Bob took full advantage of the G.I. Bill and enrolled at Southern Illinois University, not far from his home. Veda was enrolled at Murray State University, but she transferred to Southern Illinois and during their senior year they were married. Bob, like so many other veterans in college at the time, was in a hurry. He worked at various jobs while at Southern Illinois and graduated in 1948 while majoring in sociology and English. Bob was a star football player at Southern Illinois and greatly enjoyed the teamwork required to be successful in that sport. He was known as a highly competitive young man who always was encouraging his teammates to do better— a trait that was to characterize his work in student affairs throughout his career!

At the time he graduated from Southern Illinois, Bob thought he wanted to become a social worker. He had seen the effects of poverty on many people during his early years and had seen large, impersonal bureaucracies and how they often did not serve the needs of people well. "I just didn't like to see people dumped on!" Bob said, and I thought I could do something about the problems in society. But at that time, Marshall Hiskey, the dean of men at Southern Illinois, contacted Bob and encouraged him to consider a position in student affairs at the institution while pursuing a master's degree in the college of education. Bob had never thought of such a career, but the more he learned about it, the more excited he became. As a veteran, he was mature for his young years and he had been very involved in student life and realized that Southern Illinois was a fast-growing and very promising place to be. Never hesitant to express his views to anyone, Bob immediately saw some pressing needs on the campus and wrote a letter to Dr. Deleyte Morris, the president, urging him to construct a new student union. His work was so outstanding at Southern Illinois that he was asked to become the assistant dean of men; and he was responsible for such programs as campus discipline, parking, activities, and housing. He was also involved in admissions and intercollegiate athletics and became well known for his hard work, honesty, and willingness to help students. Bob loved what he was doing and was eager to learn more, wherever it might require him to go. He studied during one summer at the University of Colorado and another with E.G. Williamson and Gilbert Wrenn at

Minnesota, as Bob took the initiative himself to arrange opportunities to learn from the most outstanding leaders in the profession. He and Veda now had two young sons, and Bob was encouraged by his colleagues at Southern Illinois to pursue a doctorate. Bob traveled to East Lansing, Michigan, and met with Wayne Tinkle and John Truitt, who led the student affairs program and had close ties to the graduate program in higher education. After being strongly encouraged to come to Michigan State, Bob was granted a sabbatical from Southern Illinois, and he and his family moved to East Lansing. Bob, still in a hurry, enrolled in the doctoral program and was appointed to the position of assistant director of the men's division in student affairs. It only took him 2 years to complete his degree at Michigan State. His dissertation focused on the relationship between student affairs and university police, a subject that was to serve him well in his future career!

Bob loved learning from his colleagues and always looked for opportunities to observe their work, discuss issues of mutual concern, and speculate about future needs with them. He was able to participate as a young professional in the now famous "Allerton Conferences" at the University of Illinois, where deans met informally for 2 days and, without a formal agenda, discussed problems and issues in student affairs. As a result, Bob developed friendships with older, more experienced deans and benefited from their guidance and support. This experience at Allerton reinforced his strong belief in the importance of networking with trusted colleagues as a way to improve practice and to continue to learn in the profession.

> *Bob exercised his leadership at Miami based on his strong belief that each student deserves to be treated as a special and unique individual.*

As Bob was completing his doctorate at Michigan State, he was contacted about a position by Carl Knox, the dean at Miami University in Oxford, Ohio. Carl had met Bob at Allerton and had previous experience at the University of Illinois. Bob and Veda visited Oxford and, like so many others, loved the campus as soon as they saw it. Bob was offered the position of dean of men on this residential campus of 5,500 students, and he accepted it, beginning his duties in the summer of 1958. Bob was only 33 years old, but he had already established a reputation at Southern Illinois and Michigan State as a bright, hard-working, and caring leader. As one of his colleagues explained, "When people met Bob Etheridge, they were immediately impressed with his outgoing, friendly, and warm manner; a short time later, they also were impressed with his passion for education and for doing positive things for students."

Almost immediately, Bob was known to everyone at Miami. He was tireless in his work on the campus, visiting residence halls at night, fraternity houses on weekends, developing freshmen advising programs in the residence halls, reorganizing the campus judicial system, and advising the student senate. At a time when many student affairs professionals were relatively passive and mainly responded to student problems, Bob was everywhere on the campus, talking with students, encouraging their involvement in campus affairs, and advocating stronger roles for them in university life. He also established his reputation as a strong administrator who was not hesitant to express his views on topics of student concern and to take students and others to task whom he felt were not performing up to their potential. Bob was a motivational leader and spent a good deal of his time encouraging students and staff to do better, to work harder, and to assume more responsibility. "Perhaps it was my experience in the Navy or in intercollegiate athletics, or maybe it was that I wanted to be a coach, but I was always competitive and saw it as my job to stimulate students to get all they could from their educational experience at Miami," Bob explained. Many former Miami students can still recall the strong personal interest Bob took in them as undergraduates, prodding them to do better, no matter what the activity. They also remember that Bob was not hesitant to raise tough questions with them, or to confront them about efforts he knew were not their best. But no student ever doubted his sincere interest in their lives or in their education; and he gained the respect, admiration, and affection of thousands of students as a result.

Bob exercised his leadership at Miami based on his strong belief that each student deserves to be treated as a special and unique individual. He loved his institution, but he viewed the purpose of the university as serving the needs of individual students. When bureaucratic policies or practices interfered with students' educations, Bob worked very hard to eliminate them. He created new opportunities for students to participate in campus life, but at the same time he expected students to be prepared for their responsibilities and to perform at a high level.

When Miami decided to establish a dean of students position in 1959, Bob was asked to accept this new assignment after only 1 year at the institution, and he thus became the first chief student affairs officer at Miami, directing a comprehensive program of services and activities. Dr. John Millett, a nationally known scholar and leader, was Miami's president, and Bob considered himself very fortunate to work for this outstanding administrator. Dr. Millett had been appointed Miami's president in 1953 and was to remain in the position until 1965, when he became chancellor of the Ohio Board of Regents.

As Miami's first dean of students, Bob quickly became the most visible and well-known administrator at the institution. He and his family lived in a university house on the campus, which enabled Bob to be available 24 hours a day! He later joked that the president, whose house was less than a block away, would signal to him that he needed him late at night by turning on a special light in one of the upstairs' rooms! Miami housed all of its students on the campus and was located in a small, rural town of only 4,000 residents, so campus life was very active. It was 1959, when "pantie raids" were still not uncommon on college campuses, and Bob remembers one that involved over 1,000 students in his first year at Miami. Bob had already created a new judicial system and knew it would be tested by some of the conduct actions required after the pantie raid. Despite efforts of some influential parents to prevent institutional sanctions, Bob gained the support of his president to take the necessary discipline, and he was confident that support would enable him to develop the total student affairs program in positive ways. He acted on his belief that he needed to take the initiative on policies, procedures, facilities, and programs when working with his president; as a leader, Bob knew what he wanted and never presented a proposal to the president unless he was convinced it was the best solution. He knew his president expected him to solve problems and create positive programs—not come to him with excuses or weak proposals. Bob emphasized thoughtful preparation in working with the president, and he expected his staff to know and understand campus issues and problems so that they could be accurately represented and explained to the president.

Miami was already well known for the high quality of its undergraduate education programs and for close student–faculty relationships. This was enhanced by a freshman advising program in the residence halls, directed by senior faculty members who lived in the residence halls. When Bob came to Miami he became very engaged with this program and, to his dismay, he discovered that it was not actually working well because of the disinterest of the residential faculty, most of whom were older and had been living in the halls, performing the same functions for many years. Student views of the advising program were largely apathetic, as they had little experience in knowing what they could expect from it. Bob became convinced that the program had to be changed and improved, as he knew the students were not being served well, despite the many years the program had been in place. But he needed to have an alternative plan, not just a list of problems with the current system. He worked very closely with the provost and the dean of the school of education, and he was able to convince them to allow him to create a graduate program in college student affairs administration and to assign bright and eager graduate students in this program as academic advisers in the residence halls. He was met with opposition from the long-time faculty who were serving in these positions already; but over a period of less than 4 years, Bob was able to transform and energize this program and substantially improve freshman academic advising at Miami. This program remains in place in the year 2000. As a leader, Bob recognized a problem that few other people were willing to acknowledge, decided to propose needed changes, convinced others that the plan he conceived could work, and implemented it successfully. There was risk involved for him and the student affairs division, for if he failed then other aspects of his program would suffer as well.

Miami University was founded in 1809, making it one of the oldest public institutions in the country. Its solid academic reputation, active campus residential life, and strong alumni support made it a very attractive choice for large numbers of student applicants. Among many other responsibilities, the Office of Admissions came under Bob's direction. Beginning in the early 1960s and increasing in intensity each year, Miami became one of the most highly selective public institutions in the country. It had enjoyed the flexibility of admitting almost 30 percent of its undergraduates from states outside of Ohio, and it considered this very important in achieving its goals of academic quality and diversity. Miami was the only Ohio public institution able to attract such a national student body, but it found itself under considerable pressure to admit larger numbers of Ohio residents as demand increased. Miami's board of trustees was able to retain the authority to admit a significant percentage of out-of-state students, but at the same time they permitted the enrollment to increase. Indeed, during the first 15 years of Bob's tenure at Miami, its enrollment doubled to more than 10,000 students. Bob was a strong advocate for high academic standards and for Miami's long tradition for highly personalized, residentially based undergraduate education. Miami's unique tradition of not allowing students to have automobiles at the institution contributed to the close and informal nature of campus life, and even in the 1960s this restriction did not discourage large numbers of students from wanting to attend Miami. Bob was also responsible for the residence halls, and he knew that substantial numbers of new halls would need to be constructed to keep pace with the increasing enrollment. Thus, a good deal of his time was devoted to planning, building, and financing these residence facilities during the period of 1959–1975. Bob was strongly committed to Miami's mission of personalized undergraduate education and knew that it was essential to have high-quality residence halls on the campus to achieve this goal.

The decade of the 1960s, of course, was filled with turmoil, due to the Vietnam War, the Civil Rights movement, and the revolution in student freedoms. Bob and his staff at Miami were close to students and worked with them throughout the decade to maintain good communication and trust. Major problems were avoided until April 1970, when a large number of Miami students moved into the campus armory to protest the war. Bob and his staff were there, of course, and despite his efforts to involve faculty and others in the crisis, many students had to be arrested, and 76 were suspended from the institution. It was a difficult time for young people and for Miami, which had worked for so long to create positive, trusting relationships with its students. But Bob was the person acting on behalf of the institution; after he realized that certain students would continue to break the law, he was not hesitant to take the necessary action. While he faced criticism from some faculty and students, he retained the respect and admiration of the great majority who knew him and understood what he had to do. Bob, long convinced of the educational nature of student discipline, urged the use of the student–faculty appeal process, and as a result most of the suspended students were eventually readmitted to Miami and earned their degrees.

Some calm returned to the campus until the May 4, 1970 tragedy at Kent State. Miami, after fires and bomb threats, was forced in the interest of safety to close the university. The issues of the day were, in the best traditions of the collegiate community, discussed and acted upon through normal channels. Unheralded in this was the use of a group of student leaders, who were called on as consultants to assist and promote the reopening of the university. Bob was responsible for developing this strategy and was successful in convincing faculty from many academic disciplines to teach a new course, "The Role of the University in Community Life," the next semester.

As Miami continued to grow, Bob knew that the various student affairs offices and programs needed better coordination. He strongly believed in a holistic approach to students, and he knew that students made no distinction among various departments at the institution—to them, "everything was Miami" and he was convinced that was the way it should be. He brought career planing and placement functions together while still respecting the individual needs of the various colleges and assured that the counseling services complimented these functions instead of duplicating them or competing with them. He brought the student union in closer contact with the residence halls programs and with student activities. He phased out gender-related student affairs offices but greatly enhanced service and support programs for women students, especially in the student health service. He built a student affairs organization that was lean but well coordinated; he accomplished this by hiring outstanding new staff and by working closely with them as a team. Bob was a strong believer in professional development as essential for continuing staff learning, and with his staff he designed a program that brought outstanding leaders to the campus to engage in discussion about new ideas in the field. He also strongly encouraged his staff to participate in professional associations, and as a result various Miami staff became well known as leaders within the profession.

Bob also was convinced that students needed a centralized facility on Miami's growing campus where they could conveniently obtain various services. After persisting in his attempts for many years, Bob succeeded in making the Warfield Student Services building a reality on the Miami campus, which brought together most of the student affairs departments and continues to provide excellent services to students in one location. Bob emphasized the importance of persistence in his role as a leader. "Good ideas are abundant on a college campus and are relatively easy to conceive; however, a good idea will remain only that unless someone takes a hold of it and builds support for it and makes it a reality," Bob suggested. He argued that a leader must persist with a proposal, sometimes for several years, until the timing and conditions come together and make it possible to happen. He added that leaders can often become discouraged because their proposals are not met with instant acceptance, and then they assume there is no support for them. "Most of the things I was able to accomplish at Miami," Bob said, "were ideas and proposals that took time to sell to others!"

A key example of Bob's persistent leadership style at Miami was in the area of student recreation. Although Miami had lots of outdoor space for student recreational activity, it did not have a centralized indoor facility, and Bob knew the institution was not keeping pace with other colleges and universities in this growing and popular area of campus life. The Miami program was organized under the Department of Physical Education, and it was not given much priority by the faculty in that area. Bob had a clear notion of what needed to be done to improve this situation, and he worked with the president and the Provost for a long time before he was able to convince them that responsibility for the program should be shifted to student affairs and that a major new facility needed to be constructed. After almost 10 years of effort, Bob succeeded, and Miami students and faculty now enjoy one of the finest and most extensive recreation and fitness programs in the country. Bob convinced student leaders of the need for a new facility and gained their support for special student fees for this purpose. Bob commented, "The road to accomplishing something like this is not straight and is always lined with obstacles; however, if leaders are to achieve anything of lasting merit, they have to be willing to fight for what they believe and convince others that what they are proposing will be of real benefit to the institution." Bob's tenacity for students and their education at Miami remain very well known.

> *Bob insisted that it was important for all of his staff not only to listen carefully to what students and faculty were saying, but also to have good and reliable information themselves about campus life.*

Miami's board of trustees consisted of 27 members and the board met in Oxford or Cincinnati several times per year. Bob worked very closely with the board during his years as the SSAO at Miami. He helped members of the board's committee on student affairs to understand changes taking place in student life, informed them about admissions and financial aid issues that were critical to student success, and helped them understand the need for greater racial diversity at the institution. Bob was fully aware of his obligations to support his president in all matters associated with the board, but Bob's strong views about student needs were well known and respected by board members. Many of the board members were Miami graduates, and Bob invited them to participate in various campus student programs, which enabled them to gain a greater appreciation of the changes taking place in student life. Bob talked with them informally on many occasions, especially during the decade of the 1960s, about the impact of the 18-year-old vote, the dissolution of the in *loco parentis* doctrine, and the increasing litigation that was affecting campus life. Bob retained his basic commitments to individual students, regardless of new laws and practices, but knew that board members needed to understand the implications of these important changes as they formulated major policies for the institution.

Bob was asked by President Phillip Shriver to serve as Miami's first vice president for student affairs, in 1967. Dr. Shriver succeeded John Millett as president in the mid-1960s; and while Bob's basic responsibilities did not change from his dean's title, his recognition as a vice president clearly signaled and confirmed the support he had earned for student affairs as a significant part of the institution's management team. Bob's leadership flourished with the support of President Shriver, who shared Bob's commitment to personalized education and was also very visible on the campus with students. Bob emphasized that a Council on Student Affairs, consisting of outstanding student and faculty leaders, should advise his division on policies, programs, facilities, and practices. Bob was assigned to chair this council himself, and it proved to be a very valuable mechanism for the rational consideration of problems and issues. Bob insisted that it was important for all of his staff not only to listen carefully to what students and faculty were saying, but also to have good and reliable information themselves about campus life. Thus, he established one of the first student life research offices in the country as part of a student affairs division; and this office produced highly valuable information about student needs and expectations, student reactions to policies and programs, and student educational growth and development. Although Bob never argued that such research information should decide policies and practices, he used it effectively as a tool in making decisions and in helping others understand what was actually happening with students on the campus.

The Miami campus in Oxford, Ohio is quite isolated and all student needs have to be addressed by the institution, as the community is too small to accommodate them. This was particularly true with student health, and Bob recognized early in his tenure at Miami that the old infirmary was outdated, both in its physical structure and in the scope of its medical services. After a great deal of hard work and persistence, Miami constructed a model student health service from student fee support. Bob and his staff knew the needs in areas such as sexually transmitted diseases, drug and alcohol abuse, sexual assault and abuse, and AIDS; and they hired new staff and developed outstanding programs and services to address these needs. Perhaps reflecting his own lifelong commitment to exercise and athletics, Bob was enthusiastic about the wellness concept and helped to establish programs that supported this concept in the student health service.

Miami has had a tradition of encouraging its undergraduates to study abroad, and in the 1960s the institution was able to set up a permanent study center in Luxembourg, where almost 100 Miami students matriculate for one or two semesters during their junior year.

Bob was an enthusiastic supporter of this program and traveled to Luxembourg to meet with education and government personnel to organize the program, including important student affairs services. He maintained close contacts with the program, its faculty, and its students during the next 2 decades; and this highly successful program continues in operation today.

Certainly related to his own positive experience in the United States Navy, Bob assumed administrative responsibility for the NROTC program at Miami and did this for almost 30 years. When faculty and student protesters demanded that the institution eliminate this academic and officer training program during the Vietnam War years, it was Bob who took most of the criticism and personal insults. He knew that the best way to prepare Naval officers was in high-quality colleges and universities, and he was a strong advocate for retaining the program at Miami. President Shriver and the Miami board of trustees supported this position, and the program continued to flourish and remains strong today. Students, faculty, staff, and board members were not surprised to see Bob take a strong public stand on a highly volatile issue and withstand the bitter criticism as well. He had already established himself at Miami as a leader who was willing to speak and to act on what he thought was right, despite the personal consequences. Bob's leadership in NROTC activities was recognized outside of the Miami campus as well, as he was later elected the president of the Association of NROTC Colleges and Universities. Bob also experienced great personal satisfaction, as Mike Etheridge, one of his sons, became a Navy pilot, and now flies commercial jets around the globe.

Miami University was included in a highly select group of institutions called the "Public Ivies" in a 1988 book of the same name. This did not surprise anyone associated with the institution, as the outstanding academic programs and the high quality of student life were well known to them. This national recognition increased the applicant pool again, and Miami continued to cope with the pressures of intensely competitive admissions. This recognition and increased visibility for the institution took place at the same time Miami was working diligently to attract additional minority students, especially African Americans. The admissions office reported to Bob; and he dealt effectively with the often conflicting demands of faculty, alumni, student groups, and board members. Bob was again outspoken regarding what he thought was right, and he insisted that no student should be admitted who did not have a reasonable chance of academic success. His long-time principle that "I just don't like to see any student dumped on!" served as his guide in this volatile admissions situation. Bob knew what kinds of services and support underprepared students needed, and he and his staff were ready to do whatever they could to provide such support. However, Bob understood very well how academically competitive Miami had become. As a result, Miami admitted students who could succeed, and the institution made steady and positive progress in recruiting and graduating minority students as a result.

Miami was also selected in the 1990s as one of a small group of institutions for the "Involving Colleges" project. Miami was included because of the high quality of its student life programs and the extensive involvement of undergraduate students in all aspects of the institution. This recognition affirmed the strong leadership Bob had given to the student affairs division for 30 years, and it brought more attention to the institution. Since the release of the *Involving Colleges* book, Miami's student life programs have been studied by dozens of institutions, and many student affairs professionals from other campuses have visited Oxford, Ohio to observe student life.

Bob was an active leader in NASPA throughout his career, served as vice president of the association, and in 1983 was the recipient of its highest recognition—the Scott Goodnight Award for outstanding performance as a dean. Reflecting his commitments to young professionals and their development, Bob was concerned that NASPA's organizational structure was no longer meeting the needs of the growing number of its members. He proposed a new regional structure, designed to multiply the opportunities for members to participate in the affairs of the association. This was very controversial at the time, as it seemed to threaten the traditional way of doing things by those who had been in charge of the association for many years. Bob was comfortable in this kind of activity; he was again advocating for what he thought was right and was willing and able to accept the criticism of others and defend what he was doing. That the regional structure of NASPA now is the foundation of its success is a tribute to Bob's insightful and persistent leadership.

Bob Etheridge made the decision to remain at Miami, despite many opportunities to go to other institutions, including invitations to become a president. He believed in Miami's values and understood its history and traditions. He was one of the primary builders of its stunning success during the 30-year period he served as the SSAO. He served under four presidents during his tenure and adjusted to the changes demanded by new presidents and especially by the changes in society. But he never wavered in his commitment to students and always viewed himself as a teacher more than an administrator. He said that he taught the "three Rs—reality, reason, and responsibility" and enjoyed personal relationships with students more than any other aspect of his work. As a leader, he motivated and inspired others by his actions and his commitment to humane values. He viewed leadership as a privilege and as an opportunity. He also understood that leadership comes with a price—a recognition that one might fail. Bob was always willing to pay that price at Miami, and the quality of student life there now stands as evidence of his great success. One of his presidents, Phillip R. Shriver, said, "Bob Etheridge served Miami for more than 30 years as our principal student affairs administrator. His legacy includes one of the nation's finest humane and human-scale residential campuses, a galaxy of inspiring traditions, and an emphasis on academic excellence. After his retirement, generations of his former students helped endow the Etheridge Center for Reflective Leadership at Miami, which continues to reflect his legacy" (Shriver, personal communication with author, 2000).

Chapter 8

Anne E. Golseth
Ohlone College

A nne Golseth greets everyone with a warm smile and a contagious good humor. She loves adventure and world travel, and she always seems to be on the move! At the same time, she is widely known and respected as a quiet and effective listener—a leader who succeeded because of her ability to relate well to others and to bring people together. A pioneer in the student affairs community college movement, Anne built a highly successful program at Ohlone College in Fremont, California, where she excelled for 20 years as the senior student affairs officer (SSAO).

Anne Golseth earned her B.A. degree in English literature from the University of Colorado in 1959; her M.A. degree in student personnel administration in 1962 from Cornell University; and her Ed.S. in guidance in counseling in 1968 from Michigan State University. She earned her PhD in higher education administration from Michigan State University in 1974. She worked as an office assistant in the Counseling and Testing Center at Stanford University from 1959–1960 and then moved to Cornell University, where she was a graduate assistant and a director of a residence hall from 1960–1962. From 1962 to 1964, Anne served as the assistant dean of students at Mills College in Oakland, California. After a year of travel and work as a social worker in the Arizona State Hospital in Phoenix, Arizona in 1964–1965, she became the assistant dean of women at Kent State University. In 1967–1968, she moved to Michigan State University, where she worked as a graduate assistant in the Counseling Center. She then moved to the position of dean of women at the University of North Dakota, which she held from 1968–1971. At the end of that year, she returned to Michigan State and completed her PhD, serving in various graduate assistantships in student affairs from 1971–1974. She was then appointed the director of advising services at the University of California at Davis (U.C.D.), a position she held until 1977. She was appointed dean of students and professor at Ohlone College in Fremont, California in 1977 and later became the institution's first vice president for student services. She held this position at Ohlone College for 20 years and retired in 1997. While she was an undergraduate at the University of Colorado, she was elected to membership in Phi Beta Kappa and Mortar Board, and she is a member of many other educational organizations and honoraries. She served as a member of the board of directors of the National Association of Student Personnel Administrators (NASPA) and as a member of the national committee that wrote *A Perspective on Student Affairs* in 1987. She was a long-time member of the American Association of University Women and served many times on accreditation teams for the Western Association of Colleges and Schools. She has been a member of the editorial board of the NASPA Journal, and she chaired the Code Committee and served as vice chair for the Commission on Athletics for the 107 community colleges in the state of California. In 1995, Anne was presented with NASPA's highest honor, the Scott Goodnight Award for outstanding performance as a dean.

Anne Golseth was born in Edina, Minnesota shortly before the outbreak of World War II. Her grandparents had immigrated to the United States from Norway, Sweden, and England; and her parents met in Minneapolis while they both were attending the University of Minnesota. Her father had grown up in North Dakota, and her mother was from St. Paul. Anne has three brothers and was the second child born to her parents. After graduating from Minnesota, her father accepted a position with the Cargill Grain Elevator Company in Minneapolis and, because the grain industry was defined as critical to the war effort, was exempted from the service. The town of Edina was rural during Anne's youth, and much of the area was still undeveloped. She now laughs about Edina, as it changed to an affluent suburb of Minneapolis many years later. She remembers the war years, the rationing, mock air raids, and the saving of tin foil, but mainly she recalls a very pleasant childhood. Her mother had majored in English, and her father had studied Economics at Minnesota. Education was always strongly emphasized in her family. Anne and all three of her brothers graduated from college.

Reflecting a lifelong love of adventure, Anne enjoyed outdoor activities in Minnesota, especially sledding, skiing, and skating. Her brothers were very active as well, and Anne joined them in their sports and games. Her father enjoyed bird hunting and had hunting dogs, which most likely stimulated an avid interest in animals during Anne's life.

When she was 9 years old, Anne's father was offered a job with a company in Chicago, and the family moved to Elmhurst, Illinois, a suburb outside the city. Anne attended the public schools, excelled in her academic work, and became very active in the Girl Scouts. She attended Girl Scout camps in Wisconsin during the summers, and as she recalled later she enjoyed a secure and happy time during the early 1950s. She attended York High School in Elmhurst for 2 years, and then the family moved again as her father received another promotion with a grain company in Danville, Illinois, about 130 miles south of Chicago. Moving to another community in the middle of high school is never easy, but Anne adjusted well and became very active and successful in her new setting. She was a reporter for the school newspaper, a member of the Y-Teens, and a participant in many school activities. Always an avid reader, Anne loved the lively discussions among her family at dinner each night about current issues of the times. Her father frequently brought well-educated visitors to the house, and as a result Anne was exposed on a regular basis to new ideas. Danville, Illinois was much more diverse than the communities Anne had lived in before, and she remembers developing her social conscience during her teenage years. One of her father's professional associates was an African American scientist, and his house was bombed during the early 1950s; such incidents were bound to have a strong effect on her thinking and on her values. She remembers the move from Elmhurst to Danville as an important transition in her life, and this experience certainly was related to the emphasis she placed on students' transitions to college during her career.

Anne graduated from Danville High School in 1955, and in her family going to college was a given. She was excited about going to college, but it was mainly the next logical progression in her life. She had worked during summers at camp, and always seemed to be looking for adventures. She took flying lessons while still a teenager, worked in a riding stable in order to get free horseback riding lessons, and dreamed about traveling to the West Coast. She thought she would enjoy the mountains, so she applied to the University of Colorado at Boulder. Always a fine student, Anne was accepted right away and decided to attend, although she had never visited the campus. She boarded a train by herself when she was 18, headed for Boulder, and enrolled as a freshman in the fall semester of 1955. While she thought she might like to become a journalist, she actually had no clear idea of what she wanted to do in her future career. She loved ideas and reading, and she eventually majored in English literature. She became very active and successful at Colorado and loved the college experience. She joined a sorority, Gamma Phi Beta, was active in the Associated Women Students, became a resident assistant in the residence halls, was active on the *Yearbook,* was stage manager for a student review, and was elected president of her residence hall. She also loved the surrounding mountains and became an enthusiastic skier and hiker. While few students challenged existing standards during the middle 1950s, Anne questioned some of the practices of her sorority and expressed concern about the lack of integration in campus life. The University of Colorado was the site of a world affairs conference while she was there, and she found the intellectual climate of the campus very stimulating and challenging. Her excellent academic achievement was recognized when she was invited into membership in Phi Beta Kappa, and her service and leadership were recognized by induction into Mortar Board.

When Anne graduated from Colorado in 1959, she was ready for more adventure and did not feel as bound by the traditions of the times as most of her friends. After considering various employment opportunities, she decided she would move to San Francisco and look for work there. Anne's dream of moving to the West Coast became a reality! Without knowing where it might lead, Anne accepted a position as an office assistant in the Counseling and Testing Center at Stanford University. While not a professional position, Anne quickly became familiar with the Center's various services. The staff members recognized her intelligence and insight and invited her to join in professional development activities. Reflecting her long career as an administrator, Anne later joked, "I was only there 1 year, but of course, I completely reorganized the filing system for the Center and made sure it was working properly!" The Center's staff warmly accepted Anne, and she became good friends with many of the graduate students associated with the Center as well. As a result, she learned about graduate programs in student personnel administration, and she became quite excited about this field as a potential career. Again reflecting her interest in seeing new areas of the country, Anne looked to the East and applied to graduate programs at the University of Vermont, Syracuse University, and Cornell University. Cornell offered her a position in the residence halls, which would provide her with financial support during her master's degree program, and she decided to go to Ithaca, New York in the fall of 1960.

Anne found her first year at Cornell to be quite challenging. She was stimulated by her graduate courses and liked working with the students in the residence hall, but after a year in San Francisco she was not very enthusiastic about the frigid Ithaca winters. But she did so well in her work that her supervisor, Dr. K. Patricia Cross, promoted her to the position of hall director the next year. Dr. Cross was then serving as the dean of students at Cornell, one of only two women appointed at the time as SSAOs at major universities. Anne also enrolled in a graduate course taught by Dr. Cross. This outstanding leader was to serve as an important role model for Anne throughout her career. It was 1962, and much change was taking place in American society and on college campuses, and Anne loved being part of this. She attended conferences of the National Association of Women Deans and Counselors (NAWDAC) and met some of the outstanding leaders of that time, such as Marion Sheldon, Elizabeth Greenleaf, and Esther Lloyd-Jones. As a result, Anne decided that her career goal was to become a dean of women. She completed her M.A. program at Cornell in 1962 and attended the NAWDAC conference in Chicago, where she interviewed for various positions. Always seeking an experience that would represent a new challenge, Anne accepted a position as assistant dean of students at Mills College in Oakland, California. At Mills, her responsibilities included residence halls, student government, student activities, and international students. At this prestigious, residential college for women, there were marvelous opportunities for the students and a genuine college community for faculty and staff. There was great turmoil in American society by this time and, during her second year at Mills, President Kennedy was assassinated and the Free

Speech Movement protests occurred at Berkeley, only a few miles away. Although Anne loved being engaged in the social change of the times, she was uncertain about where she might be heading professionally. After extensive discussion with her Dean, Patricia Brauel, she decided to leave Mills in the summer of 1964. Anne said later, "I think I just needed some time to assess where my career might take me." With her love of adventure and her confidence that solitude and a new experience would bring renewal, she traveled to Scandinavia, England, and throughout Europe for the next 4 months on her own. As she had done everywhere over the years, she made many new friends and found the experience exhilarating. In December 1964, she returned to her parents' home in Danville, Illinois to relax and to contemplate her next move.

It took Anne only about 3 weeks before she packed her car and headed to New Mexico—a place she had not been, but wanted to see and experience. After exploring opportunities in Albuquerque, she decided to visit one of her brothers, who was living in Tucson. She took state exams in Phoenix and accepted a position as a social worker at the Arizona State Mental Hospital. She worked with teenagers and had challenging and rewarding experiences with the troubled patients. She quietly noted the incredible contrast with her previous work at Mills College, and she did so well in her work that her supervisor strongly encouraged her to enroll in a graduate program in social work at Arizona State University. But after a year away from college student affairs work, Anne was now clearly committed to the field. She felt very fortunate to be offered a position at Kent State University as assistant dean of women. She worked with Elizabeth Anthony, the dean, and with other outstanding professionals on the staff, such as Ronald Beer and David Ambler, both of whom would become long-time colleagues of Anne's as future SSAOs. At Kent State, Anne had full-time residence hall directors reporting to her; and she was involved with new student orientation, judicial affairs, and Greek affairs. While there was some unrest at Kent State during the period of 1965–1967, when Anne was on the staff, the institution's major turmoil was to come later, in 1970. Anne established herself again as a leader by building trusting and personal relationships with students, faculty, and staff. Others learned quickly that Anne's intelligence and insight into educational issues were very valuable, and students particularly found her to be a friendly, warm, and accessible administrator. Anne became quite active in Ohio NAWDAC activities and became a close colleague of Dr. Judith Chambers, dean of women at Mt. Union College. Judy was later to become president of NASPA, and she and Anne both became SSAOs in California during the1970s. It was mainly through her professional association colleagues that Anne became convinced that she should pursue additional graduate studies in the field. So, in the fall of 1967, Anne left Kent State University and enrolled in the specialist program in higher education at Michigan State University.

During her year at Michigan State, Anne worked in the Counseling Center and became a close colleague of many of the student affairs staff. The 1967–1968 academic year was probably the watershed year of student protests in the country, and the unrest and turmoil at Michigan State was very unnerving. Anne remembers very well the NAWDAC convention in Chicago in 1968, the tragic assassination of Dr. Martin Luther King, Jr., and the American College Personnel Association conference in Detroit, during some of the worst riots of the century. It was an extremely challenging time to be a student affairs administrator, but Anne was determined to remain in the field. She completed her educational specialist degree at Michigan State in the spring of 1968 and, although her advisers on the faculty urged her to remain in East Lansing and complete her PhD, she was anxious to get back into direct contact with students as an administrator.

After considering several opportunities, Anne decided to accept the position as dean of women at the University of North Dakota in Grand Forks. Although she had already been at Colorado, Stanford, Cornell, Mills, Kent State, and Michigan State, Anne was still only 31 years old; and it was an outstanding accomplishment to be appointed to this position at such a young age. It was the fall of 1968. She reported directly to the president at North Dakota, Dr. George Starcher. She loved the institution and its strong values of community and openness. While she was there, the university was awarded the Alexander Meikeljohn Prize by the American Association of University Professors, in recognition of the institution's strong support for academic freedom. In her highly visible position, she had responsibilities for residence halls, student judicial affairs, Greek affairs, and student activities. There were demonstrations on the campus regarding the Vietnam War and Civil Rights issues; and Anne learned that she could handle the pressure of the job and the frequent criticisms from students, faculty, and community members. She established close relationships with students and helped to establish a student exchange program between North Dakota and Grambling College in Louisiana. Her excellent skills in human relations were again a valuable asset to the university in resolving differences with students. She was the adviser to the Association of Women Students, and in the spring of 1970 she took a group of women student leaders from North Dakota to a national conference in Tuscaloosa, Alabama. Anne had the highest respect for the genuine, caring values of the University of North Dakota, and her years there as dean of women were very gratifying to her. She exerted her leadership by building positive relationships with students, faculty, and staff; and by demonstrating through her own hard work and integrity that trust could be established on the campus. When President Starcher retired from his position in 1971, Anne listened to many of her colleagues, who had been urging her to return to Michigan State University and complete her PhD. With some reluctance, Anne decided to leave her position as dean of women at the University of North Dakota in late 1971, and she returned to East Lansing to complete her doctoral degree.

While she was back at Michigan State, Anne thought she would concentrate full-time on her studies, but her close relationships with student affairs staff members there resulted in a full-time job in the Dean of Students Office. She also assisted with master's degree students in the graduate program. She helped cope with the unrest that permeated the campus, especially concerning the Vietnam War and Civil Rights issues. She completed her PhD at Michigan State in 1974 and was enthusiastic about getting back to a major administrative position in student affairs.

> *Anne had achieved success in all of her previous leadership positions and understood the value of listening to others and learning the institutional culture before she made too many changes.*

Anne's love of the West Coast was still with her in 1974, and after considering various opportunities she decided to accept the position of director of advising services at U.C.D. The U.C.D. campus was already well known for having one of the most comprehensive and effective student affairs programs in the country, and Anne was very excited about this professional opportunity to work with such national leaders as Dr. Thomas Dutton and Dr. Scott Rickard. Due to her extensive previous administrative experience, Anne was granted a great deal of freedom to develop her staff and the advising program at Davis. The institution was growing rapidly and attracted very competitive students, many of whom planned to go on to graduate and professional schools. Anne worked to establish excellent advising programs for new students and for upperclassmen and women students. She was able to hire many of her own staff as the program expanded, and her leadership and good relationships with students and faculty were well known on the campus. Anne was most impressed with U.C.D. and loved working with the large and professionally oriented student affairs staff. However, she knew she was ready to become an SSAO, and she thought carefully about the kind of institution and the type of students with which she would like to be associated. The Davis students represented the elite academic stars of the state, and many came from relatively affluent families; Anne found them stimulating, positive, and enjoyable. But she was still young and idealistic and was well aware of the exciting work being done in the California community colleges with students from very different social, economic, ethnic, and academic backgrounds. She asked herself, "Where could I make the most impact on students' education? Where was I needed most?" As a result, Anne decided to explore the possibility of shifting her career emphasis. While she did not know it at the time, this willingness to consider yet another new adventure in 1977 would become the most important decision of her career.

After reviewing various opportunities, Anne accepted the invitation of the president of Ohlone College in Fremont, California to interview for the position of dean of students. Anne recalls a meeting that day when she faced a "committee" of 15 students, faculty, and staff who grilled her about her educational ideas and leadership style. She obviously succeeded in making a good impression, as she was offered the position and decided to accept it on August 1, 1977. Ohlone had only been founded in 1967 but already enrolled 9,000 students. Anne would report to the president, Dr. William Richter, and would have responsibility for all aspects of student life, including admissions, activities, registration, student health, career advising and placement, the tutorial center, student government, financial aid, counseling, special student services, international programs, and intercollegiate athletics. She was the only female senior administrator at Ohlone College at the time and the first student affairs professional to hold her position. She was young and enthusiastic, and although she had extensive professional experience at several other institutions in other states, she had not previously worked at a community college. She knew she would have to earn the support of students, faculty, and staff. In later years, Anne joked, "I had a lot to learn!"

Ohlone College was located in Fremont, California, and the students were very diverse. Many of them came from blue-collar backgrounds, and among them were recent immigrants from India, Afghanistan, the Philippines, China, Korea, and Mexico. The geographical area was growing, and Ohlone was truly "Democracy's College" in terms of offering opportunities to everyone. Moreover, reflecting the area's economic traditions, most of the employees of Ohlone College were members of unions; for example, the maintenance staff was affiliated with the AFL-CIO. The enrollment was growing when Anne moved to Ohlone in 1977, and the expectations were that this trend would continue. However, a few months later, "Proposition 13" was passed by the California legislature, which severely reduced funds to public institutions, resulting in serious financial problems for Ohlone College. Anne realized that she had moved from the very secure and traditional U.C.D. campus into a radically different setting—a young, nontraditional community college that was striving to establish itself in the face of considerable financial obstacles! She was the SSAO and accepted the fact that a great deal was expected of her. Anne had always sought out adventures in her life; now she relished this challenge more than any in her career. She was determined to build a successful student affairs program for Ohlone College!

Anne had achieved success in all of her previous leadership positions and understood the value of listening to others and learning the institutional culture before she made too many changes. Thus, at Ohlone College, Anne met with deans, faculty members, board members, community leaders, students from all backgrounds, staff groups, union leaders, maintenance personnel, coaches, local police, and financial administrators. She worked long hours to meet the people and to gain a clear idea of their problems, concerns, and aspirations. In this process, Anne won the support and respect of the Ohlone College community for her energy, her openness, and her willingness to listen. She is a very skilled listener and can quickly understand others' needs within an organization; most important, she could also act on this understanding and make decisions that improved the education of students.

The students, faculty, and staff at Ohlone College understood that they now had a leader who not only would listen carefully to them, but also one who was able and willing to act. Anne believed in direct, face-to-face communication and did not shy away from conflicts. She became well known for her friendly, yet direct way of saying "let's deal with this!" in the face of the many difficult cutbacks faced by the college and its staff during her first few years at Ohlone. She had high expectations for her staff and insisted on quality delivery of all services and programs; and she did not transmit her messages to staff by fiat, but by her own example of hard work and high performance. In particular, Anne wanted to do whatever she could to personalize the college experience for Ohlone students, helping them develop a sense of pride in their academic and personal achievements. She assumed responsibility for the graduation program, changing the ceremony into a positive and family-oriented celebration; she developed a new student orientation program that recognized the diverse needs of the students; she initiated recognition programs for student organizations; and she gave new emphasis and visibility to the intercollegiate sports programs.

Anne says she was fortunate to become part of an administrative team at Ohlone, consisting of the president, and the three vice presidents for academic, financial, and student affairs. "We worked together very well, although not without conflicts," Anne said. "Being a member of this team, I was able to make my several proposals for improvements in student life in a direct, face-to-face manner." She was successful in achieving many new programs and facilities, including athletic facilities, a student health service, and a career resource center.

Fremont, California is a conservative community, and among the great diversity in the population, there were significant numbers of Catholics and Mormons. During the 1980s, when widespread concern about AIDS developed in California, Anne was a visible, outspoken advocate for the free and open distribution of condoms and was widely criticized by those who opposed such actions. She also continued her strong advocacy of free speech for students, and in the process she earned the respect and admiration of the Ohlone students. She continued to enjoy the support of her president and understood that this support was critical to her public actions. She was also able and willing to blunt much of the public criticism of the president by accepting it herself. She laughed later in her career,

"I didn't like to be criticized in public, but I knew it was part of my job, and luckily, I was always supporting a good cause, such as free speech!"

Anne had always loved athletics and outdoor life, and it seemed natural to her that she should do what she could to enhance the intercollegiate athletics program at Ohlone College. Her rationale was that these programs increased visibility and pride in the college, offered students healthy outlets for their energies, and increased enrollment and retention. While she later joked that she probably would be remembered as the "Vice President who dropped football!" in fact, she focused on the quality of sports programs for both men and women. Somewhat reluctantly, Anne assumed a statewide leadership role among the 107 community colleges, becoming the chair of the group that established the code that still guides the actions of the institutional sports programs. Her reputation for integrity and her abhorrence of cheating in sports resulted in others asking her to assume this leadership role. Anne was well liked by everyone as a pleasant, intelligent, and caring person; she was also respected as a person of high standards and determination who was able and willing to make difficult decisions.

> **Dr. Golseth is a true leader; she acts for the benefit of the students and nothing whatsoever deters her from reaching this goal. She is an icon and a legend all wrapped into one!**

Anne had frequent contacts with the board of trustees at Ohlone, an elected body that met twice per month on the campus. Working through her president, she kept board members appraised of the changing needs of the students and problems and issues on the campus. She realized how important it was for board members to understand student affairs, and she worked to involve them in the life of the campus.

She once described her leadership style by suggesting that she "worked at under-reaction." She says she often saw others over-reacting to problems and consequently having to spend a lot of time backtracking and correcting poor decisions. She said that the most important thing for her to do was to listen to others. At the same time, she acknowledged her own impatience for endless committee deliberations and accepted the responsibility to act and move on. She insisted on collaboration with staff, and she always gave credit to them for their work. Finally, she accepted the fact that if everything must be perfect before a leader takes any action, then nothing will ever be accomplished.

Anne became an enthusiastic advocate for the community college movement and knew her own values were an effective match with those of Ohlone College. She loved being part of the exciting, if sometimes chaotic, development of this pioneering educational movement, as it fulfilled her aspirations for adventure and reinforced the commitments of her social conscience. She was invited to consider a community college presidency, but she declined the possibility of doing this, as the constant political and financial requirements of the position were not attractive to her. She was committed to her work in student affairs, and she loved the populist nature of the students, especially the tremendous diversity characteristic of California. She became highly visible as a community college student affairs leader, not only in California, but also throughout the country. She served on the national board of NASPA, was a frequent presenter at regional and national conferences, and served as a consultant to other institutions. Her positive leadership and dedication to students and the profession were recognized in 1995 when NASPA presented her with the Scott Goodnight Award for outstanding service as a dean. One of her former students, Annette Shurn, said at the time, "Dr. Golseth is a true leader; she acts for the benefit of the students and nothing whatsoever deters her from reaching this goal. She is an icon and a legend all wrapped into one!"(Shurn, personal communication with author, 2000). And, Peter Blomerley, one of her presidents at Ohlone College said of Anne,

> I can attest to Dr. Golseth's outstanding administrative performance. Despite the challenges of operating with the chronic shortages in funding in California, she has been able to maintain a high level of student services through perseverance and innovative responses. Her support of her staff is unwavering though tempered with a realistic assessment of their individual abilities. She motivates them to maximize their personal strengths (Blomerley, personal communication with author, 2000).

After serving as the SSAO at Ohlone College for 20 years, Anne decided to retire in 1997. She built the successful student affairs program of the college and left the college with a great sense of accomplishment. True to her adventurous spirit, she has traveled to all the continents, including an exciting trip to Antarctica and a safari in Kenya. She is active in several volunteer organizations and is learning to play golf. For Anne Golseth, the adventure of life continues with the same enthusiasm that she gave to her outstanding career in student affairs.

Chapter 9

John J. Koldus III
Texas A & M University

W hile John Koldus is walking through the Memorial Student Center on the Texas A & M (TAMU) campus, he greets several students, calling each of them by name. He stops to help another student who is looking for a meeting room. "Hello, I'm John Koldus; is there something I can do to help you?" he asks. After a few minutes of chatting, while John learns the student's name, hometown, and major, John says, "It was nice meeting you, Bill; and remember, if I see you on campus and don't call you by name, I'll buy your lunch!" This story is not only true—it has become a legend on the TAMU campus, where John Koldus, vice president for student services from 1973–1993, not only remembered the names of thousands of students, but also built one of the most comprehensive and successful student life programs in the country.

John Koldus earned his B.S. degree in physical education in 1953 from Arkansas State University in Jonesboro, Arkansas. After graduation, he served as an officer in the United States Army for 2 years. Then he was a teacher and coach in the public schools of Blytheville, Arkansas for the next 4 years, during which time he completed his master's degree in education in the summers at the University of Arkansas. After teaching high school history and civics and coaching football in Amarillo, Texas for 2 years, John accepted a fellowship at the University of Arkansas in 1961 and completed his EdD in 1963. That fall, he accepted a faculty position at East Texas State University in Commerce, Texas in the Department of Health and Physical Education. Advancing rapidly through the ranks, he was promoted to professor in 1967. In that same year, he was appointed the vice president for student affairs at East Texas State University, remaining in this position for 6 years. In the summer of 1973, he accepted the position of vice president for student services at

TAMU and held this position until his retirement from the university in 1993. He has served as the president of the Texas College and University Student Personnel Association and the Southwest Association of Student Personnel Administrators. He was elected a regional vice president of NASPA in 1985, and the award for outstanding professional accomplishment in that region is named in his honor. In 1986, NASPA presented him with the Fred Turner Award for distinguished service and in 1991, with the Scott Goodnight Award for outstanding performance as a dean. One of the new student orientation special camps at TAMU bears his name, and upon his retirement the university named its new student services building the "John J. Koldus Student Services Center."

John J. Koldus III was born in 1930 in Gary, Indiana, one of four children of John, Jr. and Helen Koldus. John, Jr. immigrated to this country with his family in1913 from Hungary. His father, John, Sr. worked on the railroads in the western United States and settled in the steel-making city of Gary, Indiana, because there were jobs available there. John's mother's parents also came from Hungary, and after a time working in the Pennsylvania coal mines came to Gary for the same reasons. Their nationality group was very strong and families remained close to their language, church, and traditions. The family lived in an apartment for John's first 11 years; the public school was across the street, so John and his friends enjoyed playing various sports and games on the school grounds. Neither of his parents had been to college. His mother had worked in a stocking factory before she was married, and John's father worked for U.S. Steel. Despite being born during the beginning of the Great Depression, John's father worked steadily; there was not much money, but this was the case with almost all of his friends, and John enjoyed a happy childhood. His father was in a train accident in 1942 and lost his leg; as a result, he missed almost 2 years of work. The family moved from their apartment into its first house in 1941. John said he had very few material things except footballs, baseballs, and basketballs. He loved sports of any kind; and in this rough, working class, multi-ethnic city, growing up as a boy meant learning how to fight and to compete. Even at an early age, John loved competition and the rougher it got, the more he loved it!

John understood at an early age that if there was something he wanted, he was going to have to earn it by paying for it himself. His parents were very kind and loving, but with four children they had little spare money for nonessentials. John began delivering newspapers when he was 10 years old and joked later that he never stopped working after that. With money he earned from this job and from caddying at a local golf course, he bought his first bicycle. Gary, Indiana is close to south Chicago, so John was thrilled when he was able to attend a Chicago White Sox-New York Yankees baseball game, where he could see his hero, Joe Dimaggio! Gary was also close to South Bend, Indiana, so John grew up dreaming of playing football for his beloved Notre Dame. When John's father lost his leg in the accident he could no longer work for U.S. Steel, but he became a skilled electrician (repairing motors), a job he continued until he was 66 years old. Although his father had not finished high school, he was an intelligent man and an avid reader. John's mother and father always encouraged John in his schoolwork, although they did not pressure John to achieve. John loved school, admired his teachers and was an excellent student. Due to his father's injury, he could not serve in World War II. But John's favorite uncle was in the Army and had fought in the Battle of the Bulge. John joked later that the gasoline rationing program during the war did not affect his family, since it had never owned a car!

John continued to work after school, on weekends, and during the summers. In high school, he worked as a laborer at a steel rolling plant in Gary. He was a top-notch athlete in high school, lettering in basketball, football, and baseball. Sports were his first love; he admired his coaches and decided he wanted to become a coach someday himself. Even though John was small—5 feet, 9 inches tall, and 135 pounds—he made a name for himself as a sports star due to his determination, his competitiveness, and his toughness. He received the sportsmanship award and the top all-around athlete award when he was a senior. However, when he graduated from high school in 1948, John's dream of an athletic scholarship was not fulfilled, and he, along with many of his friends, went to work full-time in the rolling mill plant in Gary. John continued to live at home with his parents, although he paid them for his room and board costs, which was a common practice during those days. His family did not have enough money to send him to college, but John kept alive his dream of earning a college athletic scholarship. After working at the rolling mill plant for almost 15 months, two of John's former high school coaches contacted members of the football staff at Arkansas State University in Jonesboro, Arkansas, and were assured that if John enrolled for classes there in the fall, he could try out for the football team. John was extremely excited by this opportunity, even though there was no promise of a scholarship. By working in the rolling mill for 15 months after completing high school, he had saved enough money to pay for his first year of college. He was admitted to the university, his close friend drove him to Jonesboro, and John enrolled for classes. He was assigned to live in a facility referred to as the "Pig's Pen," a barracks located in the old gym, along with many other freshman athletes. On the football practice field, John discovered he was among the smallest players trying to earn a spot on the 45-man roster. He knew his chances were slim, but he was a rugged competitor and, after impressing the coaches with his furious tackling, he made the team and was granted a full athletic scholarship. He had always worked very hard for everything he earned, and this experience at Arkansas State in 1949 reinforced the belief that would guide the rest of his career in education—with hard work, encouragement, and dedication, almost anything can be achieved.

John was moved from the barracks in the old gym to a residence hall room, where he had three roommates. He loved the southern town of Jonesboro and found it to be a warm and friendly place, where everyone spoke to one another, unlike the large city of Gary, where he was raised. Through hard work and determination, John had earned his way to college, and he was going to make the most of it! He majored in education, minored in history, and decided he wanted to be a coach. He loved Arkansas State and became very active in campus life, in addition to playing varsity football. He joined the Pi Kappa Alpha fraternity and the Newman Club, and was invited to join the leadership honorary, Blue Key. He loved to dance and attended many social events. He also was enrolled in ROTC for all 4 years in college. During the summers John returned to Gary and worked in the rolling mill, while he also played in a summer baseball league. He was such a competitor that he could not resist the opportunity to enter a Golden Gloves boxing tournament while he was in college. His father was an avid boxing fan, because Tony Zale, a boxing champion of the times, was from Gary, Indiana. However, John's father would not permit him to box. But John was away at college now, and as he said, "I was from a tough neighborhood and my older friends and cousins used to beat me up all the time when I was a kid. So, I thought boxing would be fun!" So he entered the tournament, and he won his weight class! He traveled to Memphis, though, and lost a split decision in the finals (48 years later, John still insists that he won!). He jokes now that it was lucky that he lost—had he won, his picture would have been in the *Chicago Tribune* and his father would have been furious!

> **With his usual determination and hard work, John excelled in his teaching at East Texas State University, and he was rapidly promoted through the ranks, becoming a professor in only 4 years.**

Going to college at Arkansas State was a liberating experience for John; he was an excellent student, a star athlete, and a student leader. He made many friends and developed confidence in his own ability to teach, to coach, and to lead. Most of all, he loved challenges, and his success reinforced his belief in the value of hard work. In his career as a student affairs administrator later in life, John never forgot what his college experience did for him, and he worked to provide the same educational opportunities for his students.

When he graduated from Arkansas State University in June 1953, it was a proud day for John and his family. He was also commissioned as a Second Lieutenant in the Army and was assigned to basic officer's training at Ft. Sill, Oklahoma. John's great athletic skills were quickly recognized and he played both baseball and football while in the Army. He spent a short time at Ft. McClellan, Alabama, but he served most of his time at Camp Carson,

Colorado, where he was promoted to First Lieutenant. But after his 2 years of service, he knew he did not want to be a career military man, and he began searching for a coaching position. After considering various opportunities, including one at the University of Toledo (his former coach had moved there), John decided to accept a teaching position in Blytheville, Arkansas in the fall of 1955 for a salary of $3,500. He would teach history and civics, and coach football and basketball. John loved this job and living in the pleasant community of 25,000 residents. After his first year, he decided that he should take advantage of the G.I. Bill and enrolled for graduate classes in Fayetteville at the University of Arkansas. During the summer of 1957 in graduate school, when he was 27 years old, John met Mary Dell Hooker while playing tennis on the campus. She had been in medical school, but now was working as a medical technician in a local laboratory. John was completely smitten by Mary Dell, and 3 weeks later he asked her to marry him! She accepted his proposal, but they waited until the spring of 1958 to get married in Pine Bluff, Mary Dell's hometown. They lived in Blytheville, and John continued with his teaching and coaching position, and Mary Dell with her laboratory job.

In 1958, John completed his master's degree in education at the University of Arkansas. In the spring of 1959, when Mary Dell was pregnant, John decided to accept a teaching and coaching position in Amarillo, Texas. Besides teaching history and civics, John would coach baseball and football, while working for Bum Phillips, who was later to achieve fame as a head coach in the National Football League. The Koldus' first child, Melissa, was born in May 1959, and after a very difficult pregnancy, John and Mary Dell knew they were blessed. John decided to enroll in the doctoral program back at Fayetteville at the University of Arkansas in the summer of 1959, commuting the 4 hours there on most weekends. They bought their first house in Amarillo. After 2 years in Amarillo, during which time their second daughter, Cynthia, was born, they sold their house and moved back to Fayetteville in 1961, as John was awarded a fellowship to complete his doctorate. He had decided that he loved teaching and, encouraged by his major professor, George Moore, wanted to find a faculty position at a university. By the time John completed his doctorate in 1963 at the University of Arkansas, Mary Dell had given birth to their first son, John IV. On June 1, 1963, John started his full-time collegiate teaching career as an assistant professor of health and physical education at East Texas State University. He and his family moved to Commerce, Texas in the fall of 1963.

With his usual determination and hard work, John excelled in his teaching at East Texas State University, and he was rapidly promoted through the ranks, becoming a professor in only 4 years. He was greatly admired by students and became well known on the campus. Moreover, when asked by various groups to give of his time to some activity, he did so, and immediately was recognized as a leader who loved working with people. He became the faculty adviser to the student union board, chaired the University Traffic and Safety

Committee, and worked with both undergraduate and graduate students. John had incredible energy, and when he enjoyed something, he loved to give his time to it. He loved being a faculty member, and he and his family enjoyed their life in Commerce.

To John's great surprise, the president of East Texas State, Whit Halladay, called John to his office one day in the spring of 1967. President Halladay, recognizing the turmoil in society and on the campus because of the Vietnam War and racial unrest, decided to create a new position at East Texas—vice president for student affairs. He knew how much John was admired and respected on the campus, and he asked John to accept this new position. John was not interested at first, and he had never worked in student affairs before. He loved his career as a faculty member, and he thought he already had all the involvement with students that anyone could have. But President Halladay was very persuasive, and after talking this opportunity over in great detail with his wife, John decided to accept the position. It presented him with a new challenge, and there was nothing that John Koldus liked more than a challenge! He began his duties as vice president for student affairs at East Texas State in the summer of 1967.

While John knew many of the staff in student affairs, he recognized that his appointment would be viewed with some surprise by them. He immediately met with each of the department heads individually and asked for their assistance and support. That summer, he spent a week on the campuses of two experienced senior student affairs officers, Jody Smith at Oklahoma and Bill Yardley at Houston, in an effort to educate himself about his new role. He studied hard to learn more about the departments he would be supervising, including financial aid, housing, student health, counseling, placement, campus police, and the student union. He was fortunate to have the complete support of his president.

In his first semester, some of the expected racial unrest occurred; East Texas State had only become integrated in 1965, and African American students confronted the university's leadership in a packed auditorium, submitting several demands for more support and better treatment. In a very tense situation, it was John, as the newly appointed vice president, who won the trust of the students and negotiated an agreement. He said later, "There were two football players, Chad Brown and Jay Johnston, who had been in my classes the previous year, and we had a great relationship; when they saw that I was involved, they told their friends that I could be trusted, and that was all it took to resolve the situation." This experience reinforced John's long-held belief that close, personal relationships with students were the key to accomplishing positive things on the campus, and this belief became the basis for his work in student affairs.

His years as vice president for student affairs at East Texas were hectic, very challenging, and enjoyable. The Koldus' fourth child, Debbie, was born in Commerce; and John and

Mary Dell built a large house on 12 acres of land, where they could host many student gatherings, which they loved to do. John became the most visible person on the campus with students, and he created student–faculty–staff discussion groups, almost always associated with luncheons and dinners; these greatly improved student–institution relationships during this period of student protests. John said, "As a Hungarian, food was always special for us, and when we gathered around the table, we talked, laughed, and enjoyed ourselves. It was this family tradition of enjoying food that caused me to bring students and others together on the campus." It not only worked well, but also it enabled John and other invited faculty and administrators to get to know lots of students in informal, enjoyable settings. John was convinced that friendships were the key to building positive student relations. He began a tradition at East Texas as vice president that if he met a student, he would buy that student a coke if he did not remember the student's name the next time they met on the campus! This story was picked up by the student newspaper, and students discovered John was serious about this offer. He worked very hard to remember students' names, and a couple of years later he changed the offer to a free lunch! This tradition became a legend at East Texas, something that most students of that era remember from their days on the campus.

The enrollment at East Texas doubled in the 6 years John was vice president—from 4,000 to 8,000. John and his staff constructed new residence halls, restructured the division, established a successful Freshman Leadership Program, and built a new recreation center and a new student services building. He loved student affairs administration and had succeeded in establishing very positive relations with students, faculty, the president, and the community. He was elected president of the Chamber of Commerce and was frequently asked to intervene in situations where conflict was present. John's sincere, good natured, and positive approach to others resulted in others seeking his assistance when they needed some matter settled. Asked how he developed these skills, John later joked, "I had enough fighting as a young kid in Gary, Indiana growing up! You don't accomplish anything by arguing with others—you've got to look for ways for people to become friends!" When John saw two student organizations fighting with each other on a campus issue, he often would invite both groups to lunch or dinner; he knew that in such a relaxed and informal setting, he could help the students become friends and resolve their differences.

John somehow found time to teach at East Texas State while he was vice president, as he did not want to lose touch with his field. Most important, John loved to teach, and he assumed he would eventually return to his faculty role. In his 6 years as vice president at East Texas State, he had worked very hard to learn the student affairs profession. In everything else he had done in his life, he found that he could improve each year through hard work, study, and determination; and he used this same approach to his job in student affairs. He used a phrase with students and staff for years and applied it to himself as well:

"we can always get better!" He had built a strong staff, excellent new facilities, and a positive program as vice president at East Texas; and he and his family felt very good about their life in Commerce.

In the spring of 1973, Dr. Jack Williams, president of TAMU in College Station, called John and invited him to come to the campus to consider becoming the institution's first vice president for student affairs. President Williams had done his homework and knew how highly John was regarded at East Texas and how much he had accomplished there. TAMU was an institution in transition at the time and was about to experience explosive growth. A strong, new leader was needed in student affairs, and President Williams knew that John Koldus was the person he wanted. John, Mary Dell, and their four children were very happy in Commerce; and they loved their large home and their life there. John had no previous relationship with anyone at TAMU, but he was attracted to the institution because of its reputation, size, and resources. And he viewed this as another challenge—the biggest challenge ever presented to him! After some initial doubts and reluctance, his family agreed that this would be an exciting opportunity, and John decided to accept the offer, becoming TAMU's first vice president for student affairs in the summer of 1973.

TAMU had been an all-male institution until 1969, and of course it was well known for its Corps of Cadets and its emphasis on military training. Its enrollment was 17,000 in 1973, with growing numbers of women students now attending, and the academic programs were expanding and becoming much more diverse. The Corps of Cadets was still very important, but it represented a decreasing percentage of the male students. The institution was not only in an academic and cultural transition period, but also it was growing more rapidly than any other public university in the country! The student affairs program was very limited, and many of the existing services were part of academic and business affairs. Apparently, there had been an assumption at the institution for years that, because of the traditions associated with the Corps of Cadets, most student needs were being addressed through that organization. President Williams recognized that a great deal had to change in student affairs and that he needed an experienced and strong vice president to lead this new division. John saw the opportunity to do exciting things at this traditional, conservative institution, and he was very enthusiastic about this new challenge.

Following the same principles that had guided his work so successfully at East Texas State, John spent his first several weeks at TAMU learning the culture, meeting academic deans, listening to students and student groups, talking with faculty and staff, and getting to know the local community. He knew that many changes were needed in student affairs and that the staff was eager for enlightened leadership, but John understood that he needed to establish solid, personal relationships with many people before he took any major actions. During the Christmas holidays after his first semester at TAMU, John spent many hours at home, developing a draft of a long-term, master plan for the division of student affairs. When he was satisfied with it, he decided to share it with his president, the provost, and the chief financial officer of the institution. "I wanted to let them know what my plans were, and even though some of my plans might encroach on their areas in the future, I wanted to be completely up front and honest with them," John said. He had already earned the confidence and respect of these senior administrative colleagues, and they appreciated his candor, while not, of course, endorsing everything he had planned. John was a very persuasive "salesman" and advocate for student affairs, and he could clearly articulate his goals in ways that did not threaten any other administrator. The small counseling center, for example, was in academic affairs and was not given much attention or priority. But instead of fighting to obtain control of it, John was able to describe how students would be served better if his division were to lead it. He did this with student financial aid, and later with recreational sports as well. As a very competitive person himself, John was never afraid of a fight; he just knew from experience that administrative problems that could be resolved in a cordial manner worked far more effectively than those where ugly battles had to be fought. Moreover, he said that he just did not want to have to deal with the inevitable resentment that follows such battles. As a leader, John learned to use his passion and his competitiveness as an advantage—not as a fighter, but as an expert listener, friend-maker, and expert in human relations.

> **Often by sheer force of personality, John was able to inspire students to create new organizations and programs.**

After being part of the "Aggie family" at TAMU only a few months, John knew he had made the right decision. He is a strong believer in "person–institution fit" and felt that it was the right place and the right time for him to be there. His values matched those of the institution, and he was confident that his ideas and approach to leadership would be welcomed. He and his family moved into a university house located in the middle of the campus, located next to the president's home. While almost living in a "fishbowl," this made John available around the clock, and because he and Mary Dell loved to entertain students and other guests, it was an ideal place for such activity. John joked later, "Our four children grew up with thousands of student friends, right in their own backyard!"

Despite the traditions surrounding the Corps of Cadets at TAMU, John discovered that the institution was not viewed as a very warm, friendly, and welcoming place by most of its students and the public. This concerned him a great deal, and he decided one of his major goals was to change this. He had administrative responsibility for the Corps of Cadets, and his own credibility with this group was enhanced by his previous experience as an officer in the Army. John's predecessor had been a military officer and John wanted to support the Corps, while greatly expanding the vision and scope of the student affairs division. He was welcomed into the Council of Academic Deans by the academic vice president, and his plans to reorganize the division were supported by his president.

One of the traditions at TAMU was a freshman orientation camp, conducted off campus before classes began. A substantial proportion of the new students participated, but John wanted the camps to increase in number, and especially to change in their approach. The institution often had given the impression to its new students that it was so competitive that few of them would be likely to succeed in their academic programs. With the support of faculty, student leaders, and staff, John transformed these camps into positive, enjoyable, and spirit-building experiences. He emphasized the values of community, friendliness, and cooperation; and he built an expectation for success. In effect, as John said later, the camps became our best opportunity to teach the students to "become Aggies!" They became so popular and well received that outstanding upperclassmen clamored each year to volunteer to be student leaders at the camps, and participation exceeded 80 percent. They attracted the attention of many other colleges and universities and earned the enthusiastic support of faculty, administrators, parents, and the governing board. John viewed the orientation program as one of the key components in creating a warm, caring, and supportive climate at TAMU for students.

Often by sheer force of personality, John was able to inspire students to create new organizations and programs. He had lunch every day on the campus with some student group, and met for lunch or dinner each week with major student leaders. By hiring many talented and dedicated staff who reflected his enthusiasm and support for students, the largest student activity program in the country was created at TAMU, with over 700 student organizations. One of John's goals was to encourage every student to be involved in some activity that contributed to the institution or the community. His philosophy, "with hard work and determination, we can find ways to do good things," was adopted enthusiastically by students, especially in the many student leadership and community service programs that were created.

During the 20 years John served as vice president at TAMU, the enrollment grew from 17,000 to 43,000 students. He was responsible for a new student services building (which now bears his name), a new recreation building, new residence halls, an expanded Greek system, a large addition to the Student Health Center, and a large expansion of the union. More importantly, John was the single most influential leader in bringing about a positive change in the culture of the institution; his emphasis on a friendly, helpful, and caring approach to students is now the pride of the university and has become its trademark. When people walk onto the large campus at TAMU, they discover that students, faculty, and staff are genuine in their efforts to be of assistance. They all share the "Aggie pride" that John was so successful in building.

John worked for six different presidents during his years as vice president at TAMU and, of course, this required some adjustment in the way he conducted his office. He always understood that he served at the pleasure of his presidents and that it was his obligation to support them. Always determined to find the positive aspects in any relationship, John emphasized that he was fortunate to have the support of his presidents. At various times during his 20 years in the position, John assumed responsibility for the campus police, intercollegiate athletics, and other campus functions; but he always kept a clear focus on his first love and obligation—the education of students. He viewed himself as a teacher, with the campus as his classroom; and he based his leadership on close, personal, and trusting relationships with others. He was so admired by students that a former student leader later noted, "if Vice President Koldus asked us to jump over the moon, we would have lined up to do it!"

John was a leader who lived the values he was teaching every day. He emphasized to students that they should pursue a profession that gave them enjoyment and said this was the reason he stayed in student affairs for his career—he loved doing it! Students observed how he conducted his own life, especially because he lived in the middle of the campus, and this provided a very positive model for them. John somehow found time to be a national leader in his profession in addition to all of his work on his campus. He was the executive director of the Southwest Association of Student Personnel Administrators, and also its president; he was also elected president of the Texas College and University Student Personnel Association, and a national vice president of NASPA. He was codirector of the NASPA national conference in 1976, a frequent consultant and evaluator for the Southwest Association of Colleges and Schools, and a keynote speaker at many regional and national conferences. He was presented with the Fred Turner Award for distinguished service to the profession by NASPA in 1986; and with NASPA's highest honor, the Scott Goodnight Award, in 1991. The university named its new student services building in his honor when he retired in 1997. In College Station, John was the elected president of the Chamber of Commerce, and he was active in many other civic and service organizations.

John had opportunities to move to other institutions during his career, including invitations to consider a presidency. He remained at TAMU because he believed in the institution's mission, because he loved working with students, and because he felt he was making a difference there as a leader. He knows that his many years there in the same position enabled him to accomplish things he would not have been able to do otherwise. His legacy of leadership, based on hard work, honesty, friendliness, and determination, is reflected in virtually every aspect of the university today. A large number of students have praised John; two students in particular have stated,

> Dr. John Koldus is one of the most concerned and compassionate people we've ever met. He is a tremendous role model of how we all should treat our fellow human beings! He took time every day to make other people feel special. He set a standard to live up to regarding our interactions with others. For TAMU students, he is a friend, a role model, and a hero! (Bereit and Bereit, personal correspondence with author, 2000).

Chapter 10

James W. Lyons
Stanford University

I magine the following scene on the Stanford University campus....some upset students have confronted the editorial staff of the student newspaper and are demanding a retraction of an article they found insulting...Jim Lyons somehow anticipated this problem and is there. In his quiet and thoughtful way, his presence calms the situation, and in the next hour he engages the students on both sides of the issue in discussion. He is open, insightful, and occasionally humorous. He asks questions, listens carefully, and offers brief anecdotes. This is just one of the many campus settings Jim Lyons finds to teach about freedom of expression and civility. Perhaps no one in the student affairs profession has done more than Jim Lyons to help students and staff clarify their values and to help them understand that their ideas and the actions that flow from them have consequences. He celebrates and uses the "teachable moment" as his mode of teaching.

James W. Lyons earned his B.A. degree in economics and history from Allegheny College in 1954. He earned his M.S. degree in counseling and guidance in 1956 from Indiana University (I.U.) and his EdD in higher education in 1963 from I.U. During his doctoral program, he also minored in business administration. He served as a residence hall counselor at I.U. during 1954–1955, and as assistant head counselor in the residence halls at I.U. from 1955–1957. He was the program coordinator of the Indiana Memorial Union from 1957–1959, and he served as the assistant director of the Indiana Memorial Union from 1959–1963. From 1963–1972, he served as the dean of students at Haverford College in Haverford, Pennsylvania; and from 1972–1990, he was the dean of student affairs at Stanford University in Palo Alto, California. In 1984, he was appointed lecturer in Stanford's School of Education. He was named dean emeritus when he stepped aside from his position in 1990, but continued service as lecturer in education. He was also appointed senior fellow in the Stanford Institute for Research in Higher Education. After another year, he was appointed director of the masters program in higher education. He retired from Stanford University in 1998.

James Lyons has been an active leader in the National Association of Student Personnel Administrators (NASPA), a frequent keynote speaker and major presenter at national and regional conferences, and a consultant to more than 75 colleges and universities. He has been a member of accreditation teams for 26 colleges and universities; and he has written many articles for professional journals, chapters in books, and monographs. He taught graduate courses in the School of Education at Stanford University for many years, served on the faculty of the NASPA Stevens Institute, and was a visiting lecturer at three other institutions He received the Greenleaf Distinguished Alumnus Award from I.U. in 1985 and the Distinguished Alumni Award from the Indiana School of Education in 1995. In 1988, NASPA presented him with its highest honor, the Scott Goodnight Award for outstanding performance as a dean; and in 1990, the Stanford University Dean's Award for Service was renamed in his honor. Allegheny College, his undergraduate Alma Mater, in 2000 presented him with its Gold Award as an alumnus who has brought distinction to the college. In the same year, he was honored by NASPA as a "Pillar of the Profession."

Jim Lyons was born in 1932 in Jamestown, New York. His family on both sides had been in this area for several generations and originally came from Sweden and Scotland. Jim's father and uncle ran the Lyons Lumber Company, a business established by his grandfather. The business flourished until World War II, when the shortage of building materials eventually caused it to fail. Jim's maternal grandfather, James Weeks, was an attorney and served as Mayor of Jamestown. Jim's mother, Mary Weeks Lyons, attended Skidmore College. Jim's father, Mark Lyons, was a graduate of the University of Pennsylvania and the Wharton School of Business; after working in the lumber business, he became the administrator of Jamestown General Hospital for more than 20 years. Growing up in Jamestown, a city of 25,000 at the time, was a pleasant experience for Jim. Despite the severe economic strains of that decade, Jim's father remained employed and the family thrived on modest means. Education was valued and it was simply assumed that Jim would go to college.

Jim's father loved the outdoors, and had a small cabin in the woods within an hour's drive of Jamestown. There, at an early age, Jim learned to enjoy camping, hiking, fishing, and hunting—interests he maintains to this day. Jim's family was Episcopalian, but religion was not a dominating influence in his life. He learned the values of hard work and honesty from his parents and began working in odd jobs as a young boy. He delivered the Jamestown *Post Journal* on his paper route for years, mowed lawns, shoveled snow from driveways, washed cars, worked as a stockboy at J.C. Penny's, was a vacation mail carrier for the post office, and helped out at the lumberyard. He was close to his grandmother, who also lived in Jamestown, and he fondly remembers listening to the famous weekly Texaco "Saturday at the Opera" on the radio at her house on Saturday afternoons; this helped Jim develop a lifelong love of all forms of music. He was just 9 years old when the attack was made on Pearl Harbor, and he remembers hearing the news on a portable radio while at the family cabin in the woods in December 1941.

Jim liked school and was a good student, skipping the third grade. Even as a young boy, he displayed the skepticism and open questioning of authority that were to characterize his work in higher education. He remembers being chastised for his refusal to learn the alphabet in first grade, protesting that "no one gave me a reason why I should learn this, or at least one that I could understand!" Jim was cooperative, but he had to be convinced that something was right before he was about to pursue it. He might have been called obstinate; what was clear was that he always questioned everything.

Jim's parents encouraged his love of the outdoors, and he spent 6 to 8 weeks for 15 summers at a YMCA camp on Lake Chautauqua, eventually becoming its assistant director. "Little did I know it, but that was my first student affairs job!" Jim later joked. At camp he learned many leadership, organizational, and personal skills that were to serve him well throughout his career in student affairs. He cherished the opportunities he had to work with experienced leaders and teachers, as well as to take on increasing leadership responsibilities himself. One summer he was asked to become the waterfront director. A summer "boot camp" training at a Red Cross water safety training institute refined his skills for the post, and it led to a lifetime interest in swimming, including membership on his college's varsity swim team. Along the way, he developed distaste for pomposity and phoniness and a simple commitment to being real. He also loved music; sang in the school chorus; and became a very proficient trumpet player, finishing second in the New York State solo competition. He and some friends formed their own dance band and played at school functions, weddings, and parties. Jim's trumpet-playing idol was the great Harry James. When Jim was a college student, he was thrilled when he was invited to play on one occasion with the Cleveland Symphony Orchestra. Jim also sang in a barbershop quartet, and he now laughs about the time when he purchased the group's maroon sport coats!

Jim attended Jamestown High School and was involved in many activities, including a "Scotch clan fraternity," school music groups, and the honor society. He also was elected president of the student government association. Even as a high school student leader, Jim understood the differences between individual and group achievement. Perhaps it was related to the joy he experienced while singing in the choir or working each summer in group activities at camp. He loved the personal interaction and the process of working in harmony with others to achieve something greater than one could as an individual. He was a star in high school, and when he graduated in 1950 he realized for the first time that his family had very little money and that he would have to provide most of his own support for college. His father, a Penn graduate, thought Jim would like the same institution; but Jim applied to Colgate, Hamilton, Harvard, and Allegheny. Jim's mother began working as a part-time legal secretary for her brother. This helped him meet some of his college expenses. Jim, after learning of his acceptance at Harvard, decided it was too expensive and instead enrolled at Allegheny in the fall of 1950.

Jim had no firm idea of what he wanted to study or what career he would like to pursue when he entered college. He joined a social fraternity, Phi Delta Theta, became an officer of the 55-member Allegheny Singers, worked in the dining hall, earned an academic scholarship, became a resident assistant, sang in a barbershop quartet, took piano lessons, joined the varsity swimming team, and loved the college experience. He was fortunate to have some excellent professors in history and economics and thus majored in these subjects. During his college years, the infamous McCarthy hearings were being televised throughout the country, and Jim remembers this as his first serious encounter with politics and the underlying principles that animate public policies—a subject that was to fascinate him throughout his life, and which he was to use later in his career as a dean in order to teach students about ideas. Allegheny was a small college, and Jim's sense of fair play led him to question the dean of students, Charles McCracken, about the appropriateness of an off-campus housing regulation. The good dean invited Jim to write a paper on the subject, expressing his views in more detail; when Jim did this, McCracken was so impressed that he offered Jim, then a college junior, a part-time position in his office. One of his duties was to write a new off-campus student housing code for landlords, and Jim accomplished this task by setting up a series of discussions with affected students, seeking their ideas and reactions. In his senior year, the dean asked Jim to mediate a dispute between two fraternities; Jim's quiet and thoughtful ability to listen and to bring people together had already been recognized. Jim had two uncles who were attorneys, and he gave serious consideration to a career in law; but even by his senior year, he was undecided about his future. In the spring of his senior year at Allegheny, his job in Dean McCracken's office included posting, coordinating, and scheduling student interviews with employer and graduate school representatives. One day he noticed that no students had signed up to see the representative of the I.U. masters degree in business administration (MBA) program. Mostly out of politeness, Jim introduced himself to the lonely I.U. official, and after a lengthy discussion Jim decided to enroll the next fall in the MBA program at Indiana! This unlikely "decision-making process" caused Jim to remain skeptical about various "scientific" career development theories throughout his life.

Jim was able to finance his graduate studies in the business program at Indiana by serving as a resident counselor in one of the large undergraduate residence halls. In his first year at Indiana, Jim met Martha Wichser, a nursing student who was a resident counselor in a nearby women's hall. They were to be married a year later. As a result of his work in the residence hall and his association with other graduate students, Jim learned about the respected graduate program in student personnel administration. Kate Hevener Mueller was a member of the School of Education faculty, and Jim enrolled in some student affairs courses while continuing with his MBA studies. He then met Louis Stamatakos, a fellow graduate student who was to become a lifelong friend and a distinguished professor of higher education at Michigan State, and Jim was intrigued with the emerging studies and theories of human behavior and development that he was studying. He was inspired by Dr. Robert Shaffer, the dean of students at Indiana, who also taught graduate courses. As a result, Jim decided to switch from the MBA program to the student personnel administration master's degree program.

After they were married, Jim and Martha moved into another residence hall, where he became the assistant head counselor and Martha continued with her nursing career. He completed his master's degree at Indiana in 1956, and in the fall of 1957 he accepted the position of program coordinator in the Indiana Memorial Union. This was considered an important achievement, as he had just turned 25 at the time. He was also accepted to the doctoral program in higher educational administration at Indiana and was now convinced that he was fortunate to have "selected," albeit almost accidentally, the right career for himself. In 1959, he was promoted to the position of assistant director of the Indiana Memorial Union and became active in the Association of College Unions International. Jim was responsible for the Activities Center, where he managed several services and facilities, while working with several student groups. By this time, it was the early 1960s and a great deal of social change was occurring in the country. Jim found the revolution in human rights a positive opportunity to help students think through their own ideas and values, especially in regard to racial issues. He also continued to develop his mediation skills and became well known at Indiana for his ability to work effectively with difficult students and student groups who challenged the status quo. While working full-time, he managed to complete his doctorate in the School of Education, writing his dissertation on the professionalization of the college union director position. He completed his EdD at Indiana in 1963.

When Jim was a student at Allegheny College, the president's office was near the dean's office, where Jim worked part-time. The president was Louis Benezet, and Jim became well acquainted with him there, reading and reacting to some articles the president had written about liberal arts education. Nearly 10 years later, in 1963, Benezet gave Jim's name to William Cadbury, the academic dean at Haverford College in Pennsylvania. This highly selective, small, Quaker-related college was looking for its first dean of students, and president Benezet thought Jim might be a good candidate for the position. Cadbury called Jim in Bloomington and said he would be in Chicago in 2 weeks and asked if Jim could meet him at the airport to discuss the job. Jim replied, "I can't meet you at that time, as I've already made plans to go camping!" Jim laughs about this situation now, especially since Dean Cadbury appreciated Jim's candor and thought that a serious camper might make a good dean of students at this unique college. Jim did visit the Haverford campus that summer and was greatly impressed with the academic excellence, the Quaker traditions and values, and the strong sense of community among faculty and students. He liked the commitment to simplicity, honesty, and openness that characterized the college. He was offered the position of dean of students, he accepted it, and Jim and Martha moved to Pennsylvania in the summer of 1963. Jim was only 31, had just completed his doctorate at Indiana, and he was already a senior student affairs officer (SSAO)!

> *While some student affairs deans left their positions because of these unrelenting pressures, most persevered, and many of these owe a debt of gratitude to Jim Lyons for his leadership and guidance.*

Haverford is located only about 10 miles from Philadelphia, and when Jim assumed his duties there, it was a quiet, self-contained residential campus of about 700 male students. The philosophical fit for Jim with Haverford was ideal; he loved the culture of the college, its emphasis on personal responsibility, and its commitment to academic excellence. The level of student involvement was extremely high; while Jim knew all of the students individually, he also had an important sense of the whole student body. His first years at Haverford were very challenging, as the Vietnam War, Civil Rights activity, and the psychedelic movement greatly affected student and campus life. Many of the students and faculty were pacifists, and thus there was constant debate and collective action regarding the social issues of the times. The organizational structure of student affairs was not especially important at such a small college, although Jim was responsible for all aspects of student life; what was important was the quality of relationships and the effectiveness of communication among students, faculty, and staff. Jim was a major celebrant of Haverford's student founded and run honor code and powerful traditions of students accepting significant responsibility for their own affairs. He also helped to create exchange programs with Bryn Mawr (including a joint chorus and symphony!), and a conflict resolution process for which students had the major responsibility.

Jim said he was shaped as much by his Haverford experience as he helped influence the college; the importance of trust, the value of resolving conflicts in a peaceable manner, the making of decisions in an open setting, the commitment to consensus as a way of deciding, and the dignity of each person were the primary values that characterized the Haverford College culture that Jim found so compelling. Jim said that working at Haverford for him was not just a job; it was a true "calling" in that he believed so fervently in the mission of the college. Throughout his career, he spoke about the "social good" that one can contribute in student affairs and that this is the greatest reward of the profession. He remembers a proposal from Haverford students in 1970, suggesting that the entire college travel to Washington, D.C. as an educational mission to try to affect national policy on the Vietnam War. After a great deal of discussion, the consensus was to do it. One of the last items on the daily plenary meetings to plan the trip was to decide who should remain behind to care for the college. Nearly all of the office staff and custodial staff, along with spouses, wanted to participate. The trip became a very successful educational venture, and it happened at a time when other campuses were being blitzed by angry anti-Vietnam War protesters. Jim assumed an important role in this effort, and he realized that this kind of activity was only possible at a special college such as Haverford.

Jim served as the dean of students at Haverford College from 1963–1972. He and Martha had adopted their first child, Mark, in 1959; and they adopted his sister, Amy, in 1964. Their lives in Haverford were extremely busy and Jim found himself in demand by other colleges and by his colleagues in NASPA because of his insights about the dominant social issues of the times. There was great anguish and stress among most SSAOs during the period of 1965–1973, and these deans strongly needed advice about the pressing issues and challenges they were experiencing on their campuses. While some student affairs deans left their positions because of these unrelenting pressures, most persevered, and many of these owe a debt of gratitude to Jim Lyons for his leadership and guidance.

NASPA meetings during those years served essentially as opportunities for professionals to help each other cope with the daunting problems they were experiencing, and Jim was one of the most respected and sought after leaders at that time. During the 1971 NASPA conference, Jim made one of the major presentations; he talked about the importance of institutional context and "fit"—the special nature of the college and its culture and how critical it is for the dean to be in harmony with this. He also talked about the importance of building consensus on the campus and the benefits of involving students and faculty in the decision-making process. In the audience at the time was William Stone, assistant to the president at Stanford University. Richard Lyman, president of Stanford at the time, had several years earlier been a candidate for the president's position at Haverford, and Lyman had met Jim during a visit to Haverford 2 years earlier. Stanford, like so many institutions of that time, had experienced serious difficulties in the past few years because of student unrest, and there had been three student affairs deans during the 5 years prior to Jim's appointment. Before that time, Don Winbigler, an early NASPA president, had served as dean for 17 years. When Stanford contacted Jim about its SSAO position, Jim indicated that he was very happy at Haverford and loved the unifying nature of its undergraduate culture. Stanford was a large, diverse, graduate and undergraduate university with a strong emphasis on research and professional studies such as engineering, business, law, and medicine. This was much unlike Haverford and Jim at first declined the invitation to come for a visit.

President Lyman knew of Jim's strong reputation and his success at Haverford, and he was not about to give up in his efforts to attract Jim to Stanford. Jim admitted later that he had several biases about California, having spent his entire life in western New York, Pennsylvania, and Indiana. But he finally agreed to visit Palo Alto in the spring of 1972, and what he found was not at all encouraging to him. Relations between students and the university were bruised and strained by the protest years, and the student affairs staff was yearning for stable leadership. With more than a bit of irony, Jim commented years later about this visit: "It was a challenge; as the severity of the challenges unfolded, it began to look better and better!" Jim saw the biggest challenge of his career at a highly prestigious institution where the obstacles for achieving success were considerable, but the opportunities were almost unlimited. The student affairs staff was craving for more continuity of leadership and for relief from the confrontational climate of the times. After returning to Pennsylvania and discussing the job with his wife and his family, Jim decided it was so exciting that he could not say no. He accepted Dr. Lyman's offer, and in the summer of 1972, Jim and his family moved across the country, camping all the way, to Stanford University!

Jim insisted that his job title be "dean of student affairs" as opposed to "vice president for student affairs" at Stanford. He told his president that he wanted to avoid all appearances of bureaucracy in his efforts to build strong academic and student communities, and that the "dean" title would be more in harmony with that goal. Jim spent considerable time walking the campus, a habit he was to continue throughout his career, talking and listening with students and faculty, and meeting with academic deans. He discovered what he expected to discover: Stanford actually consisted of several small college-like-communities and what he hoped to do was to help create the equivalent of several small "Haverford" communities at Stanford. Jim had been dean at a very small college; but in this new, much larger setting at Stanford, he remained confident that his basic "walk-around," personalized leadership style would work well and would eventually produce positive results. Jim had to deal with a half decade of deteriorating relationships between the institution and its students. He knew that earning back the trust of the students would be a major challenge and the key to any success he might have.

In his first months as dean at Stanford, Jim made some organization rearrangements and altered some staff responsibilities. These were supported by staff and sent an early message that a new leader was in charge of the student affairs division. He also found that there were two separate offices offering traditional counseling services to students and that their efforts were not coordinated; he combined them into a new unit and informed the staff that he expected them to spend a third of their time outside of their offices, meeting with students and student groups around the campus. With the department heads in student affairs, he initiated a process he had seen work at Haverford—the sharing of all correspondence on a regular basis, with all of the department heads expected to read it all each week. This practice reinforced Jim's belief in shared governance and open decision-making; it also encouraged the staff to operate and think as a team. He began to introduce several staff development activities that were designed to help them work more collaboratively, communicate well, and deal with some of the most difficult problems they faced with students. Jim and his wife began inviting students and student groups to their house for dinners and conversations about campus issues; this was to become an almost weekly practice, which continued for all the years he served as dean at Stanford. Jim remembered a personal note he had received from Herman Wells, president of I.U., when Jim was a graduate student there. The gesture was so appreciated by Jim that he wrote three personal notes to students per day for the remainder of his career—thanking them for their contribution to a committee, their work on a project, or a letter they had written to the newspaper. Jim also knew how and when to invite his president to participate with students in campus events, taking advantage of the strengths of his president and demonstrating to students that the president was genuinely interested in their activities.

Jim and his colleagues worked very hard at Stanford to help create one of the most diverse student bodies in the nation. At the same time, he was very influential in the creation and establishment of many residential options for students in this highly pluralistic community. Faculty participation in residential life was enhanced by an increase in the number of faculty serving as resident fellows, but an even greater number did their advising and teaching in the houses. Discussion sections for large lecture classes like economics and chemistry were often organized so that students living together could participate together. Small freshmen seminars were often held in the residences themselves. Orientation was partially decentralized and lodged in residences where upperclass students and the faculty associated with a residence would assume significant responsibility. There were dozens of musical and theatrical productions in the residences that were organized by the students themselves. And several educational theme houses were organized and thrived. At the end of Jim's tenure as dean, nearly 90 percent of undergraduate students lived on campus, and the demand was still unmet. Jim counts this as one of his most significant achievements— the creation of these small, residential, learning, and supportive communities for Stanford's students. Jim is also especially proud of the many strong curricular and academic service bridges between the academic and residential programs of the university. He also hired a number of professional staff who later went on to leadership positions as SSAOs, such as James Larrimore at Dartmouth, Michael Jackson at the University of Southern California, and after Jim himself left his position, James Montoya at Stanford.

During his tenure as dean at Stanford, new undergraduate living facilities were constructed, as well as a new graduate student housing complex. The very critical policy of "need-blind" admissions was also continued, making Stanford one of the few elite, private institutions in the country able to select its new students without regard to ability to pay. Jim developed a deep respect and affection for Stanford and its students, and he understood and appreciated the tremendous intellectual resources available at the institution. His unending enthusiasm for ideas, and especially for involving others in challenging intellectual and developmental experiences, was infectious. He became a highly respected leader on the campus, yet Jim always knew that he served at the pleasure of his president. Halfway through his tenures at both Haverford and Stanford there was a change of presidents. Each time, Jim offered his own resignation as dean, feeling it was important to be "chosen" by each president. He understood that an important part of his job was to help make the president successful and he considered himself very fortunate to work for presidents whose values and leadership styles he admired and supported. Jim was evaluated each year by his presidents, although he said this evaluation was mainly informal in nature. Freedom to act in accordance with what he felt was right was of supreme importance to Jim throughout his years as dean; he placed a high value on freedom of expression and the dignity of the individual, and he was uncompromising in his defense of these concepts. Although he did not preach to students, his own value commitments, especially to honesty in all relationships, were obvious to others. He was gentle and caring with students, but he was fully capable and willing to call to task others whose actions were dishonest or disrespectful of others.

As a member of the Senior Administrative Council of Stanford, Jim played a role in setting the agenda of the board of trustees, especially of its committee on student affairs. As usual, Jim considered his primary goal to be educating the board members about the nature of student life and the value and meaning of its diverse student communities. He did this not only via personal conversations with board members over time, but also by introducing board members to students and involving them in student life programs.

In 1990, and after 18 years as dean at Stanford and another 10 as dean at Haverford, he felt that it was the right time for him to do something else. He had been in charge of the student affairs divisions at two institutions for 28 consecutive years, and he felt that his energies could best be used by sharing his knowledge with those preparing to enter the student affairs profession. So, Jim stepped aside from his dean's position at Stanford in 1990 and was appointed lecturer in the Stanford School of Education and senior fellow in the Stanford Institute for Higher Education Research. He began teaching graduate students on a full-time basis in the fall semester of 1990. In 1992, Jim also became director of the master of arts in higher education program in the School of Education, and he taught in the doctoral program as well.

> *He never used rules, regulations, or power to get things done; his authority was derived not from his position, but from his relationships and personal honesty.*

During his many years at Stanford, Jim became a highly respected national leader in student affairs. He was frequently invited to be the keynote speaker at regional and national conferences and to lead seminars and workshops at various institutes. He served as a regular member of accrediting teams for more than 20 years. He joined with George Kuh, Elizabeth Whitt, and John Schuh in collaborating on the very influential book, *Involving Colleges;* and Stanford was included as one of the institutions whose student life programs were exemplary in its effect on students. Jim was also invited to be a member of the national committee that wrote *A Perspective on Student Affairs* in 1987 in commemoration of the 50th anniversary of *The Student Personnel Point of View.* His special contribution to that document became its most important component—the "assumptions and beliefs" that guide the work of all student affairs professionals. Jim's ability to articulate the fundamental precepts of the profession helped thousands of student affairs staff understand and appreciate the values that underlie our work. In 1995, Jim worked with George Kuh, Thomas Miller, and Jo Anne Trow to write the document *Reasonable Expectations for NASPA,* which helped define and sharpen the educational compact between institutions and students. Again, Jim's ability to help colleagues think clearly about the ideas that drive our work proved extremely helpful to experienced practitioners and to young people entering the field. He was invited to write the first chapter in *The Handbook of Student Affairs Administration* in 1993; and this chapter, entitled *The Importance of Institutional Mission,* became a classic in the student affairs literature. Jim stressed the critical nature of fit between the college and the dean, arguing that the success of student affairs programs depends on the quality of this fit. Jim was in great demand as a speaker and as a consultant; and in his frequent visits to other campuses, he shared his insights about the practice of student affairs, the assumptions and beliefs that underlie our work, and the educational and personal needs of students.

Jim's way of leading may have appeared to some people as nonstructured and very informal. Although it is true that he harbored a vigorous dislike of bureaucracy, he nevertheless had clearly in mind what he wanted to accomplish as a leader and he thought very carefully about his strategy and his timing. He worked hard to understand the culture of the campus, the actual ways in which things were done, and how the organization functioned. He knew that establishing effective and trusting relationships with students, faculty, and staff was the key to any success he might achieve. He never used rules, regulations, or power to get things done; his authority was derived not from his position, but from his relationships and personal honesty. In the highly competitive academic environment at Stanford, where intellectual values were dominant, Jim was very effective in helping students and staff consider the important ideas of the times and to understand that these ideas had consequences in their lives and their careers. He understood how to use the entire campus as his classroom, and he never had any doubt about the values he was transmitting—honesty, an appreciation of differences, the dignity of the individual, respect, and personal freedom. For generations of lucky students and staff, James W. Lyons was the master teacher of the student affairs profession.

Chapter 11

Alice R. Manicur
Frostburg State University

On the beautiful campus of Frostburg State University in Western Maryland, a dignified and friendly woman greets a visiting young student in the administration building. "Hello, I'm Alice Manicur," she says, "welcome to the campus!" In no time at all, the visitor feels completely at home and knows he has found a new friend. For the past 40 years, Alice Manicur has been making friends for Frostburg State University and thousands of students have benefited from her leadership as vice president for student Affairs.

Alice R. Manicur earned her B.A. degree in business administration from Berea College in 1954, her M.S. degree in student personnel administration from Indiana University in 1955, and her EdD in student personnel administration from Indiana University in 1960. She worked as a member of the residence hall staff at Indiana University; as a freshman counselor at MacMurray College, in Jacksonville, Illinois; and on the dean of students staff at Indiana University. In 1960, she became the first dean of students at Frostburg State University, and this position title was later changed to vice president for student and educational services. She has been active in several professional associations, and in 1972 she received the Student Personnel Association for Teacher Education Meritorious Service Award. She was elected president of the National Association of Student Personnel Administrators (NASPA) in 1976–1977, the first woman to hold this post. She was a member of the NASPA Foundation board of directors, and in 1982 she was the recipient of the Fred Turner Award for outstanding service to the profession. In 1993, she received the Scott Goodnight Award from NASPA for outstanding performance as a dean. She was recognized by Indiana University with the Robert H. Shaffer Distinguished Alumna Award in 1994; and by her undergraduate Alma Mater, Berea College, with its Distinguished

Alumna Award in the same year. She has served as president of Delta Kappa Gamma and of the American Association of University Women, and she is currently a member of the board of trustees of Berea College.

Alice Manicur's father immigrated to this country as a young man in 1913 from southern Italy, where the family was engaged in farming. He was encouraged in this venture by Alice's grandfather, who had already established himself in eastern Canada. After entering the country through Ellis Island, Alice's father made his way to Honaker, Virginia and found work with the railroad, laying tracks for a living. He moved to Bluefield, Virginia, where he was still with the railroad. It was there that he married Alice's mother, after the traditional arrangements had been made by the two Italian families. Later, he was persuaded to join other relatives in the coal mines in West Virginia. Alice was born in McDowell County, West Virginia and was one of six children in the Manicur family. Alice was a coal miner's daughter, and her father was badly injured in the mines before she was 5 years old. He survived but had a permanent plate in his leg and walked with a limp for the remainder of his life. Alice developed a lifelong respect and admiration for immigrants who worked in the mines, who somehow managed to support their families while enduring dangerous conditions and terrible health hazards. When Alice was 5 years old, her father decided it would be best for the family to move away from the mines, and he was able to purchase five acres of land, which he and the family farmed. But the Great Depression had come, and her father had to continue to commute to the mines and work there to support the family.

Alice said that the family was only able to get by during those years because they could grow their own food. Their land was in Banner, Virginia, a town of 500; and Alice attended elementary school in this town, and then secondary school in the nearby town of Coeburn, Virginia. Looking back on her childhood, Alice said, "None of us knew we were as poor as we were!" She remembers wonderful times with her family and friends and the many games they would play, such as softball with sticks for bats and wound up rags for balls. She says that her love of adventure and the enjoyment of the company of others were clearly formed by these early childhood experiences. She remembers the family joy when her father purchased a radio and when each of the children would get one toy for Christmas. Her parents had completed perhaps just 4 or 5 years of school themselves, so there were few books or newspapers available in her home. However, her parents made it clear that "education was everything" to their children, and they expected Alice and her brothers and sisters to work hard in school. To her immigrant father and her first-generation Italian mother, education was the finest opportunity in this country, and they recognized it as the way to improve the lives of their children. Alice says that for her parents, the struggle was so hard that they had to believe there was a better way, and that way was through education. Alice was an excellent student, but her school's funds were so limited that in order to read a book students had to request that the teacher unlock a cabinet where the few books were kept; and for a period of 20 minutes each day, they were permitted to read.

Alice's first job for pay was in the "five and dime" store in Coeburn, and as she jokes now, "I never have stopped working since that time!" As Italian immigrants, her parents raised the family in the Catholic Church. However, in later years they attended protestant churches; and the family values of hard work, honesty, and caring for others were reinforced each week by Alice's attendance at Sunday school. Alice had great love and admiration for her father, who was determined that his children would not have to face the same hardships he did. His fondest dreams were realized, as all of the Manicur children did well in school and became successful. Alice worked as a student assistant during the day in high school and on Saturdays at the "five and dime," but she still managed to be active in clubs and activities. She graduated from high school during World War II and was encouraged to attend college by some of her teachers. Alice did not know anything about college and had never been on a campus, and she could not imagine how she could afford to go. Alice now credits the caring people in her small community, her teachers, and her parents for encouraging her to seek more education. "I was very fortunate, in that I always had people trying to help me," Alice said. This, no doubt, was a major factor in her own long career in student affairs, where she helped thousands of students.

At the suggestion of one of her teachers, who knew Alice's family well, Alice applied to Berea College in Kentucky because of its excellent reputation and commitment to talented students from very modest financial backgrounds. Alice had never heard about the college, but she was very excited about the opportunity when it was described to her. She loved mathematics and wanted to become a teacher, since she admired so many of the teachers she had in school. Alice decided she would take the bold step: after having been accepted by Berea, she took the long bus ride to Kentucky and enrolled during the summer term. She loved the institution and was thrilled by the learning opportunities, which opened up a world to her that she had not previously known. She lived in a residence hall, and like all Berea students she was employed on the campus as part of her educational program. But it was during the war years and Alice's strong feelings for her family made her feel she was not helping them while she was away at college. Her sense of obligation to help her family was so great that she decided to leave Berea and return home before the end of her first summer term. She loved the college and her professors, but she became discontented because she felt she should be working and earning money. Alice immediately got a job at the Hercules Powder Company and took a bus 40 miles per day to the ammunition plant, where she helped assemble shells to be used in combat. One of her sisters worked at the same plant, and Alice joked later, "It was dangerous work, but lots of people were doing what was necessary during those years to win the war." Alice remained in this job for 2 years, and when the war was over the plant closed down and she needed to look for another job.

She and one of her sisters purchased a part interest in a bus station café, and Alice managed this business and worked there for almost a full year. But the "big city" of Bristol, Virginia seemed to promise more opportunity; so Alice and her sister moved there, and Alice worked for the telephone company for several months while living in a boarding house. She then obtained a position with the Monroe Calculating Machine Company, where she had several functions, including assembly. She became so good at this work that she was asked to become a trainer for new employees. She loved helping other people learn and found success in encouraging others to move ahead. During these 4 years of working at the Monroe Company, Alice continued to send money to her family, helping them with their expenses, especially the education of her brothers. It was a practice that Alice would continue the rest of her life.

Alice's experiences in working for several years after high school provided her with a good deal of satisfaction. She was successful in all of the jobs she had and earned the respect and admiration of others for her intelligence, hard work, and ability to help others. When she would return to her home, her father often asked her, "Alice, when are you going back to college?" While she felt no pressure from her parents to go back to college, Alice had been thinking about it for the past 2 or 3 years and had actually enrolled in a local business college for a year of night school, preparing herself for the transition to being in college full-time. She was doing very well at the Monroe Company and was proud of the financial support she had been able to provide to her family. But she also knew that she did not want to work with calculating machines the rest of her life, so she made the difficult decision to return to Berea College in 1950. Berea was a special place for her, and she knew that was where she wanted to be. As she said many years later, "It was the best decision I ever made!"

Alice took the bus to Berea and met her future roommate on the bus. She was older than the traditional students living in the residence hall, but she quickly made friends and was warmly accepted by the other students. Like all Berea students, Alice worked as part of her responsibilities; she was employed in the dining hall and then as a janitress in the residence halls. She was still planning to be a teacher, and in her sophomore year she met Julia Allen, the dean of women, who asked Alice to work in her office on a part-time basis. Dean Allen became a role model for Alice, treating everyone with respect and caring for the lives of the students. The dean, a highly educated woman who was a Quaker and had done missionary work in China, loved nature, art, music, and hiking; and she introduced Alice to the world of higher education. Dean Allen's way of involving the students and others in decisions she made, and the genuine respect that the dean gave to others, were to influence Alice greatly in her own career.

Alice was active in campus clubs and organizations, and she majored in business and teacher education. When she returned home for the summers, she was welcomed back to the Monroe Calculating Company, where her former supervisors were very happy to have her back at her previous job. She also spent two summers during college working in a canning factory in Illinois and detasseling corn there as well. Even during her years at Berea, Alice somehow managed to help out at home as needed. In her senior year, Alice found that she did not enjoy her practice teaching experience and decided that she might benefit from exploring other positions in education. With the help and encouragement of Dean Allen, Alice discovered the graduate program in student personnel administration at Indiana University and was encouraged to apply. She took a bus to Bloomington, Indiana for her interview, and Indiana University looked huge to her. During her interview Alice impressed everyone she met and was offered a head counselor's position in a large residence hall, a very unusual offer, given the fact that she only had an undergraduate degree and no full-time student affairs experience. But Alice had already proven that she could be successful in a variety of work and academic settings, and the staff at Indiana felt very fortunate to attract her to the university.

Alice completed her master's degree in student personnel administration in only one year and excelled in her work in the residence halls. She had already made a name for herself because of her positive attitude with students, her work with her staff, and her ability to help students achieve success. As a result, she was contacted by MacMurray College in nearby Jacksonville, Illinois, and she was asked to apply for the position of counselor of freshmen. When Alice replied that she had not even completed her master's degree yet, her faculty mentor at Indiana, Dr. Robert Kinker, told her that she could complete her degree before the fall semester began at MacMurray by enrolling in 15 hours of graduate courses during the summer. Alice did this and accepted the position as counselor of freshmen. Alice, for the first time, borrowed $400 to complete her summer courses and later said, "I paid it all back within one semester!" In her position at MacMurray, Alice was to have a great deal of freedom in creating positive programs for the new students. She lived in a campus residence hall and was available around the clock to counsel and advise students. She remained in contact with her faculty adviser at Indiana, Dr. Kinker, and he strongly encouraged Alice to pursue her doctoral degree there. She was hesitant at first, because at the time she could not imagine someone from her background obtaining a doctoral degree. But she enrolled at Indiana and attended summer classes during the 3 years she served as counselor of freshmen at MacMurray. Alice was MacMurray's first counselor of freshmen, and this experience resulted in a lifelong commitment to new students, reflected in the outstanding orientation and advising programs she created years later at Frostburg State.

With her doctoral studies becoming more demanding, Alice decided that she needed to be in Bloomington on a full-time basis for at least 2 years in order to complete her degree. She applied for a John Hay Whitney fellowship and was selected for this prestigious honor, and at the same time she was invited to become one of the area coordinators for the residence hall program. Perhaps due to her positive experiences with the arts while at Berea College, Alice was placed in charge of cultural programs for students in all of the residence halls. Indiana University is, of course, one of the world's leading centers for music, dance, drama, and art; and this job was a thrill for Alice. While she did all of this, she lived in the graduate center, where she was elected the president of the Graduate Student Association. She completed her doctorate in student personnel administration in 1960, and both of her parents and family came to Bloomington for the ceremony. It was a dream come true for her father and mother, a fulfillment of their belief as immigrants in education! Her major professor at Indiana was Robert Shaffer, who was to become a lifelong friend and mentor in her work.

While Alice was at Indiana, she was encouraged to attend various professional meetings in student affairs; and in the process of doing this she met such outstanding leaders as Patricia Cross, Robert Shaffer, Betty Greenleaf, and Emily Taylor. Alice's outstanding work during her graduate program at Indiana had impressed her mentors, so it was not surprising (except to Alice!) when she received a telephone call in the spring of 1960 from Dr. R. Bowen Hardesty, president of Frostburg State Teachers College, inviting her to visit the campus and consider becoming the dean of students. Alice had never even heard of the institution and did not know where Frostburg, Maryland was located. But President Hardesty knew from his conversations with faculty and staff at Indiana that Alice was the person he wanted for the position, and he convinced her to visit the campus. So Alice, who still had never owned a car or flown in an airplane, took a bus to a professional student affairs meeting in Philadelphia, and during the trip she went to Frostburg for the interview. President Hardesty met her at the bus station in a snow storm after the 16-hour bus trip and, after talking with her about his plans to expand the programs at the 1,000-student college, offered the position to Alice that same day. After returning to Bloomington and consulting with Dr. Shaffer, Alice accepted the position of dean of students at Frostburg, and she moved there on August 15, 1960. She was the senior student affairs officer (SSAO), the first person appointed to this new position at the institution. She had just completed her doctorate at Indiana, and she knew it was highly unusual to assume this much responsibility so quickly, But she was eager, she knew she could work very hard, and she was determined to succeed.

Alice had no job description at Frostburg, but she knew she was responsible for creating and implementing a quality student life program on the campus. She was guided in this regard by the inspiring vision of her president, Dr. Hardesty, who wanted to increase enrollment and expand the curriculum. It was the early 1960s and most colleges and universities were growing, due to the baby boomers and the increased aspirations for college among young people. Frostburg State College added new academic programs, built new teaching and residential space, and hired many new faculty and staff during these years.

Alice found her job tremendously challenging and exciting; and she created new programs in the residence halls, student orientation, academic advising, and career counseling. Her previous work at MacMurray College as counselor of freshmen and at Indiana University as a residence hall coordinator proved very valuable to her in establishing these well-accepted programs. Alice took student leaders and faculty with her on trips to surrounding cities to recruit students and to increase the visibility of the college with the public. She created campus days and career days for students, established an honors convocation, and organized regular campus convocations where the intellectual and cultural life of the campus were celebrated. She personally advised the Student Government Association and established new ways for students to participate in all aspects of the university. She won the confidence of the students, and in her very first year she established the principle with them that was to be her guide for her entire career: Alice told the students, "I trust you and I believe you; you can always count on me for support, but just don't ever lie to me!" Alice loved working with the students and was very close to them, and she says that they almost never let her down. She worked very hard and her advocacy for strong student involvement in campus affairs caused some faculty and staff to criticize her. But she was committed to making things better, and she said to her staff during these times, "We're just not going to let people stop us when we know it's the right thing to do!" In her own quiet and dignified way she accomplished a great deal, and everyone at Frostburg knew that when Alice Manicur said she would do something, it would be done.

> *Reflecting her quiet determination to approach problems in constructive ways before they become unmanageable, Alice worked with her staff, selected faculty members and student leaders, and created one of the best drug education and abuse prevention programs in the country.*

Alice worked with three presidents in her first 7 years at Frostburg, during a very volatile period in the country. While most of the social unrest and violence concerning the Vietnam War and racial problems did not affect the Frostburg campus very much, these were difficult years on the campus. Dr. Hardesty, the visionary president who hired Alice, left the institution after 3 years; Alice then witnessed some of the turmoil that commonly occurs within a college upon a president's departure. The next president was Dr. John Morey, who stayed for 4 years in the position. He had such high respect for Alice that he asked her to assume responsibility for the admissions office, in addition to her duties as dean of students. With the aspirations of the college to increase its enrollment, improve services to students, and to increase residence hall space on the campus, Alice faced many tough challenges. She recalls having very few professional staff during those years, especially in admissions, and she compensated by working 7 days a week. "I always knew that I could work hard," Alice joked later, "but I never really counted on it being like this." She was able to achieve outstanding results and earned the respect and admiration of faculty, students, and staff on her campus. In the process, she gained the support to hire additional staff, and many of her staff have remained at Frostburg because of their loyalty and admiration for Alice. One of her administrative colleagues said of Alice, "Above all other stellar qualities, Alice Manicur is a professional of enormous integrity. Having worked with the alumni of Frostburg State University, I can report that Dr. Manicur is the individual that is asked about most often. She is, in many respects, the core of this fine institution. She can be credited for transforming many mediocre students into exceptional people because she demonstrated a belief in their ability" (Personal correspondence with author, March 29, 2000).

In the often rough world of higher education administration, Alice was known for her gentle and caring approach in working with students, faculty, and staff. However, she rarely left any doubt about where she stood on issues and expressed her views directly to everyone. She was effective in this regard because she always advocated for ideas and programs in a way that was entirely consistent with her values. She would take others to task (especially students!) when she found them unprepared or ill informed. She had no patience with the few people she observed in her career who tried to advance their own position at the expense of others.

In Alice's seventh year at Frostburg, Dr. Nelson Guild was appointed the new president and remained for the next 17 years in this position. She and President Guild worked very well together, and Alice's title was changed to vice president for student affairs. During this period, the enrollment quadrupled, creating the need for additional facilities. Eight new residence halls, new dining services, a student health service building, and a student union were built. Alice worked closely with student leaders to create auxiliary fees that made some of these buildings possible. She had the trust and support of the students and President Guild relied on her to assist in these major projects. In addition, Alice continued to make changes in student life by creating a resident assistant (RA) program in the halls, a campus-wide judicial board program, and a greatly expanded cultural and performing arts program. She led the move on the campus to eliminate old parietal rules and established co-educational residence halls, something that many people thought would never become a reality at Frostburg. She also hired some very outstanding staff members, some of whom became national leaders in student affairs.

Reflecting her quiet determination to approach problems in constructive ways before they become unmanageable, Alice worked with her staff, selected faculty members and student leaders, and created one of the best drug education and abuse prevention programs in the country. With support from Alice, her staff was able to acquire substantial grant money from the federal government over a period of almost 10 years to support educational, counseling, and peer programs regarding drug abuse. Her positive experiences and exposure to the arts while a student at Berea College and as a staff member at Indiana University led Alice to create similar opportunities for students at Frostburg State. A very rich cultural events program has provided students with opportunities to enjoy artists from all over the world. This co-curricular education has been characterized by an emphasis on national and international diversity. At times, this effort included bus trips to nearby metropolitan areas. Alice set an example for others, as her own early experiences in higher education had stimulated her to learn more about other cultures and especially the arts. During her career, she has traveled to all the continents and to dozens of countries, all the while sharing her experiences with her students and staff. She attributes this love of learning and her appreciation of the arts to her Berea College experience, where faculty members took a personal interest in students and invited them to culturally enriching campus events. As the SSAO at Frostburg, Alice put this concept into practice with students.

By the early 1970s, Alice was a well-established leader and was often asked to assume various responsibilities in student affairs professional organizations. She was active in the Council for the International Exchange of Scholars, the National Orientation Directors Association, the National Association of Women Educators, and the Middle States Accrediting Organization. She was a consultant to several colleges and universities and was a frequent presenter at conferences. She was a member of a NASPA advisory board in 1971 when she was asked to serve as an at-large member of that association's national board of directors. Her leadership quickly became evident, and in only 6 years she was elected president of NASPA, the first woman to hold this position in the history of the organization. While Alice was certainly aware of this fact, she never mentioned it to anyone and simply went about the business of directing the association. Her pioneering leadership opened up the association and the profession to leadership opportunities for women; in recognition of this fact, in 1996 NASPA renamed its national conference for women aspiring to become student affairs officers the "Alice Manicur Symposium." She was also honored in 1982 with the Fred Turner Award for outstanding service to the profession; in 1993 she received the profession's highest honor, the Scott Goodnight Award for outstanding performance as a dean. Both of her alma maters honored her as well in 1994, when she received the Robert Shaffer Distinguished Alumna Award from Indiana University and the Distinguished Alumna Award from Berea College. She was appointed to the board of trustees of Berea College in 1992 and continues to serve in this capacity.

Another change occurred in Alice's title in 1987 when the new president, Dr. Herb Reinhard, chose to combine student and educational services. Alice was named vice president for student and educational services, reflecting her expanded duties. Alice has always emphasized with her staff the importance of working closely with faculty and getting them regularly involved in student life. While the new president achieved several positive goals, such as getting the college name changed to "University" and creating a Frostburg State Center in Hagerstown, Maryland, the university endured a very turbulent 4 years as a result of the president's management style. Alice continued to work closely with faculty and students, while providing support to the president. The university continued to grow during these years, as the faculty, students, and staff became a strong force in making good things happen. Alice and her staff helped maintain institutional stability during this time.

In 1991, Dr. Catherine Gira was appointed the president of Frostburg State University. President Gira has provided outstanding leadership to the institution and strong support for the student affairs program. Alice and her staff have continued to develop innovative programs for the benefit of students. The student body has continued to grow, and there are plans to expand the already extensive academic programs at the institution.

> *She is a classic "hands-on" leader who spends as much time at campus events, student meetings, and community functions in support of students as she does in her office.*

Having served as the SSAO at Frostburg since 1960, Alice has been able to use this long experience to accomplish a great deal and to ensure that excellent programs continue in place. She developed the Summer Planning Conference for freshmen in the late 1960s, and this highly successful orientation and advising program remains one of the best of its kind. It involves many faculty members, and it is enthusiastically received by students and their parents. It has resulted in higher yield rates in admissions and higher retention rates of students. In conjunction with this program, Alice also developed a "Higher Education 101" course for freshmen, taught by large numbers of faculty and staff who also serve as academic advisers to these students. Alice believes strongly in the academic mission of Frostburg, which is to provide excellent educational opportunities to students from modest financial and academic backgrounds; and these two programs have achieved outstanding success. They have also cemented excellent relationships between student affairs and academic affairs, something that Alice considers critical to the success of her division.

Most of the residence halls at Frostburg State University have been built during the time Alice has served as the SSAO, and their physical design and staff organization reflect Alice's strong commitment to student learning in the halls. Professional staff, RAs, and hall governments combine to make the living experience at Frostburg part of the students' educational experience. In cooperation with faculty, Alice and her staff have pioneered in the creation of student learning communities, including some which have a residential component; and 17 of them now are in place, reflecting a variety of curricular, recreational, artistic, and cultural interests.

Perhaps reflecting her own experiences at Berea and in her own family, Alice has encouraged students to participate in community service at Frostburg—many years before this kind of activity became so popular on other campuses. As a result, Frostburg State was one of the first institutions selected to participate in the AmeriCorps program and has received grants to support its activity from this federal agency every year since its founding. With her staff, Alice established a special residence hall where the residents are committed to community service and service learning, and where many of the students receive scholarship support for their activities.

The "GOLD" program (Generating Opportunities for Leadership and Development at Frostburg State) was established by Alice and her staff to encourage students to experience an intensive leadership program in a campus residence hall. This program is linked to faculty mentors and speakers who make presentations on different aspects of leadership several times each year.

Alice emphasized the importance of developing genuine, trusting relationships with faculty, staff, students, and others as a key to her success as a leader. Her many years at Frostburg have been a great asset to her in this regard, and she indicated that the quality of these relationships was much more important in getting things done than any power inherent in her position. "A leader has to earn respect, and in student affairs we do this most successfully through building effective relationships with others," Alice said. She added that leaders must learn to make good things happen with students using the resources they have and to be creative in extending these resources as far as they can go. She had little patience for staff or other administrators who sat idle, thinking that they could not accomplish anything unless they were given more institutional resources. She recalls her early years at Frostburg, when enrollment was growing and the institution could not build new residence halls fast enough to keep up with this growth. Alice went into the community, knocked on the doors of 125 houses, and personally recruited and organized supervised off-campus housing space for students. She quickly established a reputation at the institution as a leader who knew how to get things done. "I'm a realist when it comes to money," Alice said, and "many of the best things we have done in student affairs have been accomplished with volunteers, students, parents, and community members." She has earned the respect and gained the support of her presidents over the years because of her ability to achieve positive results with limited institutional funds. At the same time, she was a tenacious advocate for additional support from Frostburg, but she recognized that her proposals for more resources would always be viewed more positively when she could demonstrate how effectively she had extended the funds she had.

While she is revered at her own institution, she continues to participate in the annual evaluation process required of all senior administrators. She believes strongly in well-defined goals and objectives for her division, she wants her presidents to evaluate her on how well she and the student affairs division have met these goals. However, she emphasized that effective leaders should know how well they are doing through the daily reactions of students, faculty, and staff on the campus; and should not depend on a once-per-year formal evaluation.

Alice decided to remain at Frostburg State as the SSAO since 1960 because she was constantly challenged by the excitement of the programs and changes in which she was so intimately involved. "I had a vested interest in seeing that something was going to get done in the right way, that a new facility was actually going to get built, or that a policy change was going to occur," she said. Above all, Alice loved the struggle of leadership and the challenges it gave her every year; she found it invigorating. The rewards were many, and primary among them for Alice was seeing the great improvements in student life and learning opportunities at Frostburg State. While the institution continued to grow, both in size and in academic complexity, she maintained a highly personal approach in her leadership at the institution. She writes many personal notes per year to students, parents, faculty, and others, encouraging them in their work or thanking them for their contributions. She is a classic "hands-on" leader who spends as much time at campus events, student meetings, and community functions in support of students as she does in her office. Her impact on the institution and on students' lives has been remarkable. Her current president, Dr. Catherine Gira, said of Alice,

> She has probably had more influence on the development of Frostburg State University than any other single individual. Fine presidents and senior academic officers have come and gone and left their marks on the institution, but none have been more visionary and responsive than Alice in developing programs to meet the needs of students. She remains a paradigm of the caring professional. To those of us who are her colleagues, she is a veritable icon (Personal communication with author, 2000).

Alice Manicur, the daughter of an Italian immigrant and a coal miner from West Virginia, was introduced to the liberating force of higher education at Berea College in the early

1950s. At that time, she never dreamed that one day she would become a member of that same institution's board of trustees and a recipient of its highest honor, the Distinguished Alumna Achievement Award. This inspiring personal story makes perfect sense to any of the thousands of her students who have known her and who have benefited from her leadership as the SSAO at Frostburg State University for the past 40 years.

Chapter 12

James J. Rhatigan
Wichita State University

I n the winter 1999–2000 issue of the Wichita State University (WSU) alumni magazine, *The Shocker,* the editors selected the 40 persons associated with the university who have done the most to change the century. To no one's surprise, listed as number 2 was James J. Rhatigan, ahead of WSU graduates and faculty who became scientists, corporate executives, scholars, philanthropists, artists, judges, entertainers, sports figures, and elected officials. Only Harry Corbin, the WSU president who achieved university status for the institution within the Kansas state system in the early 1960s, was listed ahead of him. For the past 35 years, thousands of students, faculty, and staff at WSU have benefited from the leadership, personal warmth, and wit of James Rhatigan.

James Rhatigan earned his B.A. degree in American history from Coe College in 1957, his M.A. in American history from Syracuse University in 1959, and his PhD from the University of Iowa in student personnel administration in 1965. Jim was a residence hall director at Syracuse University during his master's degree program and then worked in Washington, D.C. for Congressman Leonard G. Wolf, later returning to Iowa to help organize and conduct his campaign. After serving in the Iowa Army National Guard, he became the assistant dean of men at the University of Iowa and served in this position while he was completing his doctoral studies in Iowa City. In 1965, Jim accepted the appointment as dean of students at WSU in Wichita, Kansas. This position title was changed to vice president for student affairs in 1970. He also became professor of education in 1982. He remained as the senior student affairs officer (SSAO) until 1997, when he was appointed the senior vice president of the university. When he was appointed dean of students in 1965, he was—at age 30—the youngest SSAO in the country at institutions with over 10,000 students. He was appointed the associate editor of the *NASPA Journal,* and for over 20 years he served as the historian for the National Association of Student Personnel Administrators (NASPA). He was elected a regional vice president of NASPA in 1973, and he was elected president of NASPA in 1975.

In 1980, James was presented with NASPA's Fred Turner Award for outstanding service to the profession, and then in 1987 with the Scott Goodnight Award for outstanding performance as a dean. The annual award for the outstanding professional in Region IV-West of NASPA is named in his honor. Jim has written and published extensively in professional journals and is one of the most sought after keynote speakers in the profession. WSU presented him with its Alumni Recognition Award in 1988. In 1997, the student union at WSU was named the Rhatigan Student Center. He has been an active leader in the United Way, the American Red Cross, the Methodist Urban Ministry, and the North Central Association of Colleges and Schools. He has served as a consultant to many colleges and universities, and several of his former staff members at WSU have become SSAOs, professors, and presidents at other institutions.

James Rhatigan was born in 1935 in Monticello, Iowa, a rural community of 3,000, located about 30 miles from Cedar Rapids. His grandparents immigrated to this country from Switzerland and Ireland, and one of his great grandfathers fought in the American Civil War. His family was engaged in farming and the railroad, typical of so many of the people in the rural areas of the Midwest. Jim's parents were both from Monticello and were married there in 1933 in the depth of the Great Depression. Neither of his parents attended college, but both were avid readers and very committed to education. Jim's mother worked as a waitress and then for many years as a secretary in a law firm. Jim's father commuted to Cedar Rapids, where he worked for the Collins Radio Company, ultimately as assistant superintendent of the plant. While the Great Depression was devastating to millions of families, Jim's parents remained employed during these years, and he has very fond memories of growing up in Monticello. "It was essentially a one-dimensional town in terms of culture," Jim wryly commented, noting that almost everyone was poor, but no one thought they were. Jim had one younger brother, and his family was very close.

As a young boy, Jim understood the value of working and saving money. He began working at a clothing store, doing odd jobs before school started, then after school, and for 12 hours on Saturdays. He was a bit of an entrepreneur as a boy, selling tickets for school and community events, collecting coins, and promoting various programs, all of which enabled him to have a little spending money, buy a new bicycle, and some clothes. This interest was to remain active in his career at WSU, which developed an outstanding center for entrepreneurship education. Jim loved to read and was especially interested in politics and history. He became quite accomplished at playing the organ and, by the time he was in high school, sometimes played at three different churches. However, when he went to Coe College, he joked later, "I found out that there were many others much more talented than I was, so I went on to other things!" His interest in music has continued, especially in the history and development of hymns. He is now a collector of hymns, and while still in high school he wrote a hymn himself. He was a good student, and in high school was active in dramatic activities (he was the principal in "Our Miss Brooks" and Huck Finn in "The Adventures of Tom Sawyer!). He became the team manager for the basketball team, something he liked so much that he did this at Coe College later as well, as he was able to travel to all away games! He was the president of both his junior and senior class, and he graduated ninth in his class of 58 students in 1953, "barely squeaking into the top 20 percent" as Jim joked later!

Jim was 10 years old when World War II was over, and his main recollection of that time was when President Roosevelt died in early 1945. Jim has been a lifelong admirer of Roosevelt, and Jim wrote his master's thesis at Syracuse on "The Vice Presidency in the Roosevelt Administration." Jim, always a Democrat, though raised in a Republican family and community, joked that he picked Harry Truman to win the presidency in 1948 during a high school debate! As a graduate student at Syracuse University later in life, Jim experienced one of his greatest thrills—interviewing former President Truman in Independence, Missouri, in conjunction with his master's degree thesis. His lifelong interest in history and politics was greatly enhanced when his family took the only vacation he remembers during his youth—a trip to Washington, D.C. in 1947, where Jim became fascinated with the Smithsonian, the Capitol, and other well-known sites. Little did he know as a 12-year-old that he would return to that city 12 years later, working as an aide to a congressman from Iowa.

While Jim felt no pressure from anyone to attend college, he was among a minority of students from his high school that continued their formal education after graduation in 1953. After visiting the nearby University of Iowa campus, Jim decided that the 6,000-student institution was too large; so he and his closest friend, Jack Schmidt, decided to attend Coe College, a fine liberal arts institution of about 800 students at the time, located 30 miles away in Cedar Rapids. Jack was a basketball player, and he and Jim were roommates during their first year in college. Jack left college to get married after only 1 year. But Jim remained and became very involved in campus and academic life, and he loved the institution. He became the president of the Young Democrats at Coe, and as a result he participated as a volunteer in some area election campaigns, meeting the congressional candidate who would later hire him.

As he had done in high school, Jim worked many hours each week to pay for his college expenses. He worked as a bus boy at the Elks Club, where he was also provided with his meals, sold flowers for campus formal dances, served as a janitor in a residence hall, and in his junior and senior years became a residence hall counselor. Jim majored in American history and excelled in his studies, earning a small academic scholarship for his final 2 years of college. Again duplicating his high school experience, Jim became the student manager of the basketball team and especially enjoyed traveling with the team to area colleges, such as Carleton, Knox, and Grinnell. He was not at all sure about what he wanted to do with his life, but he received some encouragement from his faculty advisers to become an attorney. So, during his senior year, Jim applied to the law school at the University of Iowa and was accepted. But he decided not to attend law school, as one of his professors told him about the highly respected graduate program in public administration at Syracuse University; after applying there, Jim was accepted and was awarded a stipend to cover the costs of attendance.

Thinking that a career in public administration would be consistent with his interests, Jim decided to go to Syracuse University and enrolled in their master's program. After only a few weeks, however, Jim discovered that he did not like the coursework in his graduate program and decided to shift into the graduate program in American history. He served as a residence hall adviser in Watson Hall and enjoyed his work with freshmen students. He became well acquainted with some of the leaders of the student affairs staff, including Earle Clifford and Jim Carleton, later to become close colleagues of Jim's in NASPA. Jim took time to make visits to Boston, New York City, and to various colleges and universities in the East; and he spent 2 summers as a counselor for 5- to 10-year-old children at a camp in the Finger Lakes region of New York. Both in his residence hall job and his camp counselor position, Jim loved his work with young people and especially liked the personal relationships he was able to develop with the students and their families. He genuinely liked people, took an interest in them, and found that others greatly appreciated his approach to them. These close, personal relationships were to become the basis of his work throughout his career.

After 2 years at Syracuse, Jim completed his master's degree in American history and was offered a job as a director of one of the large residence hall complexes. At the same time, he was encouraged to enroll in an experimental doctoral program in social science, enabling him to combine some of his academic interests. But while Jim loved scholarship and history, he did not see himself in a career as an academician. Moreover, it was 1959, and Jim was subject to the military draft unless he was enrolled as a full-time student. After considering his options, he decided to sign up for a 6-month Army program in the Iowa National Guard in October 1959. He was sent to Ft. Leonard Wood in Missouri, and then to Ft. Knox, Kentucky.

When Jim's service in the Army was over, he was called by Iowa Congressman Leonard G. Wolf, who offered him a job in his Washington, D.C. office as an aide. Jim eagerly accepted this offer and moved to the nation's capital in the spring of 1960. After several months in Washington, Jim was asked to return to his Iowa district and help run the re-election campaign for Mr. Wolf. Jim loved this work and remembers working to arrange a speaking engagement by John F. Kennedy. When Kennedy eventually declined, Lyndon Johnson agreed to substitute. Jim was obviously very good at promotion, as the speaking engagement attracted nearly 20,000 people!

Johnson's staff members were so impressed with the arrangements that the next week Jim was called and offered a position with Lyndon Johnson, who of course was the Democratic candidate for vice president of the United States at the time. Jim was excited and intended to say yes; but at the same time, in response to an application he had submitted earlier, he received a call from the University of Iowa and was offered the position of assistant dean of men for off-campus housing. He would make $5,200 per year and could take up to 6 hours of graduate work each term toward his PhD degree. Although the political position in Texas had no salary (it did cover all his expenses, however), this was a very difficult decision for Jim, as he loved the excitement of the political process and in the back of his mind thought he might run for public office some day. On the other hand, his work in residence halls at Coe and Syracuse and his experience as a summer camp counselor in New York were so positive that he thought a career in student affairs would be very enjoyable. After a difficult time of thinking about these options, Jim decided to accept the position at the University of Iowa as assistant dean of men and begin the PhD program in student personnel administration.

> *With passion, care, and humor, he told stories about individual students and their backgrounds, problems, and aspirations in a manner that others found almost irresistible.*

Looking back at that decision now, Jim wonders what might have happened had he accepted the position with Lyndon Johnson. When Kennedy was assassinated only 3 years later and Johnson became president, the man who offered Jim the position in 1960 became Johnson's chief White House adviser, and Jim most certainly would have been working in the White House as well. Now, 40 years later, Jim has no regrets about his career, but he still occasionally thinks about this decision when he was only 25 years old.

When he began his work at the University of Iowa that fall, he was still eligible to attend law school and was not sure about what to do. But his work in student affairs, especially his association with Dr. Donald Hoyt, professor of education, persuaded him to enroll in the PhD program in student personnel administration. Jim respected the intelligence and genuine humanity of Hoyt, who was to remain Jim's most trusted mentor throughout his career. Hoyt became the president of the American College Personnel Association and was one of the pioneers of the student development movement in the profession.

In 1961 in Iowa City, Jim met Beverly Lansing, who was working at the university hospital as a cardiovascular technician. They were married in 1962 and their daughter, Becky, was born in 1964. Jim completed his PhD at Iowa in the spring of 1965, a time when the Civil Rights movement was in full swing, the U.S. involvement in Vietnam was in its early stage, and it was only a year after the famous student uprising at Berkeley. As Jim noted later, "Despite these significant events in our society at the time, virtually no one in higher education saw the tremendous changes and turmoil about to take place on the campuses."

Jim was fortunate to complete his doctorate during the "golden age" of growth in American higher education, with almost all institutions increasing their enrollments rapidly, as the generation of baby boomers began college in record numbers. Many new faculty and staff were needed across the country, and student affairs programs were expanding in scope and function. Jim had an outstanding academic record and excellent experience at Syracuse and at Iowa; thus he was a very attractive candidate for several student affairs positions. He considered opportunities at Gustavus Adolphus, Kansas State, and Kent State; but then the president of WSU, Emory Lindquist, called Jim and invited him to visit the campus. Lindquist, a distinguished historian and a Rhodes scholar, was impressed with Jim's liberal arts background at Coe and his interest in history. Jim later joked that President Lindquist must not have paid much attention to Jim's actual experience, as there were certainly many other candidates with more years in student affairs. WSU, a relatively young, but ambitious institution of 10,000 students, was growing, and Jim was very impressed with President Lindquist and his plans for the university. There really was not what could be called a student affairs division at the time, Jim recalled later. There were several offices scattered around the campus, each providing various services to students, but not coordinated in any way. After talking over President Lindquist's offer with his wife and with his faculty adviser, Donald Hoyt, Jim decided to accept the position of dean of students in the summer of 1965. He was only 30 years old!

When Jim arrived at WSU, the student affairs staff was small and there was no actual division of student affairs. The "student health service" consisted of one nurse, and there was only one staff member in student financial aid. There was an international student adviser, no minority student program, one person providing placement services, and only one staff member providing counseling to students. WSU was an urban, commuter institution with many part-time students; at the time it was not funded sufficiently to support the needed student services that existed on more traditional campuses. Jim immediately began working hard to build a strong division of student affairs. He joked later, "This was a great job and a great place to start, as the only way we could go was up!"

Jim, always an excellent listener, spent long hours each day during his first several weeks at WSU listening to students, faculty, and community leaders about their expectations and their experiences at the university. He emphasized the importance of personal "stories" and learned a great deal about what needed to be done in student affairs from listening to the personal histories and lives of the diverse student body. Later in his career, Jim was to become nationally prominent for his own ability to tell stories about the experiences of students as a way of teaching about educational values. He knew he needed real statistical information about student needs and backgrounds, and he found ways to collect this in his early years at WSU. However, he knew that it would be his own ability to persuade others about student needs that would enable him to build a student affairs division. Jim became a master at this task; and he acquired new resources, changed old policies, and created new programs by telling others about actual situations with students. With passion, care, and humor, he told stories about individual students and their backgrounds, problems, and aspirations in a manner that others found almost irresistible. As a result, Jim was able to expand all of the services, hire new staff, change policies, and reconfigure the organization.

While Jim was experiencing great success in his early years at WSU, building the student affairs division, he was also the university's point person in the very difficult student demonstrations concerning the war in Vietnam. To make matters more complex, Wichita is located close to McConnell Air Force Base. The Boeing Company, a major provider of airplanes for the war effort, is also located there. Jim's approach to the war protests was similar to his approach to everything else—it was direct, honest, and personal. He understood the value for the institution for him to be very visible with the students, making needed decisions on the spot, and saving the president only as a "trump card," as Jim described it. Jim's open and vigorous rejection of a federal effort to use undercover agents and his consistent efforts to be honest with student protestors created what Jim called a "culture of trust" at the institution. "It made my reputation at the university, and it was this trust that enabled me to accomplish most of the things I did," Jim stated. Detractors who wanted a harsher approach to the protestors subjected him to a good deal of criticism, but Jim had the support of the president and of the great majority of the students and faculty. It was during these difficult times that Jim clearly understood the importance of open, frequent, and honest discussions with community leaders.

WSU is an urban institution, and its neighbors are significantly involved in the institution. Jim became the link with community leaders by listening to their concerns, participating in their activities, and involving them in decisions. The emotional toll on SSAOs during these years was often heavy; indeed, several resigned from their positions or were relieved of their duties by their presidents because of the strain of the job and the turmoil on the campuses. Jim always appeared to be calm, rational, friendly, and even humorous in the face of this great campus unrest; but he was, in fact, not exempt from this emotional strain. He knew what was demanded of him as a leader and, through great determination, was able to remain the trusted voice of reason on the WSU campus. Jim emphasized that he was able to survive the raw emotions of those times, and the constant long days and nights, because of the support and love of his wife, Beverly. "I owe a great debt to her," Jim says; "she saved my life during those years."

> *Jim could not live with unfairness; when he saw that he could help a student, he would not rest until he had made every effort possible to correct a problem.*

Jim's first 5 years at WSU were exciting, demanding, and productive. He had won the support and admiration of students, faculty, and staff for his leadership, had expanded programs for students, had organized the student affairs division, and had handled some very difficult student protests on the campus. In this short period of time, Jim's work had become well known, and he received several invitations from other institutions to become their SSAO. Johns Hopkins, Florida State, Carleton, Nebraska, Ohio State, and University of California-Santa Barbara were among the colleges and universities that asked Jim to consider joining their staff. This was flattering to Jim, still only 35 years old. But the student deaths at Kent State on May 4, 1970 and the subsequent turmoil around the country convinced Jim to remain at WSU. "I realized then that I had already put a lot of myself into this university, and I believed strongly in what we were doing. Moreover, I saw outstanding potential at WSU, and I was convinced it was an institution where I could make a difference," Jim recalled later. Perhaps the youth, vigor, and optimism of the growing university caused Jim to stay; he decided WSU was a place that was capable of responding positively to the challenges ahead, and he wanted to be a part of this effort. In 1968, Clark Ahlberg was appointed the new president, and Jim's position title was changed to vice president for student affairs.

If the year 1970 had not already been difficult enough, on October 2 of that year the greatest tragedy in the history of the institution occurred. At 2:00 that afternoon, Jim was informed that a plane carrying WSU football players and coaches crashed in a Colorado canyon on its way to a game at Utah State, killing 34 of the passengers. No one has sufficient training or background to know what to do in such a tragedy, but Jim knew it was his responsibility to serve as a key organizer and responder during this difficult time. He and his staff, and of course many others at the institution and in the community, worked around the clock for many days and nights, trying to help the families of those who lost their lives, meanwhile dealing with the incredible grief on the campus itself. The university used experts from Wright-Patterson Air Force Base in Dayton, Ohio, and organized faculty, staff, and students to respond personally to the families. Somehow, the WSU community survived this unprecedented tragedy. Because of this situation, Jim became an adviser to student affairs colleagues on other campuses in future years, as they dealt with student deaths and other tragedies.

The city of Wichita, Kansas has a substantial minority population. But when Jim came to the institution in 1965, it had not achieved as much success in providing access to minority students as it desired, and it had very few minority faculty members. Among Jim's proudest achievements at WSU is the establishment of the TRIO programs (special support programs for disadvantaged students), due to aggressive efforts in his first few years to obtain external funding for them. There are now five separate programs, and minority enrollment has increased dramatically at the university. Just as important, participation in all campus activities by minority students and faculty has increased, and WSU now graduates more minority students than any other institution in the state. By his own direct participation in a variety of community activities and organizations, Jim has built trust and friendship for the university with minorities. Again, Jim demonstrated his leadership by listening carefully to others, understanding what needed to be done, and then built programs by finding resources to make them happen. Jim, outwardly calm and always appearing "laid back," was in fact always working very hard to make things better for students. He had little patience with those who spent their time complaining about "only if someone would give us more resources." He expected himself and his staff to do positive things for students with the resources they had, while always searching creatively for more.

Jim's commitment to individual students gave him his greatest satisfactions at WSU and resulted in legions of loyal and thankful recipients of his support. Despite his heavy administrative responsibilities, Jim admitted that it was not unusual for him to drop everything, including scheduled meetings, if a student came to see him with a problem that needed to be solved. Jim could not live with unfairness; when he saw that he could help a student, he would not rest until he had made every effort possible to correct a problem. In listening to the problems of individual students, Jim learned about what the institution should be doing to be of assistance to students. This was especially true with mature, single mothers who wanted to return to college and needed all kinds of support; and with poor, first-generation students who were struggling with academic and personal problems. Jim started using a phrase that became well known on the campus: "When the university succeeds with a student, it succeeds greatly; but when it fails with a student, it fails greatly." Jim's desire to help individual students drove him to change policies, create new opportunities, and to make things less bureaucratic. He hated taking "no" for an answer from others when he was trying to help a student, and this attitude permeated his staff and, eventually, the entire institution. One of his presidents, Eugene M. Hughes, said, "Jim was the role model for what defined the ideal dean of students—what's best for the students has always been his primary focus" (Personal communication to author, 2000).

Jim was a strong advocate for students' education and considered it essential that students be treated as trusted colleagues in the learning process. He vigorously disagreed with the notion that students were merely "customers" or "consumers of educational programs." One day, he presented his thoughts on this issue to a meeting of the faculty senate at WSU, as he felt the distinction was extremely important in the way the institution dealt with students and how it approached the teaching process. The faculty senate was so impressed with Jim's presentation that it passed a resolution, defining the student–institution relationship as he had described it.

As mentioned above, Jim used stories and humor to illustrate his points with others and recognized that he and the student affairs division were dependent on the support and participation of faculty and staff throughout the university to accomplish their goals. Jim was able to develop excellent working relationships with his business, academic, and development colleagues at the institution; and because of his ability to get things done, he was assigned many additional responsibilities at various times as vice president for student affairs. For example, when the institution's intercollegiate basketball program was scrutinized by the National Collegiate Athletic Association for possible violations, Jim was asked by the president to chair the review process, which involved many faculty, coaches, athletes, and alumni. Jim had established a reputation as a person of complete integrity who could not only represent the institution in a positive manner, but also handle difficult problems effectively.

Jim continued to be contacted by other institutions that wanted to recruit him to be their SSAO. He declined all of these overtures, but in 1982 he was faced with a particularly interesting situation when the president's position at WSU became open and over 100 faculty members at the institution signed a petition, urging Jim to apply for the job. But Jim clearly understood what his priorities were and what it was he enjoyed most in his career, and of course this was helping students. As a result, he thanked the faculty for their support, but declined to apply for the president's position.

With his ability to tell stories, his wonderful wit, his genuine interest in others, and his calm and thoughtful approach to problems, Jim made friends for the institution and for student affairs wherever he went. He insisted that he received far more credit for good things that happened at the institution than he deserved, but others disagreed. He was extremely proud of the staff he hired and nurtured, among them John Schuh, David Meabon, William Harmon, Vicky Triponey, and Lyle Gohn, all of whom who became national leaders within the student affairs field. Jim joked that he often did things at the university for which he had no authority, but he knew were right for students. He always urged his staff to do something extra for students; even when they failed to help students, the effort would be recognized and appreciated. He emphasized that the rewards of working in student affairs are many, and most valued of these is seeing the success of students who have been helped by the institution. Jim learned to accept the nasty criticism that often is directed at SSAOs, although he frequently said, "Criticism hurts more than praise helps!" He practiced this in many ways himself; and he wrote thousands of personal thank you notes to students, parents, faculty, and community members over his career. He was a great admirer of Winston Churchill; following the advice of the great British leader, Jim often tried to appear spontaneous in his comments, while thoughtfully practicing what he was going to say in advance. He had an amazing ability to communicate with students, listen to their concerns, and then help them achieve their goals. He understood and sympathized with the students' basic human shortcomings and dilemmas, and he never wavered in his faith that with education and encouragement all things are possible.

Besides being sought after by other institutions, Jim was asked to do many things within the profession. He found the time to be the associate editor of the *NASPA Journal,* the vice president of Region IV-West of NASPA, a frequent speaker at large conferences and meetings, and president of NASPA in 1975. He was among a small group of leaders who were instrumental in creating NASPA's regional structure, which has resulted in rapid growth and increased participation by members in the association. He was invited to become NASPA's first historian in 1976, a position he held until 1998. He was the first person to be recognized by NASPA with both the Fred Turner Award and the Scott Goodnight Award, a clear indication of the high regard his colleagues have for him. When the beautiful student union at WSU was named the "Rhatigan Student Center" in his honor in 1997, Jim looked out at the large audience gathered for the dedication and saw many of his former students—and recalled the individual stories that brought each of them to where they are today. In 1994, he was selected to present the closing address at the national conference, and his speech that day, entitled "Simple Gifts," was so warmly received that it has become part of the culture of student affairs professionals. Borrowing from an old Shaker hymn, Jim talked about the "gift to be simple, the gift to be free, and the gift to come down where we ought to be." He went on to say,

> Part of our role is as teacher, and in that role we recognize the importance of the development of students. We hope for them what we hope for ourselves. We do not need a hefty portfolio for this work, nor a book of law, a seat of power, nor

personal dominion over anyone. What we need is a set of beliefs; the courage to convey them; and the intellectual, collaborative, and collegial skills to make them work. This is why we need to strive for excellence. This challenge presents itself each day.

James J. Rhatigan could have been a minister, a diplomat, or a statesman. As the SSAO at WSU, he was all of these, and more. This warm, witty, and outwardly calm "Mark Twain of the Plains" was a passionate, spiritual, intellectual, and caring educator who used the bully pulpit of his office for the benefit of WSU students for 32 wonderful years.

Chapter **13**

Robert H. Shaffer
Indiana University

I n an article in the *Journal of Counseling and Development,* Robert H. Shaffer was described as "The Quintessential Do Gooder" (Kuh and Coomes, 1986). Few who have known Bob Shaffer would disagree with this description!

Robert H. Shaffer served on the staff and faculty of Indiana University (I.U.) for 40 years, and as its senior student affairs officer (dean of students) from 1955–1969. He was assistant and associate dean of students from 1946–1954. He was a professor of education and a professor of business administration, and from 1973–1981 he served as chairman of the Department of Higher Education and Student Personnel. He retired from I.U. in 1981.

Bob Shaffer's career includes so many honors and outstanding achievements that it is difficult to include all of them. He graduated from DePauw University in 1936, earned his masters' degree from Columbia University in 1939, and his PhD in 1945 from New York University (N.Y.U.). He served as the associate editor of the *Personnel and Guidance Journal* from 1948 to 1952, and he was elected the first president of the American Personnel and Guidance Association in 1951–1953. He has been a consultant and adviser for the Agency for International Development and State Department in Thailand and Afghanistan. He served as vice president of the National Association of Student Personnel Administrators (NASPA) and chairman of the Council of Student Personnel Associations in 1965–1966. From 1969–1972 he was the editor of the *NASPA Journal,* and he was the founder and dean of the Interfraternity Institute from 1970–1981. In 1973, he was the first recipient of the Scott Goodnight Award from NASPA for outstanding performance as a dean, and in 1979 he received the American College Personnel Association's (ACPA's) Distinguished Service Award. In 1980, Lambda Chi Alpha national fraternity established an award in his name, as did the Association of Fraternity Advisers. He was also recognized by the National Campus Activities Association for his many contributions.

In 1987, NASPA established the Robert H. Shaffer Award, presented annually to an outstanding faculty member teaching in a higher education and student affairs graduate program. In 1976, Bob's alma mater, Depauw University, presented him with the LL.D. honorary degree. In 1985, I.U. presented him with his second honorary doctor's degree. In 1981, friends, former students, and staff established the Robert H. Shaffer Quality of Student Life Endowment at I.U. in honor of Bob. The endowment is an "investment in values" for Indiana students. The class of 1967 at I.U. established the Robert H. Shaffer Professorship in the College of Arts and Sciences as a tribute to Bob; and they recently announced that it will soon reach its $1 million endowment goal, making this professorship into a permanently endowed chair. Bob Shaffer may have been described in a journal article as a "do gooder;" but during his career, this energetic dean became a legend in his own time for his tremendous institutional, professional, and personal accomplishments that may never be matched again by any student affairs leader.

Bob was born in 1918 in Delphi, Indiana, near the Wabash river. His grandfather had left Pennsylvania in the late 1800s, and the family settled in central Indiana. In the small town of Delphi, Bob knew almost everyone and he attributed what he called the "small town values" he learned there to his lifelong service to others. In that setting, Bob said, "I learned to be outgoing;" he also learned a keen sense of responsibility and accountability, as any trouble he might have gotten himself into was usually known and reported to his family by someone before he got home! As with almost everyone during those years, people had very little money. But Bob described his youthful years as great fun and very rewarding. He loved sports and, of course, Indiana small towns were hotbeds of high school basketball. He went to high school in Mishawaka, Indiana, where he excelled as a student and as an athlete.

During his youth, Bob was a very active member of the Boy Scouts, an association that was to have a lifelong effect on his views about education and his ideas about service. He earned the Eagle Scout status and was recognized with the coveted Silver Beaver Award. Bob graduated from Mishawaka High School in 1932, with the Great Depression in full swing. The effects of the terrible economic crisis were felt most severely in small, rural towns in the country, and Bob wondered what his future might be. To his delight and modest surprise, Bob was offered a Rector's scholarship at nearby DePauw University in Greencastle, Indiana. He had graduated third in his high school class of 210, so he was an outstanding student. This academic scholarship enabled Bob to attend DePauw, where he managed to get by financially by working for 12.5 cents per hour (plus meals!) at the Castle Café and by serving as the house manager for his fraternity, Sigma Chi. Bob continued his interests in scouting and became the president of Alpha Phi Omega, the national service group. As an officer in Sigma Chi, he actively recruited freshmen who were Eagle Scouts themselves, being convinced that these young students would make responsible members. He was elected president of the Interfraternity Council, but his proudest achievement was being the quarterback on DePauw's undefeated, unscored-upon football team! Despite going to college during the middle of the Depression, Bob loved his years at DePauw and graduated in 1936.

While Bob was an undergraduate student at DePauw, he became acquainted with Louis H. Dirks, the dean of men. Bob was an outstanding student leader and athlete, and Dirks took a special interest in him, encouraging him to consider the young field of student affairs as a career. Having grown up in a small town where he knew almost everyone, Bob was accustomed to many personal contacts and friendships; the encouragement he received from Dean Dirks at DePauw in 1935 reinforced Bob's lifelong commitment to helping others. He had received encouragement many times from family members, teachers, and friends; and it only seemed natural for Bob to do the same for others. Bob majored in social science at DePauw and planned to be a high school teacher and coach. However, upon graduation, he was offered a position in New York City with the national Boy Scouts of America organization. This was a fine opportunity for Bob and, of course, moving to New York was a major change for this young man from Delphi, Indiana!

Bob was the assistant to the director of personnel with the national Boy Scouts organization in New York, and he was in charge of recruiting and training. Bob was only 22 years old at the time, and little did he know that recruiting and training would be central to his work in the next 40 years! He loved the work with the Boy Scouts and, ironically, Bob took note as a young staff member that Scout executives worked almost every weekend, something that he thought was quite unusual! While Bob was working in New York, he followed up on the suggestion of a friend from Mishawaka, Indiana, that he should introduce himself to Dr. Harry Kitson, a professor at Teachers College, Columbia University. Kitson had Indiana ties himself, having previously served for 6 years as a professor of psychology at I.U. Dr. Kitson befriended Bob and became his first mentor, as Bob enrolled in the master's degree program in vocational guidance on a part-time basis by attending classes 3 nights per week, as he continued his full-time work with the Scouts. During this exciting time, Bob enrolled in courses with two of the best known scholars in the field, Alice Lloyd Jones and Ruth Strang. Bob completed his master's degree in 1939 at Columbia.

The Great Depression was still a reality in 1939 and, of course, terrible events were taking place in Europe. Although the United States was determined not to enter the war raging by this time, Bob and his young friends sensed that the country would be in it, soon. But while Bob remained in New York City, he was determined to make the most of his opportunities. Because Columbia University required doctoral students to enroll on a full-time basis for a full year, Bob opted for the doctoral program at N.Y.U. and studied there under the direction of Dr. Robert Hoppock. Bob was asked by his mentor at Columbia, Dr. Harry Kitson, to serve on the editorial board of *Occupations Magazine*. Even though Bob thought he was probably not experienced enough for his position, he loved the responsibility and, of course, he was to serve as editor of the *NASPA Journal* later in his career. Again, the encouragement that Bob received from Dr. Kitson convinced Bob of the value of helping others. At this time, Bob met Marjorie Fitch, a young woman who was working at the International House, near Rockefeller Center in New York City. Bob and Marge were married in 1940, and their experiences at the International House inspired Bob's lifelong passion for students from other countries. Bob completed his course work at N.Y.U. in the summer of 1941, just 4 months before the Pearl Harbor disaster shook the country.

While in New York, Bob also was active in the National Interfraternity Conference, attending some of their meetings and volunteering his time. During his involvement with the conference, he met Dr. Fred Turner, dean of men at the University of Illinois, who was a prominent leader in that organization and also the National Association of Deans and Advisers of Men. Fred Turner encouraged Bob to consider working in student affairs, and in 1941 he recommended Bob for an assistant dean's position in the School of Business at I.U. As a result, Bob decided to leave his job with the Boy Scouts, and he and Marge moved to Bloomington that fall, where Bob assumed his duties. Bob, who has always considered himself very lucky, again realized how much a little encouragement by someone can mean. Bob has maintained innumerable friendships over the years, and he remains convinced that "linkages," as he calls them, are very important in helping others.

Bob tackled his new assistant dean's job with the same enthusiasm that was to characterize his approach to everything during his career. After less than 6 months on the job, faculty and students were leaving to join the war effort, and the dean of the School of Business left as well. Bob found himself, in effect, as the acting dean! It was an unusual and difficult time, of course, with the nation plunging into the war. Bob's strong commitment to the individual guided his actions, as he worked to assist students in their academic and career decisions. It was in this position, seeing the incredibly complex and emotional strains on students, that Bob learned to work with bureaucracies and to get them to adjust to the benefit of individuals. In those days, Bob recalled, "I did whatever I could to help a student—the circumstances demanded it!" If this meant being called "soft" by some critics, it did not bother Bob; he was willing to make exceptions to rules when it was justified by the student's circumstances, and he was able to defend his decisions. Such actions were consistent during his entire career.

During this busy time, Bob managed to work on his dissertation, conducting a study of freshmen academic adjustment at I.U., while corresponding with his adviser, Dr. Hoppock, at N.Y.U. Because there were many new training programs located on the campus, Bob made housing arrangements for large numbers of Army and Navy trainees who were at Indiana for varying lengths of time. But in 1943 Bob was called for duty into the Army, and he left Bloomington for Camp Lee in Petersburg, Virginia, where he was assigned to the adjutant general's office as a personnel officer. Bob found himself assigning young men to a variety of posts, based on evaluations of their qualifications. As Bob joked, "It was one of those lucky instances when my qualifications and experience were actually used well by the Army!" Right before he left Bloomington, Bob mailed the final draft of his dissertation to Dr. Hoppock at N.Y.U. Because of his duties in the Army, the awarding of Bob's PhD degree was delayed until 1945.

> **Bob was already making a name for himself in student affairs; in the various conferences he attended, others made note of his energy, insight, and ability to get things done.**

Bob was then assigned to duty in Hawaii, where he worked in the replacement depot, assigning troops to various tasks. After a short stay there, he was shipped to New Orleans and Officer Training School, where he became a second lieutenant. From there he went to Boston and the Port of Embarkation, where he worked with the National Maritime Union, arbitrating disputes among civilians and the Longshoremen's Union. In looking back on the Boston experience, Bob said, "I guess I didn't know it at the time, but I was already doing student affairs work for the Army in Boston!" He was so good at what he was doing that he was asked to teach courses in human relations to the civilian employees of the Port. The terrible war came to an end in August 1945, and Bob was granted an earlier release than he expected, as I.U. had created a Veteran's Guidance Center and had requested that Bob to return to Bloomington to be its director. So, in November 1945, Bob left the Army and assumed his duties as assistant dean of the junior division and director of the Veteran's Guidance Center at I.U. The G.I. Bill made it possible for veterans to go to college, and Dr. Herman Wells, the chancellor at I.U., foresaw the great influx of students and wanted to be prepared to meet this challenge. Bob and others worked 7 days a week during that time, helping the large numbers of new students in literally every aspect of their lives. It was a hectic life, and Bob helped students with health, counseling, housing, financial, and academic issues.

In early 1946, Dr. Arnold Shoemaker, the dean of Students at Indiana and a former Army Colonel, asked Bob to be his assistant, directing most of the departments and handling the budget for the student affairs division. Colonel Shoemaker had been selected for his position by Chancellor Wells because of all the returning war veterans. Bob learned from the colonel and supported his work with students. Bob, alone at I.U. in having extensive professional education for student affairs, knew about the strong program at the University of Minnesota, so he arranged to visit with Dr. Gilbert Wrenn and Dr. E.G. Williamson in Minneapolis. Bob studied the Minnesota organization plan and used the knowledge gained in that visit to make changes in Bloomington.

Bob was already making a name for himself in student affairs; in the various conferences he attended, others made note of his energy, insight, and ability to get things done. He was elected the secretary of the ACPA in 1948; and during that time of great expansion of guidance and counseling programs, there was a need to unify the work of vocational counselors, school counselors, and those engaged in higher education. The American Personnel and Guidance Association was created, and Bob was elected its first president in 1951. Bob was only 37 years old. The challenges were great, and it was not entirely clear that the new association would survive financially. But Bob served as president for 2 years, and he worked hard to recruit prominent leaders to join the group. He also created Commission I of ACPA, the Organization and Administration of Student Affairs, which was attractive to members of NASPA. The organization thrived, and Bob was a leader who was able to persuade and encourage people from diverse professional backgrounds to talk with one another and work together effectively. In his professional association work, Bob was applying the same principles of hard work, cooperation, involvement, and helping others that characterized his dean's work at Indiana.

Bob was appointed acting dean of students in 1955 and dean in 1956. While Chancellor Wells hired him, Bob reported to John Ashton, the vice president for undergraduate education at I.U. Although Bob and Ashton got along well, Bob discovered that he would have to work hard to convince the vice president of the benefits of student programs and needs. Bob learned how to adjust to administrators with differing priorities; and after finding that his proposals for additional support in student activities were not supported, he decided to initiate a "faculty associates" program in the residence halls, an idea that the vice president liked a great deal. Moreover, Bob knew that Ashton liked research, so Bob proposed a student affairs research office and was successful in getting it funded. One of Bob's advisers for this program was none other than B.F. Skinner, who was an I.U. faculty member at the time. Bob was already good at the art of negotiation, and there were few people anywhere who were more persuasive than he was. He loved "selling" ideas and programs that would be of benefit to students; and he knew how to obtain support from key people on the campus, often convincing two or three departments outside of student affairs to share in the expense to support his proposals. "There is almost always a way to get something good done, but you've got to be willing to talk to lots of people and be ready to make some deals!" Bob would say of his work at this time.

During these years at Indiana, Bob continued to be an active leader in professional associations and served as the associate editor of the *Personnel and Guidance Journal.* Despite the huge time demands of his job, his association work, and his family (he and Marge now had two young boys, Bruce and Jim), Bob somehow managed to pay special attention to international students. He became legendary at I.U. for knowing the names of every international student; he and his wife hosted parties and dinners for these students throughout the year during his tenure there. Bob was an effective advocate for international education, and in 1959 he was invited by the Agency for International Development to consult on higher education issues in Bangkok, Thailand. These activities later were to take him to several other countries in a similar capacity.

In his first full year as dean of students at I.U., Bob was the subject of an extensive article in the *Saturday Evening Post* (1956), entitled "This is the Dean Speaking!" The article is quite revealing about the expectations and public perceptions of deans of students during that decade, as there was an emphasis on troubleshooting and responding to student problems. But Bob's fundamental commitment to student growth and development was evident in the article and his great humanity as well. Bob described the variety of ways he and his staff worked to help students, especially those who had experienced some academic, personal, or behavioral problem. Bob was the dean in charge of a large staff at Indiana, but he continued to work with individuals, always challenging them and helping them in any way he could. The article concluded with a quote from Bob that clearly reflects his educational values: "If we can hold ourselves to our own best aspirations, things will somehow work out. To aid in this noble striving, is, as I understand it, the first duty and the final satisfaction in the work of a dean."

In the 1950s, years before it became the norm, Bob organized the student affairs division at Indiana by function rather than gender. What seems so logical now was certainly quite controversial in 1956. Bob had the courage of his convictions, and Chancellor Wells agreed with his approach. Thus, various departments, such as residence life, orientation, financial aid, counseling, career placement, and student health were established and became the foundation of his organization.

The Civil Rights movement was building strong momentum in the country by the end of the 1950s decade. Bob, long an advocate of fair treatment and equal opportunity for all, was fully engaged with this issue on the Indiana campus, the Bloomington community, and the student affairs profession. In addition to his dean's responsibility, Bob wrote articles for professional journals and taught graduate classes in the higher education graduate program. Bob was a strong and public advocate of equal rights, and during this volatile time he was asked to serve as the chairman of the mayor's Council on Human Relations in the city of Bloomington. Through his work and leadership, problems among various groups were settled without violence.

Bob was an early advocate of "The Joint Statement of Rights and Freedoms of Students" (American Association of University Professors, 1967), which was viewed with considerable suspicion by conservative faculty and administrators at the time. He used it effectively on his campus to help ensure freedom to learn for students. The Vietnam War introduced great turmoil on American campuses during the decade of the 1960s, and Bob was in the middle of the campus unrest, day and night, for years. His strategy then, as always, was to be highly visible and accessible to students; whenever there was a protest or a demonstration, Bob was there, and he made a point of getting to know the most vociferous of the protesters. Many people at I.U. who were there during those years would say that it was Bob Shaffer's leadership that held the institution together. He was publicly criticized for his views and his actions, and during those years some of this was nasty and personal. But Bob managed to maintain his beliefs in personalized leadership and the fundamental goodness of young people. It was not unusual for Bob to be on campus until 2:00 a.m. because of the constant turmoil, and then, day after day, to report to his office the next morning at 8:00 a.m. A new chancellor, Elvis Stahr, came to Indiana in 1962. Bob, of course, had to adjust to the style of the new leader. The previous chancellor, Herman Wells, was well known to students and willingly engaged them in public debate during these difficult times. Now, Bob found that as the dean of students he would clearly be the public point person with campus problems in the years ahead. This was the most challenging time of Bob's career, but he had the confidence and the courage to work directly with students in the most troubling times in higher education.

While Bob was in Las Vegas in 1968 for the national American Personnel and Guidance Association meeting, he learned the tragic news from his wife that their son, Bruce, had been killed in Vietnam. The entire I.U. community shared in the family's grief and probably no one but Bob Shaffer would have been able to continue as dean of students, especially since he himself had been a target of the war protesters. But somehow, Bob was able to continue in his role as dean. Because of his highly personalized and completely honest ways of working with students, even the most negative of the protesters were friends with Bob and maintained the highest respect for him.

During the 1960s, Bob also found time to serve as the vice president of NASPA, and in 1965–1966 he was selected to be the chairman of the Council of Student Personnel Associations. This latter group represented an effort to bring together many of the professional organizations in student affairs, and Bob's reputation for fairness and honesty made him the logical choice for this challenging assignment.

Bob was especially proud of the faculty associates program, the effective match between theory and practice he was able to maintain, and the vigorous staff development program within his division. They have all had a lasting effect on the institution, its students, and staff. The faculty associates program was established to increase opportunities for students to learn from faculty in the many student organizations on the campus, to get faculty involved with student affairs, and to improve the overall functioning of student groups. Of course, Bob knew large numbers of faculty and was very persuasive in "selling" his faculty friends on the benefits of such involvement. Again, Bob relied on his personalized leadership style in making this initiative a success. The emphasis was not on control of student groups, as it often was at other institutions, but upon helping students learn responsibility and leadership skills. Bob also knew that most of these faculty would become willing supporters of student affairs programs once they became actively involved with student groups, and in Bob's terms this "paid off" in many ways. The faculty associates program continues to this day at I.U.

Reflecting his "can do" attitude in everything he had done since his scouting days, Bob was convinced that one of the most effective ways to teach was through practical experience. Bob had worked in a great variety of jobs since his youth, and he had seen firsthand the benefits of working during his graduate programs at Columbia University and N.Y.U. This enabled him to combine theory and practice, and Bob applied this in his staff hiring and supervision strategies while he was dean of students at Indiana. In accordance with this belief, Bob established the well-known "extern" program at I.U., placing graduate students in full-time positions at area colleges with whom Bob had made arrangements. The residence halls were staffed with talented staff who were pursuing graduate degrees at I.U., as were areas of other student affairs offices there. Bob and his staff worked hard to apply the fundamental ideas learned in the classroom to the everyday world of student affairs, and it resulted in one of the most respected and successful student affairs programs in the country. Dozens of other colleges and universities adopted the model Bob developed at Indiana.

Bob was strongly committed to the learning of the student affairs staff and demanded very high standards for all of them, expecting them to be well informed, hard working, and thoughtful. As a professor in education and in business administration, he was very familiar with the "scientific management" movement of the times; he insisted that the staff should be on the cutting edge of their profession. He organized a staff development program that involved meeting at his home twice per month on Saturday mornings until noon, which Bob explained was the only time that was not already filled on the calendar. One of the monthly meetings was devoted to a theoretical or research presentation, and a member of the staff or faculty was asked in advance to conduct that seminar. Books and articles were discussed and debated, and the most pressing educational issues facing higher education comprised the agendas. Bob continued these Saturday morning sessions for years, and the learning that took place as a result undoubtedly contributed to the high level of comradery among the staff, and to their later prominence in student affairs leadership positions throughout the nation. Bob expected a lot from his staff, and in hiring new staff he sought people who had demonstrated that they could handle responsibility and were willing to work hard. He was not impressed with formal job descriptions and wanted people who were eager to help students, without regard to the hours it took to do so.

In 1969, an opening in the School of Education occurred due to a retirement of a key faculty member. Bob, already a professor in the department of College Student Personnel Administration, decided he would step aside from the dean of students position he had held so long and pursue another professional responsibility. He was already serving as the editor of the *NASPA Journal*, had a long list of publications, had taught and advised graduate students in the program for many years, and was one of the most respected student affairs leaders in the country. He was named the chairman of the Department of College Student Personnel Administration (later, called Higher Education) at Indiana in 1969, and he served in this position until his retirement in 1981. As chairman of the department, Bob built upon the already strong reputation of Indiana and established it as the most sought after and highly rated program in the country (Sandeen, 1982). He and his long-time colleague, Dr. Betty Greenleaf, collaborated in educating an entire generation of student affairs leaders. Bob was also elected the secretary (chair) of the faculty senate, an indication of the high respect he enjoyed from his academic colleagues. He founded the Interfraternity Institute in 1970 and served as its dean for 11 years; he also served as executive director of the Center for the Study of the College Fraternity. Bob was responsible for hiring Dr. George Kuh at Indiana, perhaps the leading scholar in the field of student affairs today, and other outstanding faculty as well. Most important to Bob, many of his students at Indiana went on to positions of significant leadership in the profession. As a result of his inspiring personal leadership, Indiana graduates are well known and respected contributors to higher education throughout the country.

After Bob retired from Indiana in 1981, it was not long until he received a call from the northwest campus of I.U. located at Gary, asking him to help them with some difficult problems and to serve as acting dean for a year. Bob's sense of service just would not allow him to decline, and he spent most of that academic year as acting dean on that campus, putting together a student affairs organization and directing the programs. He commuted to Gary from Bloomington during the year, returning home whenever his campus schedule would permit.

Bob Shaffer had to deal with many extremely difficult administrative, political, financial, and social problems as the dean of students. However, he emphasized that the most difficult problems had to do with personnel. Bob believed so strongly in developing staff and in supporting them in every way possible, so when someone had to be dismissed it was very painful for him. He understood and accepted this responsibility, but he hated doing it and would have preferred to deal with a large, nasty student protest than to terminate a staff member. His greatest sense of disappointment in his work occurred when he discovered that a student leader or faculty member had lied to him; Bob was so open and honest with others that he naturally expected others would be the same way with him. This was true most of the time, but he was disheartened when someone did not tell the truth. Bob always confronted those who lied to him, as he felt this was part of his teaching responsibility, and he never abandoned a student who was deceitful. When questioned by his staff or others about this, Bob often replied, "Well, who else is going to support this student?"

> *While impressed with the great opportunities technology has presented to educators, Bob suggested that face-to-face communication and interaction will remain the most valuable form of teaching.*

While Bob was a leader in efforts to evaluate staff and did so in a very personal manner himself, he was never formally evaluated by any president or chancellor for whom he worked. He was on a year-by-year contract in a highly volatile job, and he understood that he served at the pleasure of the chancellor. Bob was very confident in what he was doing and said he sensed from the chancellors for whom he worked that they were pleased with his actions, but he never asked for a formal evaluation. Bob stated, "I loved what I did, and I believed what we were doing was right; if my boss didn't like what we were doing, I know he would tell me!"

To no one's surprise, Bob Shaffer had many other professional opportunities during his career, but he decided to remain at I.U. He had invitations to become a senior academic officer or a senior student affairs officer at many institutions, and a president at several colleges. He also had opportunities to join the corporate world in major leadership positions. His basic commitment to working with students, his active involvement with all aspects of life at Indiana, and his engagement in community affairs in Bloomington convinced him to remain at I.U. He and I.U. have been virtually synomynous for many years!

Bob Shaffer is optimistic about the future of student affairs and speculated about how his highly personalized approach to leadership on a large, complex campus might work today, with all of the specialists and the technology in place. He expressed his hope that student affairs leaders will not forget the basic commitment of the field to the whole student, and he voiced his concern about the evident splintering of student affairs organizations into so many specialties. While impressed with the great opportunities technology has presented to educators, Bob suggested that face-to-face communication and interaction will remain the most valuable form of teaching.

Bob Shaffer did not follow any set formula in his leadership as dean of students during his long tenure at I.U. Bob served during the period 1946–1969, an era characterized by incredible growth and social and political change in American society. While he had very clear ideas about education and student development, he fully admitted that most of the major issues he faced at Indiana as dean of students were imposed upon the institution as a result of external events. He was a national leader in moving the student affairs field from its perception as being concerned with control to being focused on student development. Due to his strong academic credentials, teaching, and writing, Bob also led in the application of theory to practice.

Bob Shaffer was the epitome of the personalized leader, known and respected by everyone, visible, and tireless in his efforts. He pursued policies and programs with great enthusiasm and a positive attitude, and he did things because he felt it was right to do them. He strongly rejected any notion that student affairs consisted of the application of simple techniques, rules, or gimmicks. He was a tenacious champion of the individual, willing to advocate passionately for the underdog in the face of any uncaring bureaucracy. He was supremely confident in his ability to get things done, which he often did simply by working harder and longer than others. He was a fierce defender of human rights who was able to stand up to frequent public criticism because of the strength of his own convictions. He built one of the most successful student affairs programs in the country by his belief in others, his commitment to staff, his unflagging optimism and honesty, and his willingness to take risks. He was a supersalesman for education who knew that what he was doing as an administrator was teaching. Bob Shaffer's view was always that "the heart of student affairs work is the heart."

Chapter 14

William L. Thomas, Jr.
University of Maryland

William L. ("Bud") Thomas, Jr. is a very well-known person at the University of Maryland. A colleague said, "If you want to be sure that something gets done, and gets done right, then ask Bud Thomas to do it!" This affable, tall, handsome man has been getting things done with quiet dignity and determination for over a quarter of a century as the senior student affairs officer (SSAO) at the University of Maryland.

Bud Thomas completed his B.S. degree in social science in 1955 at the University of Tennessee, and he obtained an M.S. degree in educational administration and supervision in 1965 from the same institution. His PhD was earned in higher education administration in 1970 from Michigan State University. From 1955–1959, he served as an officer in the U.S. Army, Infantry, spending most of his time in Germany. He taught high school in Knoxville, Tennessee during 1960–1961, and then served as the head resident and manager of Hess Hall at the University of Tennessee during 1961–1964. For the next 2 years, he was the administrative assistant to the director of residence and food services at the University of Tennessee, and from 1966–1968 he was the director of residence halls and assistant dean of students at the University of Tennessee. During the period 1968–1970, Bud Thomas was an area director and assistant director of residence hall programs at Michigan State University. After completing his PhD at Michigan State University in 1970, he moved to Greeley, Colorado, where he was the director of housing and assistant professor in the College of Education at the University of Northern Colorado. He became the director of residence life at the University of Maryland in 1972, and the next year he was named the acting vice chancellor for student affairs. In June 1974, he was appointed vice chancellor for student affairs at the University of Maryland, a position he still holds. His position title at Maryland was changed to vice president in 1998.

For almost 20 years, he has served as the National Association of Student Personnel Administrator's (NASPA's) representative to the Council for the Advancement of Standards (CAS) and, for 16 years, as secretary of this group; CAS develops and publishes standards and guidelines for student services and development programs. He served as director of the ACE-NASPA Summer Institute for Chief Student Affairs Officers in 1987 and 1988, and he was the president of the NASPA Foundation board of directors in 1998–1999. He has been active in Commission III of the American College Personnel Association, a member of the editorial board of the *Journal of College and University Student Housing,* and a member of NASPA's national board of directors from 1981–1983. He has been a member of the National Vice President's Group since 1980, a member of the board of directors of BACCHUS (Boosting Alcohol Consciousness Concerning the Health of University Students), and a member of the editorial board of Synthesis: Law and Policy in Higher Education. He has been a frequent speaker at regional and national meetings and a consultant to several colleges and universities. In 1986, Bud Thomas was presented with the profession's highest honor, NASPA's Scott Goodnight Award for outstanding performance as a dean. In 1999, he was presented with NASPA's Fred Turner Award for outstanding service to the profession.

Bud Thomas was born in 1932 in Knoxville, Tennessee in the early years of the Great Depression. Bud's family came from Irish, Scottish, and German origins; and they migrated from both Kentucky and North Carolina to Tennessee. Along with many other descendants of the Cumberland Plateau region, Bud claims that Daniel Boone was related to at least one member of his family! Bud's father was employed as the bookkeeper for a local lumber company and was the only one on either side of the family at the time who completed high school. However, Bud describes his father as a voracious reader and an extremely intelligent man who probably should have been a college history professor. His father's lifelong interest in education was an early source of stimulation and encouragement in Bud's career. His mother was Bud's main source of inspiration, because of her wisdom, insight, independence, and strong sense of self. Despite having only a third grade education, she was very intelligent and talented in many areas. Both of Bud's parents were gifted singers. His sister sang, played the piano, and later taught music. As a result, Bud developed a love of music as a young boy; he was active in church choirs, school groups, barbershop quartets, and other groups. He was the church's choir director before he was out of high school and sang in an octet during college, which helped pay part of his expenses at the University of Tennessee. He continues to sing in various groups today and is convinced that the musical experiences in his youth gave him the confidence to speak effectively to public groups later in his life. Perhaps related to his singing talent, Bud's voice is resonant and powerful, making him a very attractive speaker within the student affairs field.

Bud describes his family life as close and loving, with his parents not placing any noticeable pressure on him to achieve. However, their own love of learning and their active participation in music activities naturally stimulated Bud to be a good student. He joked that his older sister, who was an excellent student, a gifted singer, and very beautiful, made it possible for him to get by just on her reputation! Bud was hard working and active as a boy, and he remembers making $15 selling soda pop at University of Tennessee football games when he was 12 years old. His parents instilled a strong work ethic in him; even when he was mowing lawns in his neighborhood, Bud insisted on doing the job very well, paying attention to detail. It was to become a habit throughout his career. While he was on the nearby campus quite often, he never really thought about going to college during his youth. Despite growing up during the Great Depression, Bud's father remained employed and the family, although poor by current standards, got along quite well. Bud was only 9 years old when the United States entered World War II, but the war did not affect him a great deal.

Bud attended Young High School just outside of Knoxville; and he was active as a class officer, a star basketball (and sometimes baseball) player, and a frequent participant in musical and dramatic activities. As a result, he believes now that these activities led him to associate with a small group of friends who were interested in college. At this county school, in contrast with the city high schools, only about 25 members of Bud's 1950 graduating class of 167 initially attended college. The University of Tennessee, of course, was easily available, and Bud decided to enroll. Moreover, tuition was only $25 per quarter, and he could continue to live at home.

Bud sensed that he was in college because he should be and because others expected this of him, but he was not at all sure of what he wanted to do. He was a member of the freshman basketball team, but he was not much involved in campus life as a freshman; he lived at home and took a bus to the campus each day. All male students at this land-grant institution were required to enroll in the Reserved Officer Training Program, and Bud excelled in this area. He loved his political science courses and became very interested in learning more about world events. The Korean War was just under way, and Bud tried to enlist in the last quarter of his freshman year, but there were waiting lists for all the desirable branches of service in his area, so he decided to remain in college.

Bud continued to participate in church activities. At one time, he was the director of the choir, in which both of his parents sang, and his older sister was the church pianist. Bud later joked, "It was truly a family affair, and it is said the music never has been as good since that time!" Given his strong involvement in the church, some family friends anticipated that Bud might become a minister. But Bud never saw himself going in that direction, and his parents did not try to push him into it. Although Bud was not at all sure of what job he wanted to have someday, he was comfortable with himself, trusted his own feelings, and generally knew what his personal values were. He thinks he was influenced in this regard mostly by his mother, and these traits were to serve him very well as a student affairs leader throughout his career.

After his freshman year at Tennessee, Bud was invited to join the Kappa Sigma social fraternity, and this provided quite an education for him. He did not drink alcoholic beverages during college, and there was never any alcohol in his home. In his fraternity, he observed some of his friends making bad decisions and discovered that there were a few students who frequently engaged in negative behavior. Moreover, Bud hated the hazing that was a prominent part of his fraternity initiation, and he also questioned the exclusionary clause in the organization's membership rules. He eventually became the pledge trainer, was successful in eliminating most of the hazing, and later became an officer of his fraternity. He is convinced that this experience helped him learn to work constructively with people whose actions and values were opposed to his own, something that he would have to do during his entire career as a student affairs leader.

Bud decided not to continue with basketball after 1 year in college. He said, "The varsity coach had no interest in my continuing!" So, he became involved in other campus activities. He became an officer in the Scabbard and Blade society within the ROTC unit; and he was elected president of the University Singers, a 50-member musical group that traveled around the state, presenting concerts. He was still not sure of what he wanted to do as a career, but he liked English classes, world history, and especially political science. He was very good at speaking, enjoyed writing poetry, and was an avid reader. His various interests and experiences eventually convinced him that he should become a teacher. He loves to relate that he did his practice teaching in Severville, Tennessee, at Dolly Parton's alma mater! He also became interested in photography, a lifetime hobby at which he became good enough that his work has been recognized at a regional competition. Bud anticipated going into the Army as an officer. At his graduation ceremony at the University of Tennessee in 1955, he was commissioned a second lieutenant in the U.S. Army. His family was all present; it was a happy day, especially because he was the first member of the Thomas family to earn a college degree. However, in Bud's matter of fact way, he did not view it as a dramatic event, but as a natural progression in his life. He was looking forward to "getting out of Knoxville" and into his Army service; for his first duty, he was sent to Ft. Benning, Georgia.

Bud met many good people in the Army and liked his experiences. In his first unit assignment, he was a platoon leader, in charge of 81-millimeter mortars at Ft. Lewis,

Washington. After being transferred to an armored infantry unit at Ft. Hood, Texas, Bud was sent to Germany, just South of Heidelberg. He was very successful and became the Assistant S-3 for operations and training program in his battalion. After 2 years in Germany, Bud decided he did not want to embrace the mission of an armed force and its routine as his life's work, so he made the decision to leave the service in 1959 after 5 years. His interest in teaching was still strong, and his Army experience as an officer convinced him that he liked to be part of the decision-making process in organizations and that he could contribute positively as a leader. He had heard about the Graduate School of Education at Teacher's College at Columbia University and thought he would try to enroll there when he returned to the states, knowing that a graduate degree would enhance his opportunities for securing a leadership position. But his father became seriously ill, and Bud returned to Knoxville to help his family. Bud enrolled in the master's degree program at the University of Tennessee in educational administration and supervision, fully intending to become a high school principal. He liked the idea of being in charge, and he was confident that he could make a difference in such a role.

Bud was 28 years old and during that first year of his master's degree program, Bud said, he had the defining experience of his professional life. He enrolled in a philosophy course, and it caused him to think seriously about what his values were and how he had formed them. He realized that he had essentially "coasted" on important values issues during his Army years, but now he confronted his own beliefs and was able to feel comfortable with himself. As a result, he had little doubt about his desire to work in education and make a difference in the lives of young people. One of his graduate school professors was Dr. Howard Aldmon, who was later to become the vice president for student affairs at the University of Tennessee and a close colleague during Bud's career. Dr. Aldmon encouraged Bud in his work, and before Bud actually completed his degree he was convinced to take a position as teacher and assistant principal at Halls High School in Knox County, which is in East Tennessee. It was 1961, Bud was 29 years old, and the position paid $3,650 per year. Bud taught geography, world history, and English for seven periods of each day; 30 minutes were allotted for lunch. He also served as assistant principal and said that he worked most nights and weekends to get everything done. He loved the work! He also found that even in his first year of teaching, many of the other teachers came to him with their problems, because he was a good listener and as he later joked, "I apparently appeared more knowledgeable to them than I actually was!"

After only 1 year of serving as a teacher and assistant principal at Halls High School, Bud was offered the position as principal. Bud's maturity, intelligence, organizational skills, and speaking ability impressed the superintendent. Bud was to receive many similar invitations to leadership positions during his career after others observed his work for only a short period of time. But one of his later advisers at the University of Tennessee, James

McAulliffe, persuaded Bud to return to the campus to become the manager and head resident of the new, 1,032-bed Hess residence hall. The position included room and board plus a salary and, since Bud had not yet completed his master's degree thesis, he decided to accept the residence hall position. During his first year back on the campus, Bud met Betsy Ann Woods, who was serving as the program director for student activities in the student union, and they were married in 1962. A few years later, their children, Will and Marcia, were born.

> **He felt increasingly confident in confronting problems, whether fiscal, personnel, programmatic, or policy related; and he was effective in reaching consensus with others.**

Bud found his work very challenging, and after Dr. Charles Lewis came to Tennessee to fill a newly created position as executive dean of student affairs, Bud was personally introduced to the professional field of student affairs. Again, Bud's outstanding leadership was recognized, and in 1964 he was appointed the administrative assistant to the director of residence and food services. At a time of rapid growth of the university, the job had great opportunities to learn about many things. Bud demonstrated a remarkable ability to get things accomplished, while also bringing people from previously insulated areas of the campus to work together. Bud later joked, "It may have been my experience as a choir director in church that got me through some of these tasks!" He found the work very stimulating. During these years of rapidly increasing enrollments and social change, he was instrumental in restructuring the organization of the residence hall division, developing a new plan for resident assistants and professional staff, and integrating and streamlining some aspects of the financial structure of the division. He attended the initial meetings of the Southeastern Association of College and University Housing Officers and traveled to other campuses to learn more about how to make residence halls an important part of students' learning.

In 1966, the University of Tennessee recognized again that Bud was such a valuable leader that he was appointed the director of residence halls and assistant dean of students. The position brought together management and programming, as well as men's and women's halls, into one organization. His reputation as a highly effective leader was already known in the profession. Bud was also offered a dean's position at Ohio University, but he declined, feeling that there were plenty of challenges and excitement at Tennessee.

Enrollment was increasing rapidly at Tennessee, and the climate for change was very positive. But this also meant that outstanding professional staff were moving to other institutions as new positions were created. Dr. Lewis, the SSAO at Tennessee, moved on to the same position at Penn State after only 3 years at Tennessee, and the dean of students, Win Martin, left as well. Dr. Lewis had urged Bud to apply for the National Defense Education Act (NDEA) special year-long institute, and Bud was one of 40 persons accepted into this prestigious program. In this program, Bud became acquainted with a dynamic professional who was to become his primary mentor in his career, Dr. Melvene Hardee of Florida State University. She was one of the faculty in the NDEA Institute, and her leadership and commitment became an inspiration to Bud. Among other activities, the program included three seminars at various locations in the southeast, and Bud's acceptance in this program stimulated him to complete his doctoral degree.

After visiting with faculty, Bud decided to enroll in the doctoral program at Michigan State University, where he was also offered an area coordinator position in the Division of Residence Hall Programs. He took a leave from his position at Tennessee, and he and Betsy (who was pregnant with their first child at the time) moved to East Lansing. Bud worked with Donald Adams at Michigan State and was intimately involved with the new living-learning residence halls and one of the three new experimental colleges, all located in the residence halls. Bud was a man in a hurry during these years, and he completed his PhD in administration and higher education in 1970, as he was able to transfer in some of his advanced course work from Tennessee and from his NDEA Institute experience.

When Bud completed his PhD at Michigan State in 1970, he considered various options. After visiting various campuses, Bud decided to accept the position as director of residence halls and assistant professor of education at the University of Northern Colorado in Greeley. He was impressed with the staff and felt attracted to what this innovative institution was working to accomplish with its students. Bud and his growing family (Betsy was pregnant with their second child) moved to Greeley, Colorado, and he loved this new experience. He also gained additional confidence in his own approach to leadership, as he realized that others looked up to him and expected him to make difficult decisions, something he was comfortable doing. He felt increasingly confident in confronting problems, whether fiscal, personnel, programmatic, or policy related; and he was effective in reaching consensus with others. He also found that leaders need courage and noticed that some administrators were reluctant to make decisions, especially when the outcomes were risky. Bud was able to influence and implement changes in the administrative structure, the student life programs, the fiscal management, and campus policies in his leadership role at Northern Colorado. And again, others noticed his work, and he was in demand by other institutions.

He was asked to consult with the residence hall division at the University of Maryland and did this twice during 1971. Maryland was experiencing serious problems, and the vice chancellor there was so impressed with Bud's leadership that he tried to get Bud to take the position of director of residence life. Bud was comfortable in Greeley and declined this offer, as well as an offer to become the director of residence halls at Florida State University. But the University of Maryland called him back again in 1972, and after a lengthy visit Bud decided to accept the position of director of residence life at the University of Maryland. Now, many years later, he realizes this was the most important professional decision of his career. He enjoyed his work at Northern Colorado, but the challenges of a much larger university beckoned him; and Maryland was, of course, quite similar in size and structure to Tennessee and Michigan State. Bud knows now that he has always been attracted to professional challenges where he thinks he can make a difference, and this is what he saw at Maryland. He knew he could compete in his profession and achieve positive results in difficult circumstances, and he was very attracted by the opportunity to "fix things." When he and his family moved to College Park, he discovered that there were plenty of things that needed "fixing!"

Bud plunged into his job as director of residence life at Maryland in the summer of 1972. There had been three different student affairs vice chancellors in the past 4 years at the institution, reflecting the volatile political, social, and racial climates of the times, as well as some questionable personnel decisions. Bud found a passive attitude within the student affairs division and low morale. He also found reluctance on the part of some staff to assume what he considered to be obvious professional responsibilities. When three student suicides occurred, Bud assumed the leadership role in handling them, including the painful notification of the families. Bud was again realizing that basic human weaknesses are often exposed in situations that call for leadership, and that institutions suffer as a result of the reluctance of administrators to do what they should. Bud never saw himself as anything special in this regard, but he took his obligations as a leader very seriously; as a result, other staff, administrators, and students developed high respect for him. Bud, however, felt he was just doing the things that needed to be done.

After Bud had been at Maryland for less than a year, the vice chancellor for student affairs, who had been in the position less than a year himself, found it necessary to leave. The chancellor had already noticed Bud's outstanding leadership, so he asked Bud to serve as the acting vice chancellor for student affairs in 1973.

Even though he was in an acting role as vice chancellor, Bud decided to handle the position as a leader in the same way he had approached his other positions in student affairs administration—by straightforwardly and honestly assessing the problems, working closely with students, and especially by making decisions that were needed to move forward in positive ways. Thus, during his 9 months as acting vice chancellor, Bud reorganized the student affairs division; hired new professional staff; and convinced the Residence Life staff, the Student Union, Campus Activities, the Counseling Center, and the Student Health Service to become more visible on campus and to work more closely with each other. He asserted his authority as vice chancellor with the other vice chancellors, something that his predecessors had not done effectively; he developed sound professional relationships with them, but reminded them that he, as they, reported directly to the chancellor; and when he was not able to reach agreement with any of them on what he needed for his division, he would not hesitate to ask the chancellor to intervene. The campus quickly learned that there was a solid leader at the head of the student affairs division—a person with ideas, but also a person who was getting positive things done! Bud knew he had the support of the chancellor to make the changes he initiated, and he used this freedom to his advantage. He loved the opportunity to make things better, and he was very comfortable with being in this highly visible leadership role where much was expected of him.

When Bud went to Maryland in 1972 as director of residence life, the thought of becoming the vice chancellor of the entire student affairs division there had not occurred to him. But his performance as acting vice chancellor was so outstanding that Chancellor Ed Bishop asked him to accept the permanent position in June 1974. Again, Bud found himself thrust into a major leadership role primarily because others asked him to do so. In less than 1 year as acting vice chancellor, Bud had earned the support and respect of the student affairs staff, the students, the other vice chancellors, and the chancellor. Despite his limited tenure at Maryland and the fact that he had only completed his doctorate 3 years earlier, Bud was confident that he could make a difference at Maryland and was very excited about the challenge. He decided to accept the vice chancellor's position in the early summer of 1974. The freedom to do the things he believed needed to be done was most important for Bud, and he knew he had the support of his chancellor in this regard. He was comfortable at Maryland, as the institution's mission and size matched Bud's educational values.

Bud Thomas can be described as a leader who is goal-oriented and very well organized. He also is a person whose work and ways of dealing with others result in respect and loyalty from them. Staff who have worked with Bud are comfortable with him in charge, as his actions are up-front, honest, and clear. While never dominant or authoritarian, Bud is a strong leader who makes others believe they have important ideas to contribute and who always gives the credit to others for what is accomplished. As a result, Bud has not only accomplished a great deal at Maryland, but also earned a reputation on the campus as a person who gets things done effectively. Thus, various chancellors and presidents over his 27 years as vice chancellor have added new responsibilities to his division, ones not typically found in most student affairs divisions. For example, Bud has responsibility for the bookstore; the university golf course; campus guest services; parking; and, for an interim period, intercollegiate athletics. Moreover, after he was appointed vice chancellor, some student support offices that reported elsewhere were brought into the student affairs division. All of this happened because others on the campus, especially the six chancellors or presidents for whom Bud has worked, had confidence in Bud's leadership, knowing that positive things would happen if he was in charge.

Bud emphasized the importance of having the chancellor's support. But as a general rule, he did not need close supervision from any chancellor for whom he worked. Bud saw it as his job to make decisions, build positive programs, and handle difficult problems while keeping his chancellor informed and well prepared. Bud would not have remained in his position as vice chancellor for very long if he would have had to respond to detailed direction from his chancellor. The key question of "who decides?" was critical to Bud, and so long as he was vice chancellor, the answer to that question for his responsibilities was that he or his staff needed to decide. He acknowledges that he was fortunate to work for six chancellors who allowed him great freedom to decide; however, it is obvious that Bud's actions and ability to lead successfully earned this freedom.

Despite an outward appearance of calm confidence, Bud confessed that he has worried a good deal about issues on the campus, relationships with his chancellors, and how well his division was functioning. As his division grew in size and complexity at Maryland, Bud had more to worry about than many SSAOs; but to students, staff, faculty, and administrative colleagues, he remained a steady and dependable source of strength.

> *Bud worked very hard to establish programs in advising, counseling, housing, and student life that would make Maryland an attractive and successful place for students from all backgrounds.*

Bud takes his greatest pride in the high quality of professional staff he has hired (and retained!) at Maryland, making the student affairs division there one of the most respected in the country. Many of the Maryland student affairs staff are national leaders in their specialized fields and have flourished under Bud's tutelage. Bud was also instrumental in establishing Maryland's graduate program in college student affairs administration as among the best in the nation. His cooperation with the faculty in the College of Education, his own teaching, and his division's support for the graduate program have attracted outstanding graduate students and faculty to Maryland's program.

Bud understood that it was important to the division of student affairs that he would be a key participant in campus-wide administration and a respected member of the chancellor's cabinet. As an example of how well Bud accomplished this goal, he served for many years as the chairman of the powerful finance committee for the campus. At Maryland, this committee makes most of the important decisions regarding allocations of resources, and Bud's central role was another indication of his leadership ability. Bud is especially proud of the many new and renovated facilities at Maryland that were built on his watch. The impressive residence halls, new student union, dining facilities, recreation center, family housing areas, and bookstore all are there in some appreciable measure because of Bud's persistent leadership. However, he emphasized that getting new facilities takes time and patience and often requires the support of student groups. He is convinced that his long tenure as vice chancellor at Maryland enabled him to persist with his plans and to make them a reality. Although not considered a typical student affairs function, student transportation was a significant problem for years at Maryland. Bud assumed this responsibility and helped create a highly popular and financially sound campus shuttle bus system that gained national attention. Again, Bud demonstrated his leadership by his willingness to tackle a problem others had not addressed, and he turned it into a success for the institution. While giving the credit to others who did much of the work, everyone knew it would not have happened without Bud's leadership.

Bud served as vice chancellor and vice president during three very different decades: the 1970s, 1980s, and 1990s. His institution, located close to the nation's capital, was not only highly visible, but also often a stage where many of the most vexing social issues in the country were acted out and tested. Most prominent among these issues were race relations; and Bud, a person with very strong commitments to equal opportunity, fairness, and civility, was a key leader at Maryland in developing a positive campus climate for diversity. Bud worked very hard to establish programs in advising, counseling, housing, and student life that would make Maryland an attractive and successful place for students from all backgrounds. He was often viewed as the most trusted institutional leader in this area, one who could be counted on for his honesty and his willingness to deal openly with problems that were too often avoided by others.

At the same time that Bud was so active building a strong student affairs program at Maryland, he was also a very visible leader within the profession. For instance, he was a member of the national board of NASPA and an active leader in the Association of College and University Housing Officers and BACCHUS. Bud was also the director of the prestigious NASPA Summer Institute for Chief Student Affairs Officers in 1987 and 1988. Since its beginning, and for many years, he has been active in CAS in Student Services and Student Development Programs, and he served on its executive committee since 1979. The *CAS Standards* have had a profound effect on the profession. Bud has been a frequent keynote speaker at regional and national conferences, a consultant to many colleges and universities, and since 1994 has been a member of the NASPA Foundation Board. In 1998, he was elected the president of this Board. In 1986, as an indication of the high regard his peers have for his leadership, he was presented with the profession's highest honor, NASPA's Scott Goodnight Award for outstanding performance as a dean. Bud had several invitations to consider other senior student affairs positions during his career, and a few opportunities to pursue a presidency, but he declined them all. He was committed to the University of Maryland, the excitement of the Washington, D.C. area, and was stimulated by the constant challenges of his position. He also referred to the benefits of what he calls the "refreshed longevity" of being in his position for many years, considering it "worth its weight in gold" in exerting leadership on the campus.

Bud loves being in the center of the action. But he emphasized that this was not always the case when he was young, and he did not believe early on that he was destined to become a leader. He insisted that he "grew" into leadership over many years, probably beginning with his church responsibilities as a young man. "Leadership is something that you learn, a little bit at a time, over many years," Bud said. He described his progression of leadership from church, part-time jobs, school, college, the Army, teaching, and student affairs administration as an enjoyable journey. Along the way, Bud learned how organizations work, how people respond in various situations, what students need, and how to make decisions. And he claims that he is still learning these skills. But he says the most important aspect of leadership for him is to believe that what you are doing is important—education is an infinite good, especially the education of students. This basic commitment to a worthy task is what drove Bud in all of his actions, and he emphasized that this was made possible by his good fortune to be able to work for an institution whose values he admired. "The university is not perfect, of course, but if I were to put my faith in any social institution in our society, it would be the university," Bud said. His ability to identify problems and to work effectively with others in addressing these problems, his ability to describe issues clearly and persuasively, his obvious professional competence, and his courage to make tough decisions made him one of the most successful SSAOs in the country.

Bud Thomas, viewed by many people as the consummate administrative leader, is a man with a strong passion for education. A voracious reader who loves the arts, he treasures the higher learning, civility, and integrity, but also recognizes the fragile nature of individuals and of society. He sees education as the best hope against the long time human enemies of ignorance, prejudice, chaos, and the abusive power of ill motivated authority. "Education is truly a noble profession," Bud says, "and I have been privileged to be part of it!"

Chapter 15

Carol A. Wiggins
University of Connecticut

When Carol Wiggins was a first-year teacher, one of the senior teachers referred to her as "Beave," short for "Eager Beaver." Always diligent in everything she has done, the nickname characterized her work throughout her career. As she walked across the lovely University of Connecticut (UConn) campus in Storrs, it was difficult for others to keep up with her pace; Carol Wiggins was moving quickly; she had things to do, and everyone knew she would get them done!

Carol A. Wiggins received her B.A. and M.A. degrees from New York State College for Teachers at Albany in 1958 and 1959, majoring in social studies and minoring in mathematics. She earned another M.A. degree in 1964 from UConn in guidance, counseling and personnel, and her PhD was awarded in 1972 in guidance, counseling and personnel from the same institution. She was a high school history teacher in Delmar, New York for 4 years and then served UConn in a variety of positions for 32 years until her retirement in 1997. Her work at the university began in 1965 as a head resident. She progressed to assistant dean of students, then dean of students and assistant vice president, and then from 1981–1997 was the vice president for student affairs.

She served as the elected chair of the Council on Student Affairs of the National Association of State Universities and Land Grant Colleges, served as a member of the board of directors of the National Association of Student Personnel Administrators (NASPA), and the NASPA Foundation board of directors. She received the Distinguished Alumni Award from the State University of New York at Albany in 1985, and NASPA's highest recognition, the Scott Goodnight Award, for outstanding performance by a dean in 1994.

She is a member of several academic honor societies and was asked by the Connecticut Commissioner of Higher Education to serve in key leadership roles on committees dealing with racial diversity and AIDS education. She also received the Outstanding Educator Award in 1997 from the Beta Sigma chapter of Pi Lambda Theta, the national honor and professional association in education.

Carol Wiggins was born during the Great Depression years in Newburgh, New York, a city of 35,000 in the Hudson valley. She was an only child, as both of her parents had been. Neither of her parents had earned a high school diploma, although Carol described them as highly intelligent and well read. Her father was a fireman for the city of Newburgh, and her mother was a housewife. She was very close to her two grandmothers and a grandfather, who lived in the same town. Her mother had a heart attack when Carol was only 13, and she was not expected to live more than 10 years. She told Carol that she hoped to live long enough to see Carol graduate from junior high school; happily, she lived until 1973 and was present when Carol was awarded her PhD degree from UConn! Carol's father was very skilled at building and fixing things, but she was perplexed by his apparent difficulty in completing projects. She is convinced that her lifelong determination to get things done is partly a reaction to her father's reluctance to do the same. Carol's mother was very active in the Methodist Church, so Carol spent a good deal of time as a young girl in church activities and became president of the church's youth group. Carol attended Chestnut Street elementary school in Newburgh and immediately fell in love with learning and excelled in her studies. She had so many interests that now she wonders if she had Attention Deficit Disorder before this was formally known! Carol was involved in many things in school and church, including sports, and was even captain of her sixth grade softball team. She insisted that she was not competitive and that her motivation to excel was driven by a simple admonition that she referred to in her work with students throughout her career: "Do your best!"

Carol attended high school at the Newburgh Free Academy and, not surprisingly, was the valedictorian of her class of 276. She was co-editor of the student paper, secretary of her senior class, and president of the YWCA senior club. She visited Skidmore College in New York when she was a junior as a member of Girl's State. At the end of her senior year, she was the recipient of the American Legion Award for her excellent leadership and service. She loved history and math courses, and there was never any doubt in her mind that she wanted to be a teacher. Carol worked each summer during high school as a cashier at the city swimming pool and later as a bank clerk, saving her earnings in order to attend college. Since she wanted to be a high school teacher and was paying for her own education, Carol applied to only one college, New York State College for Teachers at Albany, just 80 miles from her home in Newburgh. She enrolled in the fall of 1954. She lived in a freshman residence hall, was elected president of her hall, and became acquainted with the resident assistant (RA) and others working in student affairs, including Dr. Ellen Clayton Stokes, the dean of women. This enthusiastic young woman, who had been valedictorian of her high school class, graduated from New York State College for Teachers at Albany in 1958, Magna Cum Laude, majoring in social studies and minoring in mathematics. Her outstanding achievements were a great thrill to her family, but Carol again insisted that her motivation was simply to "do her best." Indeed, Carol was doing just that!

Carol decided she wanted to pursue a master's degree and returned to Albany in the fall of 1958. To support herself through this additional year, she became an RA. For her, the position was a means to an end, a master's degree, and a permanent teaching certificate. She realized later, however, that her work as an RA had a major effect on her ultimate career decision—work in student affairs! During her graduate year at Albany, one of her professors, Dr. Kendall A. Birr, urged her to apply for a Woodrow Wilson fellowship that would lead to a college teaching career. Carol declined, however, because she wanted to teach high school.

Carol took a job at the Bethlehem Central Senior High School in Delmar, New York, in the fall of 1959, and loved teaching history there for the next 4 years. She also advised the junior class and the Keyettes and found that many students came to her with their problems and personal concerns. Although she had no formal training as a counselor, she discovered that students responded very positively to her and many benefited directly from the assistance she provided to them. She was greatly admired by her students, and in her fourth year of teaching the students dedicated their annual yearbook to her. Part of the dedication was reflected throughout the remainder of her career: "Devoted and patient, teaching and learning with your students, and always quick to catch the humor of a situation."

During the summer of 1962, after her third year of teaching, and as a reaction to so many of her high school students coming to her with their personal problems, Carol decided to enroll in summer school in the graduate program in educational psychology at UConn. She knew of the program at Storrs because her former student teaching supervisor earned his doctorate from UConn. She liked the program so much that she decided to teach for one more year and then leave high school teaching. In 1963, she enrolled on a full-time basis in UConn's M.A. program in guidance, counseling and personnel, and she earned her degree in 1964.

Carol continued in a doctoral program. After a year of full-time study, she ran out of money and took the position of head resident in the new, large, and first co-educational residence hall at UConn. In this full-time position, she formed the ideas of what was to become her basic commitment throughout her work in student affairs—she was a teacher first, a counselor second, and if she did those roles well then she believed the administrator role would fall into place. Reflecting the strong commitments to the education of students she had as a high school teacher, Carol saw student affairs as an ideal setting to teach responsibility, leadership, respect for others, and public service. She was also inspired by the opportunities student affairs afforded her to help students with their character development. Her own traits of caring, kindliness, and respect served as a model for students in her first position as a head resident and for later generations of students throughout UConn.

> **As a leader, Carol did her homework, learned the issues well, studied the political and cultural climate, involved key people in developing a plan, and pursued it with great determination.**

Carol's work was outstanding and was quickly noticed by others at the university. When she completed her doctorate, she was promoted to assistant dean of students. She visited other institutions to learn more about their student affairs programs, and these visits reinforced her belief in the comprehensive, public university as the type of institution where she felt most comfortable. She also taught courses in the College of Education's graduate program. In 1975, she was asked to become the dean of students and assistant vice president for student affairs. In this role, Carol was responsible for a large portion of the total student affairs program on the campus. She consolidated the business and student life aspects of housing into one department, expanded the counseling center's programs, and developed new opportunities for student organizations in leadership development and community service. She loved this position. In 1981, after a national search, Carol was appointed the vice president for student affairs at UConn by President John DiBiaggio. She was the first female vice president at the university since its founding in 1881. Initially, Carol did not plan to apply to be vice president. She loved what she was doing as dean of students and assistant vice president and did not want to distance herself from students. But she had high respect for Dr. DiBiaggio, saw the needs at the institution, and recognized the leadership challenge the position offered. Moreover, her colleagues at the university expressed strong support for her, urging her to apply. When she was appointed, she was confident that her past experiences as a teacher, residence hall director, assistant dean, and dean and assistant vice president had prepared her well for the position.

As the new vice president, Carol carried out her responsibilities in the same way she had in all of her previous professional positions—she put students first, treated everyone with respect, put in long hours, and developed a team concept with her staff. She placed a priority on the hiring of high-quality professional staff and encouraged their development; four of them became presidents of national associations during her tenure as vice president! She was strongly committed to attracting more minority students to the university, and with her staff she developed excellent programs to help students learn about and appreciate diversity. She was asked by the commissioner of higher education to chair a task force on the recruitment and retention of minorities throughout Connecticut's public higher education institutions. In advocating for students on her campus and throughout the state, she argued for what she called the "three R's—recruitment, retention, and responsiveness to student needs."

As a leader, Carol did her homework, learned the issues well, studied the political and cultural climate, involved key people in developing a plan, and pursued it with great determination. As a result, she was able to accomplish a great deal and became well known and respected for her ability to get things done, especially in a manner that brought people together. She was not afraid of making decisions and recognized that she would face criticism no matter what direction she would take on various issues. But she also understood that she had to maintain good working relationships with a wide variety of students, faculty, administrators, and others in the process. Her caring attitude, genuine affection for others, and willingness to listen were great assets in her ability to get things done. Also well known to those who worked with her for years was her sense of humor, which Carol used effectively with students and staff alike to place issues in perspective and to remind everyone not to take themselves too seriously.

Carol succeeded the university's first vice president of student affairs, who was not viewed as a strong leader on the campus and who had spent a good deal of time away from the university in various political activities in the state. She recognized when she accepted the position that the staff was ready for some steady leadership from a person they knew and could trust to be there and to represent them well. Carol also understood that she would have to establish herself as a competent leader with the other vice presidents and the campus deans, who had not seen much evidence of strong direction from her predecessor. She approached the position with confidence, ever aware of the high expectations for her from her staff and students.

Carol worked for four presidents during her career as a vice president, and she found that this necessitated changes in the way she approached issues and problems. When one president expected to be informed about almost everything happening on the campus, Carol spent more of her time defending and justifying policies and programs than she would have liked. She also protected her staff by accepting a good deal of criticism and struggled with decisions that might not be acceptable to the president. With presidents who granted a great deal of freedom to her and did not expect to be involved in student affairs decisions, Carol was able to accomplish a great deal. She developed a model student rights and responsibilities statement, hired new staff, established a new student conduct code, supported a relationship statement between the university and the sororities and fraternities, and encouraged student participation on university committees and councils.

Under her direction at UConn were the departments of admissions and orientation, residential life, dean of students, counseling, career services, student health, student union and activities, cooperative education, and dining services. At the time of her retirement in 1997, the division's annual budget exceeded $42 million. Carol commented that she could have spent all her time simply as a manager, making financial decisions and working with the directors of the departments; but she knew this was only a part of her responsibility. She knew she needed to be the most visible advocate for students at the university, especially with the other vice presidents and academic deans. She also was determined to remain visible with students and student organizations—not usurping the role of her own staff, but supporting them with her regular presence at campus meetings and events, especially in the evenings and during the weekends.

Carol put in many long hours during the years she served as vice president, but she loved what she was doing and never regretted the time she spent. She knew that a significant part of being an effective leader was to know what was happening on a first-hand basis, and she wanted to remain personally involved in campus life. Her title may have changed several times at UConn in the 16 years she served in various positions before being named vice president, but she knew she was the same person and worked hard to treat everyone in the same manner, regardless of rank or position. She said that the title of vice president did not make her a leader, but did give her the opportunity to help her staff and others do the things they were hired to do. Her leadership style was to make others feel appreciated for what they did, feel pride in their accomplishments, and give them the credit for their positive contributions.

Carol became well known by members of the board of trustees for her knowledge about students, her ability in handling problems, and her success in managing large departments. Carol had very positive and cordial relationships with almost everyone, but she was also known as a person with strong convictions about educational issues, especially the rights and freedoms of students to learn. Because she was well prepared for her presentations, knew the issues very well, and had earned the respect of others for her fairness and integrity, Carol realized a good deal of success in working with the board, actively working with the board's committee on student affairs.

In the 1994–1995 academic year, Carol experienced a very difficult challenge, when a group of new board members, responding to budgetary problems, decided to reorganize the administrative structure of the institution. After a lengthy review, one of the recommendations submitted to the board was to eliminate the student affairs division by reassigning the various departments to other vice presidents. This, it was argued, would streamline the university's administrative organization and save money. Carol understood that the motivation to suggest this unprecedented action had little if anything to do with student affairs or its effectiveness. She was not naive about the politics that can often invade university governance. She had never backed away from a battle and was well known for her ability to argue for what she thought was right. However, in this situation, with the local newspapers describing the recommendation in a way that would essentially eliminate her position, she did not want to appear to say anything publicly that could be viewed as trying to save her own job. With no suggestion from her, staff and students became outraged. Several hundred students rallied on her behalf and on behalf of students affairs to the board at a specially called meeting. Staff and alumni also inundated the board with letters of protest. Carol had the support of her president and the other vice presidents and deans. The recommendation was set aside.

Carol emphasized the importance of working closely with her vice presidential colleagues in academic affairs and finance and administration during her years as a senior student affairs officer (SSAO). There were three different academic vice presidents during her tenure, and Carol spent a good deal of time informing them about her ideas, her goals, and the needs of students. She knew that some of her own responsibilities overlapped with academic affairs, and she felt comfortable with this. She worked to establish a holistic approach to students' educational experiences on the campus.

Carol worked with four finance and administrative vice presidents during her years as the SSAO and watched their responsibilities change when new presidents came into office. She knew she had to demonstrate her skills as an effective financial manager in such key areas as residential life, student health services, and dining services. She scrutinized her departmental budgets on a regular basis. The majority of the financial resources in the student affairs division were generated from student fees, and Carol understood that she needed the support of the vice presidents, student leaders, and her president to continue to gain the backing of the board of trustees. She believed that the best strategy to accomplish her financial goals was to be a good manager and to share all financial information, up front, with everyone. She thus earned the trust and confidence of all of these groups, and this proved critical in the success she was able to achieve at the university. Her respect and credibility on the campus were acknowledged when she chaired the search committee for the vice president for finance and administration in 1984.

There was legislation in Connecticut that provided protection to campus auxiliaries. These funds could not be used for other, nonrelated purposes at the university. However, the board of trustees wanted more flexibility in the use of all funds at the institution and argued its case successfully before the legislature in the early 1990s. Legislation was passed that enabled all campus funds to be used for any purpose deemed appropriate by the president and board. This was generally good news for the university, but it made some of the departments under Carol's control vulnerable to the financial needs of other, nonrelated areas. She was worried about what might happen if fund balances and reserves in dining services and residential life, so critical to the departments' future growth and development, might be redirected. This important shift in institutional decision-making required Carol to become more diligent in managing student affairs departments, especially the auxiliaries. It also required her to be able to defend the continued use of fund balances for the benefit of the departments that generated them. Discussions on these issues among vice presidents often become heated and difficult, but Carol was successful in maintaining the financial support she considered necessary.

UConn had run its own large dining program for many years, and Carol and her staff took pride in this operation and worked hard to ensure that it was meeting the needs of the institution. Carol argued that it was closely coordinated with other student development programs in the residence halls. In an effort to save money, some members of the board of trustees initiated a study to explore if the institution might be better served by contracting this service to a private vendor. After the board studied this matter, Carol argued successfully to retain institutional responsibility for the dining service.

Carol had to deal with many difficult issues during her tenure as vice president, and one of her most challenging problems involved significant budget cutbacks during lean years in the legislature. She worked with the other vice presidents in developing plans that were designed to retain the most important aspects of educational and service programs at the university. This required Carol to understand the budgets and goals of university functions outside of student affairs, something she considered important in her leadership as a vice president. She understood that she could not be effective if she argued exclusively for her own narrow interests in student affairs. She was part of the institution's top management team, headed by the president, and it was this same team concept she had built within her own student affairs departments that she knew was critical to the success of the institution. She also gained the respect of her administrative colleagues during these difficult budgetary times by the actions she took within the student affairs division. In one year, for example, Carol combined the Cooperative Education and the Career Services departments in order to save funds. She knew that it was always preferable to take the initiative on budget decisions oneself, rather than waiting until the president has to dictate what has to be done. Moreover, she knew this was her obligation as the leader of the student affairs division.

Carol was also very active in convincing the university to confront the problem of alcohol abuse. This was a continuing issue; Carol argued that if any success was to be realized in decreasing alcohol abuse, a campus-wide commitment was necessary. She was able to broaden the discussion on this topic to include faculty, administrators, students, and members of the student affairs committee of the board of trustees. A comprehensive policy resulted that included education, prevention, and adjudication.

> *Carol often talked with students and staff about respect, initiative, pride, and excellence as the necessary ingredients for success. Her commitment to these values was entirely consistent with the way she conducted herself as the SSAO at UConn.*

During her tenure as the SSAO at UConn, Carol's leadership resulted in renovations in the residence halls, the student health service, the student union, and the dining halls. Long-range facilities' plans were also developed by her departments. She understood that one of her roles as a leader was to "tell a story clearly" about student needs. She became known on the campus for her ability to persuade others about various issues and needs. This ability to "sell" was a function of Carol's excellent planning and her strong belief in the ideas and programs she was proposing. Carol said, "You never win all your arguments; but you've got to try and keep on trying!"

A dramatic illustration of the effective team Carol had built at Connecticut took place on Mother's Day in 1993 on the campus, when three students were diagnosed with meningitis. On that Sunday, Carol called in her entire staff, and with volunteers from around the university and representatives from the Connecticut Department of Health and the Centers for Disease Control, organized a mass inoculation program for 13,000 students. Her president at the time, Dr. Harry J. Hartley, commented, "The way in which Dr. Wiggins mobilized her staff and quickly disseminated accurate information about meningitis became a national model used in training materials by the American College Health Association." Dr. Hartley went on to say that

> No one was a better team player than Carol Wiggins. When describing results, she said "we," not "I;" and she assembled a very competent management team that supervised a large, diverse, and outstanding division of student affairs at UConn. She was simply the best! (Hartley, personal communication, 2000).

While understanding that student affairs is impossible to quantify, Carol was a strong advocate of planning. She worked hard to involve her staff in planning efforts and knew that this process produced some of the best ideas they had for the campus. She knew that good programs emerged from rigorous discussion and debate about ideas, and she used this model for most of the plans she pursued. In 1989, she and her staff developed programming and planning initiatives that included specific goals for each department and four division-wide challenges: promoting campus pluralism, supporting health and wellness, augmenting weekend student life, and enhancing campus pride. Carol understood the value of having her staff develop ownership of this process; as a result, considerable success was realized from the planning effort.

Carol and her staff were very close to the students. She always insisted that it was necessary to get out of the office, attend student meetings, and talk with students where they live in order to understand the various student cultures at the university. She understood that as the vice president, her presence at many evening and weekend events was important; she did not consider this a burden on her time, but something she genuinely liked. She also never claimed that the staff in student affairs had some exclusive insights about students. She knew faculty were a tremendous resource as advisers and cultivated this support whenever she could. Carol also placed an emphasis on research about students, and she encouraged her staff to conduct surveys of student needs and assessments of their experiences on the campus. On the national level, she served for 3 years as director of the Division of Research and Development for the NASPA.

Carol had high expectations for others. She was very demanding of herself, and she understood that this was necessary as a leader in order to encourage excellent performance in her staff. She was able to withstand criticism from others and accepted it as an inevitable part of her role as a leader. She joked, "If you need to be liked or popular, don't become a vice president for student affairs!" In fact, her staff say she was the most popular and admired administrator at UConn for a long time, and among the reasons for this was that she was open, honest, and well known to students.

Carol often talked with students and staff about respect, initiative, pride, and excellence as the necessary ingredients for success. Her commitment to these values was entirely consistent with the way she conducted herself as the SSAO at UConn. Student affairs for her was the most effective way to teach young people, and it enabled her to pursue her goals with compassion and great energy. She worked especially hard during her tenure for increased diversity on the campus.

She never sought leadership opportunities at other institutions. Carol decided to remain at UConn, and her 32 years there were a labor of love. She believed in the mission of the institution and felt she could use her knowledge of the campus and experience over many years to enhance the quality of student life. When she decided to retire in 1997, students, faculty, staff, community members, and alumni joined in thanking her for her outstanding leadership and the tremendous effect she had on so many lives. An entire issue of *The Daily Campus,* the student newspaper, was dedicated to her; and on "Carol Wiggins Day" on May 7, 1997, hundreds of T-shirts were worn by students, staff, and faculty. The T-shirts were adorned with a photograph of Carol and her well-known credo, "Students are our bottom line!"

Carol's leadership extended beyond the campus, and she was recognized by many organizations for her work. She was elected the chair of the Student Affairs Council of the National Association of State Universities and Land Grant Colleges. She was a member of the NASPA board of directors, and in 1994 she was the recipient of the organization's highest recognition, the Scott Goodnight Award for outstanding performance as a dean. In all of the leadership positions she had and in all of the recognitions she received, Carol honestly asked, "Why me?" She always gave credit to others when good things happened and expressed sincere surprise when she received recognition. For Carol, the greatest joy gained from her work was to see a student grow in a positive direction. She took her first teaching position in 1959, and she remained a great teacher throughout her career.

Chapter 16

George W. Young
Broward Community College

George Young became the first vice president for student affairs at Broward Community College in 1969. When he retired from that same position some 28 years later, everyone associated with the college was convinced that George Young and Broward Community College represented a "match made in heaven!" The phenomenal growth and development of the college during his career clearly reflected his influence and leadership in all aspects of the institution.

Dr. George W. Young served as the vice president for student affairs at Broward Community College from 1969–1997. Previous to this assignment, he was the dean of student affairs at Valdosta State College from 1966–1969, the director of the Counseling Center at Florida State University from 1964–1966, and a residence hall director at Florida State University from 1963–1964. He earned his B.A. degree in psychology from Florida State University in 1961, his M.A. in experimental psychology in 1963 from Florida State, and his PhD in higher education administration in 1966 from Florida State. Dr. Young was the elected president of the National Association of Student Personnel Administrators (NASPA) in 1979–1980, and he was the recipient of NASPA's Fred Turner Award for distinguished service to the profession in 1994. He served as the chair of the State of Florida Council on Student Affairs and as the chair of the statewide Commission on Community Service. He has been a prominent leader in the American Association of Community and Junior Colleges and a frequent consultant to colleges and universities in the United States and abroad. During Dr. Young's 28 years as vice president for student affairs at Broward Community College, the institution expanded to four campuses, the enrollment increased from 2,800 to 60,000, and the academic and service programs grew to be among the most extensive of any community college in the country.

George Young was born in Ft. Lauderdale, Florida in 1938. His grandfather had been a ships carpenter in Northern England and decided to emigrate to the United States in 1909 at age 22. As George describes it, "My grandfather got on the train in New York and ended up in Ft. Lauderdale because that's as far as the train went!" His grandfather had no money but was a hard-working, talented, and determined young man. The population of Ft. Lauderdale was only 500 in 1909, and George's grandfather lived for 2 years in a tent on what is now the downtown Ft. Lauderdale site of Broward Community College. Grandfather Young began a construction business and became well known in the area for the quality of his work and for his personal integrity. George's father was a superior student at Ft. Lauderdale High School and was offered a scholarship to study engineering at the Massachusetts Institute of Technology (M.I.T.). But it was the early years of the Great Depression, and George's father was not able to attend college, a decision that was to affect George's own thinking in significant ways in future years.

George's mother, Virginia Young, was a reporter for the *Ft. Lauderdale News* and became an active community leader in the days before most women assumed such responsibility. Mrs. Young had a strong interest in education, and she ran successfully for the Broward County school board, later becoming its chair. She was later elected to the position of mayor of Ft. Lauderdale, and seeing his mother as an active leader in community affairs and his father as a task-oriented, honest contractor had a profound influence on George in his youth. George's reputation as a community service-oriented leader who could always be counted on by others to get things done was a direct reflection of these traits in his parents. George's father was denied, by economic circumstances, the opportunity to attend M.I.T. So perhaps as a reaction, George and his wife strongly encouraged their three children to pursue higher education; all three of them earned graduate or professional degrees.

George was a good, but not outstanding, student at Ft. Lauderdale high school. He spent most of his time working in construction projects for his father and playing high school football. He did not give much thought to college; since he had such high respect for his father, George wanted to be a building contractor. During the several summers he had worked for his father, George had proved to himself and his peers that he could work hard, learn fast, and get things done while getting along well with others. Because his mother was active in politics, she sometimes had business in the state capitol, Tallahassee, and George accompanied her on some of her trips. As a result, George became familiar with Florida State University and decided to enroll there as a freshman. Following the interests of his father, George decided to study engineering, and during his first year he also was a member of the freshman football team. George enjoyed himself, pledged a fraternity, and made many friends; however, his grades were undistinguished, and he found he had little interest in his engineering and math courses. He enrolled in a beginning psychology course, taught by Dr. Larry Chalmers, a professor who was later to become the president of the University of Kansas. Dr. Chalmers recognized George's intelligence and asked him why he was not doing better in his classes. The personal interest and concern expressed by Dr. Chalmers was to have a major effect on George. Dr. Chalmers believed in George and convinced him that he could do anything he wanted to do in higher education. Taking a similar, personal interest in students became a hallmark of George's own career as a student affairs administrator. George changed his major to psychology and as his confidence and interest increased, his grades soared. He joined Alpha Phi Omega, the service fraternity, and with another member, developed a Boy Scout troop for disabled elementary school students. Following the example of his parents, George saw a need for a service and took the initiative to do something about it, something that was to characterize his entire career in higher education.

George was invited to become a house fellow in the residence halls by John Blackburn, who was one of the residence hall directors in the housing program at Florida State. John was later to become vice president for student affairs at the University of Alabama, president of NASPA, and a lifelong friend and mentor. George loved working with students in the residence halls and joined the Phi Kappa Tau fraternity. He injured his knee during his freshman year while playing football and decided that he no longer had sufficient interest in the sport to continue it, especially since he was now so stimulated by his studies in psychology, his volunteer work in the community, and his job as a house fellow in the residence halls.

The director of housing at Florida State during this time was Edith McCollum, who provided excellent guidance to George. She recognized his excellent potential and encouraged him to attend graduate school. She offered George a graduate assistantship in her office, working with various residence halls and the fraternities. In this position, George learned about late hours, student conduct problems, and direct assistance to students. George was accepted into the graduate program in experimental psychology and was encouraged by both Edith McCollum and his undergraduate adviser, Dr. Chalmers, to pursue a doctorate as well. George was stimulated by his graduate studies in experimental psychology, but he was even more engaged with his student affairs work in the residence halls. He and Dawn Wilson, his high school sweetheart, decided to get married in 1960. While Dawn interned in a local elementary school, George continued with his graduate program. George had financed almost all of his undergraduate expenses by working, and he and Dawn continued this effort during graduate school.

George was intrigued by the research programs he was involved with in his graduate program in experimental psychology, but he began to recognize that his main interests were moving in the direction of student affairs. He decided to talk with Dr. Melvene Hardee, professor of higher education administration at Florida State. This meeting with Dr. Hardee proved to be a very significant occurrence in his career, as he decided to transfer from experimental psychology to the higher education program and pursue student affairs as a career. Dr. Hardee was to become his major adviser and a significant influence throughout his career, as she was with so many other subsequent leaders in the profession. George, recognized by others again for his intelligence and leadership, was invited to become the assistant director of the Counseling Center during his graduate program, and he accepted. George did so well that he was promoted to director of the center in 1965, and he completed his PhD in 1966 at Florida State. George was convinced he had done the right thing by selecting student affairs, and he began exploring various positions. He attended his first NASPA meeting in 1965 in Washington, D.C. and met with representatives of other institutions there. He was offered the position of dean of students at Valdosta State College in Georgia and decided to accept. He, Dawn, and their two young children, Jenifer and George, III, moved to Valdosta in the summer of 1966; and George began his new role as dean.

George loved the challenge and considered himself very fortunate to work with Walter Martin, the president of Valdosta State, who gave his support to George and expected him to build an effective student affairs program. George was able to reorganize the division along functional lines, build three new residence halls, a student health service, and a student union. Above all, George loved to build programs and create new services, and Valdosta State provided him with an excellent opportunity to exert his leadership skills. He instituted new ways to involve students in decision-making, established close relationships with the campus and city newspaper, and worked closely with community leaders. This was the late 1960s, of course, and it was a very volatile period in the country. George and his staff spent long hours with student groups in planning constructive activities. George was also responsible for admissions, registration, the campus police, and intercollegiate athletics. He hired new staff and developed new strategies to reach out to area high schools, and the enrollment at Valdosta State increased significantly. He was strongly committed to student learning and worked with faculty to involve them in residence halls and student organizations.

George was very good at assessing problems and needs on the campus and involving others in this process. Once George was convinced of what needed to be done, he was a strong and tireless advocate for his cause or project. He was also willing to confront those whose opposition was based on misinformation or power struggles. He remembered a conflict with the senior business officer regarding a plan to construct a new residence hall, finding that his strong advocacy and commitment to honesty was eventually appreciated, resulting not only in the residence hall being built, but also a much closer and more trusting relationship with the senior business officer. George earned the respect of those he worked with for his honesty, his knowledge, and his ability to get things done. He was a very effective advocate for the things he wanted to establish on the campus and was not afraid of controversy or conflict. He knew that sound financial management was important to his success, and his ability to handle money, perhaps learned from his father's experience in the construction business, earned George the confidence of his president and his fellow deans. George taught his staff about fiscal management and frequently used the phrase, "You've got to know where the money is!" Knowing where the money was, and especially how to compete for resources and manage them wisely, enabled George to build extensive new student facilities at Valdosta State, create new programs, and hire new staff that increased the institution's enrollment and academic quality.

> *He achieved a great deal in a relatively short period of time because he had the support of his president, the willingness to make difficult decisions, the ability to build new facilities, the courage to dismiss some staff and hire new professionals, and the willingness to put in long hours on the job.*

George remembers a meeting with one of his mentors, Melvene Hardee, who was visiting with George in Valdosta. Mel asked George, "What is it that you are teaching here?" George responded by saying that he and his staff were all teachers and what they were teaching was leadership, responsibility, dignity, and respect for others. George, clearly reflecting the strong values of his parents, was always a fierce opponent of racism and bigotry in any form. During the time he was dean at Valdosta State, Lester Maddox was the governor of Georgia, and there were many citizens of the state who did not welcome African American students to higher education. George was a visible and strong advocate for the rights of minority students and worked with faculty and community leaders to create a supportive campus environment for all students. George was always willing to take a strong, public stand for what he knew was the right thing, especially when it involved educational opportunities for students. This was often difficult to do during these tense years in Georgia, but George was willing to take the criticism he knew would be directed toward him. George was very effective in getting along with almost everyone, but he could also be a tenacious fighter for what he knew was the right thing to do.

George worked to develop a new student judicial system at Valdosta State, one that clearly stated the expectations for student behavior and also granted to students a significant role in the process. It reflected the principles of the *Joint Statement on Rights and Freedoms of Students* and was considered quite liberal for the times in his state. By that time, George already had extensive experience at Florida State University in handling student discipline, and he knew that it could be a positive educational experience for students if handled in the right manner. When a case George affirmed on his campus was appealed by a student's father to the statewide board of regents, it was upheld, and the system George had created became a model for the other state institutions. More important, George insisted that the student conduct system retain its educational purpose; and many former students who encountered difficulties during their undergraduate years have affirmed this concept, as they have thanked George for his personal concern, his faith in their future, and his insistence on honesty and taking responsibility for one's actions.

George knew what he wanted to accomplish when he accepted the dean's position at Valdosta State, as he was able to assess the needs of the campus, the competence of the staff, and the institution's potential for growth. He achieved a great deal in a relatively short period of time because he had the support of his president, the willingness to make difficult decisions, the ability to build new facilities, the courage to dismiss some staff and hire new professionals, and the willingness to put in long hours on the job. Above all, George loved the opportunity to move the program forward and was greatly stimulated by the challenge. In working with his staff, George was convinced that they could do more than they thought they could, and he gained great satisfaction in seeing them accomplish things beyond their own expectations. The phrase he often used with his staff was "You'll grow to the extent that I give you something to do that is outside of your job description!" He spent a lot of time in building a staff team, and he did this through frequent retreats where goals were set, strategies were developed, and plans of action were decided. He viewed himself as a motivator, a leader who could earn the respect and support of his staff to accomplish significant change on the campus. He required and expected staff to work hard and put in long hours, and he led in this regard by personal example. George loved to get things done; even before one project was completed, he was already preparing for the next one. One of his former staff members at Valdosta State said, "George Young was an inspiring leader—a man of action, and he expected a lot of all of us. It was very exciting to be on his staff, as there was always something happening and we knew we were moving in the right direction."

In 1969, after George had been the senior student affairs officer (SSAO) at Valdosta State for 3 years, he received a phone call from Dr. Hugh Adams, the newly named president of Broward Community College in Ft. Lauderdale, Florida, George's hometown. Dr. Adams invited George to consider becoming the dean of students at this small community college of 2,800 students. George thanked him but indicated that he was not interested in leaving Valdosta State, where he thought he might remain for the rest of his career. He loved his job, and he and his family were active in the very pleasant local community. Moreover, George had never worked in a community college and admitted to himself that he did not have high regard for 2-year colleges. He was well aware of Broward Community College of course, because it was located in his hometown; and the thought of moving back to Ft. Lauderdale was somewhat attractive, but not enough to make him leave his dean's position at such an exciting and growing institution as Valdosta State. But Hugh Adams, whom George described as a visionary leader, was very persistent and convinced George to come for a visit.

President Adams described his plans for the community college and talked about the future, emphasizing opportunity, growth, and egalitarian values. He described the opportunity for leadership at the college and the lack of bureaucracy and traditional structures that were often impediments to change in older, 4-year institutions. Obviously, Dr. Adams knew George well, because these were the conditions that would excite George and convince him that he would have the freedom to build, to improve, to create, and to move ahead rapidly. Knowing that a move to a nontraditional college at this time would be a major shift in his professional career, George thought long and hard about the offer to go to Broward Community College. George was only 32 years old, had already been a successful dean at Valdosta for 3 years, and his future in student affairs looked very bright. Why would he want to move to a virtually unknown community college whose future was very uncertain? George declined the offer but agreed to meet again with the very persistent President Adams in Ft. Lauderdale. George purposely took a train on the 400-mile trip from Valdosta, as he knew this would give him time to think carefully about this professional opportunity, which continued to gnaw at him.

Dr. Adams proved to be successful, as George accepted the position at Broward Community College as dean of students in the summer of 1969. He and his family moved to Ft. Lauderdale and began a journey about which George had both excitement and apprehension. George was close to his president at Valdosta, and it was difficult for him to leave that institution. The state system office was in Atlanta, and George was asked to travel to that office to meet with one of the system-wide officers about his planned move to Ft. Lauderdale. When George took the occasion to inform the officer that there was far less bureaucracy at Broward Community College and that he would be able to get more things done more quickly as a result, his comments were received with surprise and resentment. But George was used to honesty and candid comments, and he was not timid about pointing out the problems with organizations when he saw them. When he left Valdosta State, the faculty held its own reception for George, expressing its appreciation for his excellent work and leadership and presented him with a gift. This willingness to tell the truth and to take a strong stand on issues was appreciated by the faculty at Valdosta, and it was to characterize George's work for the remainder of his career.

George knew the Ft. Lauderdale community and understood that the future success of the college was heavily dependent on how well he and Dr. Adams might earn the community's support. George also knew his move to Broward Community College was a professional gamble on his part, but he had high respect for Dr. Adams, confidence in his own leadership ability, and a love for a challenge. While George was well known for his organizational ability, he was much less interested in administrative structure than he was in freedom. What attracted him most of all to Broward Community College was the freedom President Adams had given to him to build a student affairs program. George loved to see positive developments from his efforts and knew that his own leadership style required freedom to make decisions quickly without having to deal with layers of bureaucracy. Broward Community College and Dr. Hugh Adams presented George with this opportunity.

Broward had its own board of trustees and, with Dr. Adams' support, George quickly became directly involved with board affairs. When he found that the board members had almost no real contact with students, George brought students to board meetings for presentations on their activities, invited board members to student leadership retreats, and began a systematic program of educating board members about student affairs issues and policies. George always insisted that frank and honest discussions would take place between students and the board; he knew that "public relations" approaches would not only be misleading, but also would prove to be counterproductive. He was confident that by sharing real problems, issues, and concerns with board members, greater support and understanding would eventually result; and the board would be better prepared to lead this rapidly growing and highly diverse student body.

George enjoyed the strong support of President Adams at Broward for almost 20 years. During this time, George was able to hire large numbers of new staff, create outstanding student support programs, develop a huge financial aid and scholarship program, build one of the finest student leadership programs in the nation, get thousands of students involved in community service programs, and develop effective and trusting relations with a diversity of leaders in Ft. Lauderdale. During this period of incredible growth, enrollment increased to over 40,000 students and three additional campuses of Broward Community College were established. George set up the student affairs support programs on each of the campuses and thus spent many extra hours traveling from one site to another, assuring himself that programs, policies, and staff were effectively in place for the students. Reflecting his commitment to equal opportunities for each student, George insisted that all Broward students, regardless of what campus they attended, would have the same access to the programs available.

George's leadership philosophy was clearly reflected in the types of professional staff he hired at Broward Community College. He emphasized intelligence, creativity, and a sincere care for students; he looked for staff willing to be entrepreneurial in their work, and for those who were able and willing to move "outside the lines" of conventional job descriptions. George viewed community college work, especially in the 1970s and 1980s, as democracy's best effort to provide opportunity to a wide variety of people, and he wanted strongly committed educators who had a passion to carry out this mission. While Broward Community College attracted significant numbers of very talented, traditional-age college students, it also was a place that welcomed persons of any age who needed and wanted a second chance and who were willing to work for it. This institutional mission proved to be the perfect match for George's enthusiasm, his concern for students, and especially his determination to get things done. George confesses to his own impatience, and believes he was very fortunate to find an institution that allowed him so much freedom. He seriously doubts that he would have been able to work as long in a more conventional university, with its strong traditions and layers of bureaucracy.

Recognizing that rapid enrollment growth at Broward would necessitate greatly expanded student affairs programs and services, George called in consultants from other colleges; traveled to other campuses to observe their organizations; and met with staff, students, and community leaders to assess the needs of his growing institution. But he also understood that there would always be limitations to conventional institutional support. As a result he encouraged, and later expected, his staff to become effective grant writers and administrators in order to expand their services to students. By 1980, Broward Community College was among the nations' leaders in grants to community colleges, much of it from the Fund for the Improvement of Postsecondary Education. This support enabled George and his staff to provide extensive programs in orientation, student aid, counseling, community service, and leadership development.

George gained his greatest satisfaction over the years in seeing his staff extend themselves beyond where they thought they could, achieving results that surprised them. He was strongly committed to working as a team, and his staff retreats at his home and at other locations in the Florida Keys are legendary now among his remaining staff. "George always pushed us to do more and told us we could do more. Sometimes we fought with him, but in this free atmosphere of respect and honesty we always knew he would support us. When we decided as a staff what we were going to do, we were confident that we would succeed," said one of his former staff. His staff respected him and were very loyal to him, not only because he showed the same respect and loyalty to them, but also because his staff knew George had the courage and strength to represent them well and to take honest and tough public stands on issues that needed to be addressed. "George might not win every single battle on our behalf, but he won most of them, because he was right; moreover, I can't think of a more caring, capable, or committed person who could argue our case!" said another staff member.

During the early 1970s, after George had been vice president for only about 3 years, he became so frustrated with the poor traditions of the student government that he decided to abolish it altogether. He had the support of President Adams and his own staff for this dramatic move, but he only did it with the understanding and commitment that he and his staff would help build a high-quality student leadership program, involving far larger numbers of students than before. "We can do better," George told everyone at the college, and he challenged the students to do just that. Although he encountered hostility and skepticism at first, the students recognized his commitment to excellence and his insistence on high standards and integrity. Within 2 years, George and his staff had created new policies, new structures, new organizations, and many opportunities for students to participate in the life of the college. He convinced both the students and his president to create special fees to support facilities, programs, and services. He also created a permanent student activities board and granted it considerable authority in allocating fees and making policy decisions. The outstanding student leadership development program, which included credit classes, retreats, conferences, diversity training, and community service, produced a significant core of students who learned from their experiences and contributed greatly to the quality of student life at Broward.

> *As a leader, he emphasized the importance of knowing and understanding where his institution has been, where the students have come from, and what major value changes are taking place in society.*

While Broward Community College is very large, has a large percentage of part-time students, and includes four campuses in a huge population area, George Young was convinced that the intercollegiate athletics program was very important and contributed to student pride in the college, esprit de corps, and greater visibility in the state and nation. But competitive athletics are expensive, and there was a move within the college to eliminate the program. George was the leading campus advocate for intercollegiate athletics and was able to convince the president and the board to retain the program. George was responsible for the athletic program, and under his direction he worked to obtain significant student fee support, enabling it to continue. His advocacy for this program was not always popular, but he was willing to accept the criticism because of what he knew the program meant to the college.

In his first 3 years as vice president, George developed a model statement on student rights and freedoms at the college, and this was accepted by the board of trustees and continues in practice today. It describes the basic relationships between the student and the institution and clearly indicates the roles and responsibilities of each. As an administrative leader, George knew the volatile times necessitated such a statement and took the initiative to create it; he did so by inviting key faculty, administrators, students, and community members into the process. Convinced that institutions need to understand and clarify their own values, George anticipated the benefits of such a statement that served as the benchmark document from which other policies and practices developed.

The "Competitive Edge" student leadership development program that George and his staff established had a tremendously positive effect on the quality of student life at Broward. Several hundred students participated in this program each year; by involving faculty and administrators in it, George was able to increase support and understanding for student affairs at the college. When this program included a community service component, George knew that getting a diversity of students at Broward to participate would contribute to more positive racial relations on the campus. Many of the students engaged in these programs indicated that it was their most significant learning experience while at the college.

George also created an extensive internship experience for students in the "Competitive Edge" program, whereby these students worked several hours per week in various campus offices, including the president's. This program became very popular with students and administrators, and it resulted in positive learning for the students and additional support for student affairs. It also led to an expanded mentoring and internship program for Broward students with state legislators in Tallahassee, the state capital, and to the nation's capital as well.

While George Young was developing the highly successful student affairs programs at Broward, he became very well known and respected far beyond his campus in Ft. Lauderdale. He was elected the chair of the Florida Council on Student Affairs for the 28 community colleges in the state, and he was often asked to represent the community college system before legislative committees in the state capitol. George was respected not only for his knowledge and experience, but also for his willingness to take strong stands on controversial issues and to urge lawmakers to address the most important issues of the day. Probably reflecting his extensive experience in the construction business as a young man working for his father, when George learned to "tell it like it is" and to be completely honest, he was not hesitant to confront others when he felt their views or actions were incorrect. But George always insisted that this was his responsibility as a leader—to advocate for what he knew was right for the education of students. George Young was one of the most persuasive leaders in student affairs; and he earned the respect and admiration of others for his passion, honesty, and competence. He loved being in the arena where the action was; indeed, he created a good deal of the action himself. He was not afraid of controversy and could disagree with others while remaining good friends with them. As a leader, he always remained focused on what he thought was best for the education of students, and he fought hard for what he believed.

George was invited to serve in a variety of leadership positions with professional and community organizations and became the elected president of NASPA in 1979–1980. He also was the recipient of NASPA's highest honor for professional service, the Fred Turner Award, in 1994. He was also elected as the president of the Florida College Personnel Association. His long-time leadership in community service was recognized when he was asked to chair the state of Florida's Commission on Community Service. He was invited on several occasions during his career to consider accepting a president's position in higher education, but his commitment to student affairs and to Broward Community College were always his first priority, so he declined many opportunities to leave for other positions. He firmly believed that working as a student affairs leader was a great privilege and that it was a passion similar to a religious conviction.

George Young, formally educated as a psychologist and higher education administrator, is a careful student of history. As a leader, he emphasized the importance of knowing and understanding where his institution has been, where the students have come from, and what major value changes are taking place in society. He stressed the critical nature of timing regarding the introduction of change and the willingness to take risks to accomplish goals. He was able to work successfully through changes in presidents, incredible enrollment growth, new campuses, and especially changes in society over a period of almost 28 years as the SSAO at Broward Community College. His many years in this position enabled him to have a special effect on the institution and its students. While enormous changes were taking place during his years at Broward, it was his uncanny ability to relate to students, faculty, staff, administrators, board members, and community leaders that enabled him to be the leader he was. As his president, Willis Holcombe, said, "George Young is part of the culture of Broward Community College. He has defined the Student Affairs Program" (Holcombe, personal communication, 1996).

Appendix A:
Interview Guide

INTERVIEW GUIDE

1. Please describe where you grew up, your family life, and its effect on your values.

2. What factors caused you to enter the student affairs field?

3. Who were the people who had the greatest influence on your decision to enter the field?

4. At what point in your career did you decide that you would like to be a senior student affairs officer? What influenced you to do this?

5. When you first accepted the position, what were your thoughts and expectations?

6. Please describe your work as an institutional leader: how did you decide which issues to address, and how did you develop your strategy for change?

7. Please describe how you went about hiring key staff.

8. Why did you stay in your position at one institution for such an extended period of time? What were the advantages and disadvantages of doing this?

9. How did you respond when a new president was appointed and you had to work for a new leader?

10. Could we talk about three major accomplishments you would identify during your years as a senior student affairs officer at your institution? What was your role in accomplishing your goals, and what were some of the obstacles you had to overcome before you could succeed?

11. Please discuss how you worked with the senior academic officer at your institution, both in terms of budget and in terms of improving student learning.

12. Please discuss how you worked with the senior financial officer at your institution.

(Interview Guide, continued)

13. How important was it to establish good relationships with the other senior administrative officers at your institution in accomplishing your goals? What obstacles did you have to overcome? Was genuine cooperation possible when you were competing with them for resources?

14. Please discuss your views of working with presidents and the importance of earning their support. What did you do when your president did not support your suggestions for change?

15. How were you evaluated, if at all, in your work? How did you know you were doing a good job and whether or not your work was appreciated or making a difference?

16. Would you be willing to discuss the interaction of your job and your personal life? Were the demands of the position so intense at times that you considered doing something else?

17. Please discuss the most difficult problems—either issue-oriented, personnel-related, or problem—based that you faced during your career as a senior student affairs officer and how you handled them.

18. What were (are) the most gratifying aspects of your years as a senior student affairs officer?

19. Please discuss your professional preparation for your work as a student affairs officer. How did it contribute to your success as a leader? Would you pursue the same graduate degree if you had it to do again?

20. What experiences, issues, ideas, or events shaped your style as a leader? What gave you the confidence and determination to believe you could "do it?"

21. What were the rewards of your position?

(Interview Guide, continued)

22. Was it an asset for you as a leader to have been in your position for many years? If so, in what ways, and how did you take advantage of this in accomplishing your goals?

23. When you stepped aside from your position, how did you make this decision? What factors influenced you in this decision?

24. Were there other professional opportunities you had during your career? If so, what were they and why did you decide to continue as a senior student affairs officer?

25. Institutions' needs change, depending on major societal conditions such as social turmoil, economic downturns, war, or prosperity. Are different kinds of student affairs leaders required for different times? What enabled you to survive and thrive as a leader as major changes occurred on your campus?

References

American Association of University Professors. (1967). *Joint Statement on Rights and Freedoms of Students.* Washington, D.C.: AAUP.

Astin, A. W. (1993). *What Matters in College: Four Critical Years Revisited.* San Francisco: Jossey-Bass.

Baldridge, J. V., Curtis, D. V., Ecker, G., & Riley, G. L. (1978). *Policy Making and Effective Leadership.* San Francisco: Jossey-Bass.

Bereit, D., & Bereit, M. Personal communication with author, July 24, 2000.

Blomerley, P. Personal communication, October 27, 1994.

Bloom, A. D. (1987). *The Closing of the American Mind.* New York: Simon and Schuster.

Bok, D., & Bowen, W. G. (1998). *The Shape of the River: Long Term Consequences of Considering Race in College and University Admissions.* Princeton, New Jersey: Princeton University Press.

Bolman, L., & Deal, T. E. (1997). *Reframing Organizations: Artistry, Choice, and Leadership.* San Francisco: Jossey-Bass.

Bryan, R. A., & Tucker, A. (1991). *The Academic Dean: Dove, Dragon, and Diplomat.* 2nd Edition. New York: American Council on Education.

Coll, E. E. Personal communication with author, March 1, 2000.

Drucker, P. F. (1996). *The Leader of the Future: New Visions, Strategies, and Practices for the Next Era.* San Francisco: Jossey-Bass.

Ferrari, M. J. Personal communication with author, May 15, 2000.

Gira, C. Personal communication with author, March 23, 2000.

Hersey, P., & Blanchard. K. H. (1984). *The Situational Leader.* Escondido, California: Center for Leadership Studies.

Holcomb, W. Personal communication, September 25, 1996.

Hughes, E. Personal communication with author, April 19, 2000.

Keller, G. (1983). *Academic Strategy: The Management Revolution in American Higher Education.* Baltimore, Maryland: The Johns Hopkins University Press.

Kernan, A. B. (1999). *In Plato's Cave.* New Haven, Connecticut: Yale University Press.

Kerr, C. (1989). *The Guardians: Boards of Trustees of American Colleges and Universities: What They Do and How Well They Do It.* Washington, D.C.: The Association of Governing Boards.

Kouzes, J., & Posner, B. (1987). *The Leadership Challenge: How To Get Extraordinary Things Done in Organizations.* San Francisco: Jossey-Bass.

Kuh, G., & Coomes, M. D. (1986). Robert H. Shaffer: The Quintessential 'Do-Gooder.' *Journal of Counseling and Development, 64,* 614–623.

Kuh, G., Schuh, J., & Whitt, E. (1991). *Involving Colleges: Successful Approaches To Fostering Learning and Development Outside the Classroom.* San Francisco: Jossey-Bass.

Meyer, J. H. Personal communication with author, June 15, 2000.

Nanus, B. (1992). *Visionary Leadership: Creating a Compelling Sense of Direction for Your Organization.* San Francisco: Jossey-Bass.

O'Toole, J. (1995). *Leading Change: Overcoming the Ideology of Comfort and the Tryranny of Custom.* San Francisco: Jossey-Bass.

Pascarella, E. T., & Terenzini, P. T. (1991). *How College Affects Students: Findings and Insights from Twenty Years of Research.* San Francisco: Jossey-Bass.

Rosovsky, H. (1990). *The University: An Owner's Manual.* New York. W.W. Norton.

Sandeen, A. (1982). Professional Preparation Programs in Student Personnel Services in Higher Education: A National Assessment by Chief Student Affairs Officers. *NASPA Journal, 20* (2), 51–58.

Sandeen, A. (1991). *The Chief Student Affairs Officer: Leader, Manager, Mediator, Educator.* San Francisco: Jossey Bass Publishers.

Senge, P. M. (1990). *The Fifth Discipline: The Art and Practice of the Learning Organization.* New York: Doubleday/Currency.

Shein, E. H. (1992). *Organizational Culture and Leadership.* 2nd Edition. San Francisco: Jossey-Bass.

Shriver, P. R. Personal communication with author, February 28, 2000.

Shurn, A. M. Personal communication, October 31, 1994.

Upcraft. M. L., & Schuh, J. H. (1996). *Assessment in Student Affairs: A Guide for Practitioners.* San Francisco: Jossey-Bass.